Baseball

America's Diamond Mind
1919-1941

Baseball

America's Diamond Mind
1919-1941

Richard C. Crepeau

A University of Central Florida Book

UNIVERSITY PRESSES OF FLORIDA
FAMU / FAU / FIU / FSU / UCF / UF / UNF / USF / UWF
Orlando

The Sporting News, a weekly newspaper published in St. Louis, Missouri, by Spink Publications, now a Times Mirror Company, and for almost 100 years the official repository for professional baseball in the United States, has made the writing and publication of this book possible. Its columns from the years 1919 to 1941 are the principal record source for the social and cultural history of American baseball during this period. Writing from those columns constitutes the central core of this narrative and is the source of every unidentified quotation appearing in the text of this book.

University Presses of Florida is the central agency for scholarly publishing of the State of Florida's university system. Its offices are located at 15 NW 15th Street, Gainesville, FL 32603. Works published by University Presses of Florida are evaluated and selected for publication by a faculty editorial committee of any one of Florida's nine public universities: Florida A&M University (Tallahassee), Florida Atlantic University (Boca Raton), Florida International University (Miami), Florida State University (Tallahassee), University of Central Florida (Orlando), University of Florida (Gainesville), University of North Florida (Jacksonville), University of South Florida (Tampa), University of West Florida (Pensacola).

Library of Congress Cataloging in Publication Data

Crepeau, Richard C.   1941–
    Baseball: America's diamond mind, 1919–1941.

    (A University of Central Florida book)
    Bibliography: p.
    Includes index.
    1. Baseball—United States—History. I. Title.
GV863.A1C7   796.357′09   79–16237
ISBN 0–8130–0645–7

Typography by American Graphics Corporation
Fort Lauderdale, Florida

PRINTED IN U.S.A.

Acknowledgments

A NUMBER of people and institutions have been extremely helpful in gathering the materials for illustration. I would particularly like to thank Lorrie Lindsley of the University of Central Florida Library, Helen Struthers of the Orlando Public Library, Richard Spencer of the Photography Department at the University of Central Florida, and the Wilson Library of the University of Minnesota. Special thanks go to Joseph J. Sullivan of Seattle, who provided cartoons from his private collection.

Epigraphs are quoted with publisher's permission from Robert Coover, *The Universal Baseball Association, Inc., J. Henry Waugh, Prop.* (copyright by Random House, Inc.).

Quotations from James T. Farrell, *My Baseball Diary* (copyright by A. S. Barnes & Co., Inc.) are with publisher's permission.

Contents

Preface / ix

Wars and Scandal / 1

Democracy and Character / 24

Community and Rural Roots / 48

Superstar / 73

Commercialism and the Corporate Player / 102

Novas / 126

Problems and Tensions / 150

Crisis, Change, and Continuity / 173

Baseball Diplomacy / 196

Bibliography / 219

Index / 225

Preface

History: in the end, you can never prove a thing.

BASEBALL reigned supreme during the Golden Age of Sport in the 1920s and 1930s. If there ever was a time when it was the undisputed National Pastime, it was during these years between the world wars. The baseball establishment made this claim seriously and put it forward at every opportunity. Sportswriters assigned to cover major-league baseball assumed that it was entitled to this designation. Baseball management repeated it on every possible occasion. To prove that baseball was the National Pastime it was necessary to demonstrate that American cultural values and baseball were intertwined. To those in baseball the "proof" was overwhelming.

What was American about baseball? Those in baseball needed to answer this, but the question implied another: What was American? The way in which baseball people answered the first question provided an indication of what they perceived to be the answer to the second. A study of baseball, therefore, should reveal what the people connected with the game saw as important personal and national characteristics, beliefs, and values. Such an ethos emerges from the baseball literature of the Twenties and Thirties. Concepts like democracy, opportunity, and fair play permeate the literature of baseball, identified both with the game and with those who played it.

As the National Pastime, baseball also became a means of expressing American nationalism. The nationalist spirit, although not confined to wartime, is more clearly and intensely expressed then and during other times of national crisis. The Golden Age of Baseball began and ended with world wars that provided ample opportunity for nationalist display. During the 1920s great emphasis was put on what was called "100 percent Americanism." The 1930s were marked by the national crisis of the Great Depression. Clearly there was no dearth of opportunity for the expression of nationalist and patriotic spirit, and baseball took full advantage of these opportunities.

These years were a time of change in American culture. Different changes had varying impact and significance. The obvious but minor changes such as Prohibition and the coming of Sunday games had a significance for baseball that was anything but profound. Changes such as the advent of radio and night games made a strong impact on baseball, but their social significance was less obvious. Changes in social order, such as the new roles for women and the challenges to the old roles for blacks, had varying significance for baseball and little immediate impact. Finally, there were the deeper and broader changes in American society that were clearly reflected in baseball. One such major change was the evolution of American society from a rural-agrarian society to an urban-industrial one, which had been going on since the mid-nineteenth century. By the 1920s the process was nearly complete. Like all changes it produced problems and tensions, and baseball reflected both the changes and the tensions.

The change from a rural to an urban culture might be met in several ways. It might produce a clinging to the rural past and rejection of the urban culture. (The Scopes "Monkey Trial" was an example of such a reaction.) However, the change might produce a rejection of the rural past and the enthusiastic embracing of the urban present and future. This happened, too, as exemplified by the pseudo-sophistication of the flapper and her beau. Or it might be met by a combination of these responses: holding onto the values of the rural past while, at the same time, embracing the new urban society.

This was America's most common response. John William Ward has shown this to be the essence of the reaction to Charles Lindbergh's solo flight. It was also the most common response to change in the baseball world.

This book is not a history of baseball. It is an attempt to look at one segment of American society as it saw itself and as it reflected the larger society. The major source for such a study must be the sports pages of the nation. With the passage of time much of the material has become humorous; some was also contrived and seems today to lack subtlety. But all of the material is pure Americana. As such it should recall essayist M. de Crevecoeur's question, "What then is the American, this new man?" This was a question without a definitive answer in the eighteenth century, and it still is. It is also a question of prime and timely importance, at least to Americans. A study of baseball may provide some direction in the search for an answer.

It was in the sports sections of their newspapers that most Americans "saw" major-league baseball. A weekly newspaper published in St. Louis, The Sporting News, the self-styled "Bible of Baseball," devoted itself entirely to the National Game. This journal printed reports from writers who covered all the major-league teams for the local press. It also offered editorial comment and feature stories from around the nation and from its own staff writers. The value of The Sporting News is enhanced by the fact that much of the writing was of an incestuous nature; that is, one writer tended to write the same thing in different columns, and the writers tended to borrow freely from one another. Therefore, The Sporting News, with its cross section of sports writing and opinion, serves as the heart of this book. Quotations from editors and sportwriters not otherwise identified are from the pages of The Sporting News. The quotations that precede each chapter are taken from Robert Coover's excellent and insightful novel, The Universal Baseball Association, Inc., J. Henry Waugh, Prop.

I would like to thank a number of people who have been of great assistance in the preparation of this book: Dr. William Miller, whose direction and friendship have guided me throughout; Dr. James P. Jones, who provided his historical and baseball expertise; the inter-library loan staffs at Florida State University and Florida Technological University (now the University of Central Florida); The Florida Technological University Foundation (now The University of Central Florida Foundation), which provided funding for the final preparation of the manuscript; Mrs. LaVerne Ryan, who typed the final manuscript and caught many little errors. Special thanks go to Pat Crepeau, who assisted in the preparation of the final draft and made many suggestions for improvement in style, but who, most important, shared for four years the joys and anguish evolving from this project.

1

Wars and Scandal

> "You know, Lou," Henry said, "you can take
> history or leave it, but if you take it you have to
> accept certain assumptions or ground rules
> about what's left in and what's left out."

IN so many ways it had been such a wonderful war that it might have been called the last of the great fun wars. The idealism, the slogans, the music served to create an atmosphere that was one part Woodrow Wilson and one part P. T. Barnum. George Creel's Committee on Public Information, the propaganda arm of the federal government, provided instant patriotism in which all could equally share. No walk of life, no age group, neither sex was overlooked. It was an ironic equality, this equality of shared hysteria which was forced on a people who were out to make the world safe for democracy. Participation was nearly universal. There were few brave souls who would protest against the possible alienation of civil rights in the face of the infamous epithet "slacker." Truth, justice, and the American way were real and pervading concepts. These were words with tangible meanings that all Americans intuitively understood. The eternal verities still stood, and they would meet the test of the "barbaric Hun."

Nothing was more a part of the American way than baseball in 1919. The National Pastime did its bit in the war and came away knowing that war had been good for America, good for the world,

1

and good for baseball. Sportswriter I. E. Sanborn commented that the return of the players from the army would "do more than anything else to restore professional baseball to favor in the eyes of the public and the government."

The 1918 season had been cut short, and the World Series was played in early September. A boy named Babe Ruth was the winning pitcher for the Boston Red Sox in two of the games as they beat the Chicago Cubs four games to two. No home runs were hit in the entire series. By October nearly 50 percent of the players on major-league rosters were in the service of their country in what they thought of as an even more important World Series. It was proudly claimed that few players sought "bulletproof jobs." Even those in the shipyards were not necessarily slackers, as was demonstrated by the case of Chief Bender, who worked the yards fourteen to eighteen hours a day and suffered a nervous breakdown in the "greatest cause that ever was."

For the soldier–ball player the war was over almost before he could change his spikes. Only a few players saw action "over there." But baseball could still play an important role for the men in uniform. In February 1919, Ban Johnson, president of the American League, announced that the first shipments of *The Sporting News*, the self-proclaimed "Bible of Baseball," were about to be sent to the returning soldiers. Pointing to the significance of this event the editors of the publication predicted that it would be a treat for those men who hungered for something "real American" and make the trip "to home and mother a joy." It would serve to remind the soldier that "his game—the Only Game—remembers him and is getting ready to receive him again with the rest of a proud nation." For those not yet returning, Clark Griffith's Bat and Ball Fund provided YMCA representative Bill Lange with baseball equipment to distribute to American bases overseas. Lange claimed that Americans had shown the Europeans how to fight; now they would show them how to play. The American boy would demonstrate through baseball how quick he could think, how fast he could run, and what a good sport he was. "They will see the fastest, fairest, cleanest game ever invented, played by the lads that invented it," claimed Lange.

For those already back home there was adulation. A theatrical syndicate offered Hank Gowdy, the first major-league player to volunteer for the service, $1,500 per week for a thirty-week swing around the vaudeville circuit to tell everyone how he beat the Hun. Johnny Evers—second baseman in the Cubs' Tinker to Evers to Chance combination—went on the lecture circuit to relate his wartime experiences as a worker for the Knights of Columbus in France. And there was Tom Herbert, an usher at the Cleveland ball park, who was one of the first pilots to go overseas. He had been shot down and, after a stay in a London hospital, returned to a hero's welcome in Cleveland.

War memorials would long remain a part of the baseball scene. One was erected at the Polo Grounds in honor of the brave deeds of Eddie Grant, the New York Giant infielder who died October 5, 1918, facing the enemy in the Argonne Forest. In 1921 the American League created Hospital Day to honor war veterans, "lest we forget." *The Sporting News* used the occasion to comment on the importance of baseball to the national defense, as it had "proved a very essential thing in sustaining morale during the dark days. It's proving no less essential now, when others seem to forget. Baseball is still doing its bit."

With the war out of the way, attention turned to the 1919 major-league baseball season. The fans looked forward to the new season with enthusiasm. According to *Literary Digest*, American League president Ban Johnson felt the war had created new fans: thousands who had never before played baseball had come into contact with it in the service. Letters from overseas indicated the boys were eager to return home and get out to the bleachers. The players too were eager to get back to their civilian employment. As Maj. Branch Rickey, manager of the St. Louis Cardinals, said, "I don't think there is a more patriotic, virile or enthusiastic body of men anywhere than the baseball players in the service. And they're coming back to help the game, too."

Not only had the players contributed to the process of making the world safe for democracy, but that experience had contributed to the betterment of the players themselves. There was the case of Walter

Ruether, star pitcher for the Cincinnati Reds in the 1919 season. Prior to the war Ruether had not shown much for the Reds. But during his tour of military duty, army training and discipline helped him to realize that life was not just a joke but a serious business. Ruether decided that when the war was over he would—if he got the chance—work hard and make good. *The Sporting News* reported: "Thanks to Uncle Sam's methods of dealing with men and making them better Ruether had convinced himself that he had the goods. It didn't take him long then to convince the world. The result is ... one of the greatest winning pitchers in baseball." The army did build men.

Major-league baseball faced the 1919 season having made its contribution to the war effort, having been improved by the war experience, and standing ready to help the American people readjust to the postwar world. On the eve of the 1919 opening, the owners received this piece of advice from *The Sporting News*:

> Remember, baseball magnates dear,
>   If in your hearts some feud is flickering,
> This year is Get-Together year
>   The fans are sick of war and bickering.
> Fans will not hear the old old yaps
>   About the grudge some magnate nurses
> So get together all you chaps
>   If you would fill your purses.

Despite this plea, 1919 was not a peaceful season for the nation or for the baseball world. With the war over and the Hun no longer a threat, new outlets for the proponents of superpatriotism unleashed by the Creel committee were not difficult to find. A threat loomed large from the East, such people felt, in the form of the Bolshevik, who had collaborated with the cursed Hun, practiced free love, and hated free enterprise, motherhood, and God. For those who were looking for them, there were signs that this new enemy was moving to the shores of America: bombs in the mails, the International Workers of the World, a "Soviet in Seattle," strikes, violence, race riots, unemployed veterans—even liberals, suffragettes, and the League of Women

Voters. It seemed as though the entire nation was coming apart at the seams. Of course not all Americans had gone overboard. There were those who kept their balance and were out at the ball game instead of out in the streets. In fact, baseball was touted as the perfect tonic for these disturbances. One May Day in Cleveland offered a case in

point. A group of 100,000 people were in Public Square "knocking in each other's heads" over political issues while thousands of others out at the ball park watched the exploits of Ty Cobb and Tris Speaker and cursed the umpires. The lesson was clear: in these "ticklish times," the ball park was the place to be "for safety sake and to keep a lot of us out of trouble."

If there was turmoil in the nation and the world, the same could be said of the baseball establishment. The governing structure of organized baseball was collapsing as the National Commission, the existing ruling body (which consisted of a chairman and the two league presidents), went through a dismantling process that would eventually lead to the rise of Judge Kennesaw Mountain Landis as commissioner of baseball. The executive officers of the major leagues were at war: Ban Johnson, president of the American League, was at the center of the conflict; August Garry Hermann, chairman of the National Commission, had lost most of his power and effectiveness; and John Heydler, president of the National League, did not want to get involved. The basic issue was power. Who ruled the major leagues—the individual owner of each team? the owners working as a body? the league presidents? the National Commission? Everyone had his own opinion.

The case of Carl Mays, bad-boy pitcher of the Boston Red Sox, who jumped his team and demanded to be traded to the Yankees, became the issue that led to the near destruction of the American League. Mays was traded to the Yankees in accordance with his demands, but Ban Johnson ruled the trade invalid and suspended him. Yankee owner Col. Jacob Ruppert then got an injunction against the American League president, allowing the Yankees to use Mays. Ruppert was supported by Harry Frazee, owner of the Red Sox, and by Charles Comiskey, owner of the Chicago White Sox. At one point the three owners threatened to withdraw from the American League and join the National League. This dismal situation detracted from an otherwise successful season. Joe Vila, New York correspondent of *The Sporting News*, decried the developments: "The mud throwing has worked great harm and doesn't belong in a clean sport. Baseball is enjoying a wonderful revival and the public cares only for the work of the players on the field." The crisis ended in February 1920, when the New York Supreme Court made its injunction against Johnson permanent; a week later, at the winter baseball meetings in Chicago, Johnson capitulated. An uneasy and unsatisfactory truce was concluded, but the damage done was irreparable. The Mays case so weakened the structure of organized baseball that it was unable to respond when the rumors of a "fix" circulated at the 1919 World Series.

Gambling had long plagued the National Pastime. Warnings of the danger were frequent. In June 1919 the *New York Evening Sun* reported that gamblers were in evidence in the Polo Grounds and commended the Yankee management for trying to clean things up. Editorials in *The Sporting News* stressed that the integrity of baseball must never be in doubt. The gamblers were an "obnoxious and objectionable" element to club management and to loyal fans. Despite these attacks and the efforts of Yankee and Giant management at the Polo Grounds, the gamblers were not deterred. At the beginning of the 1920 season efforts to clear out the gamblers continued on orders from the American League president. Joe Vila applauded this action and called for the barring of any players involved in betting. "The fans who love baseball for its honesty are up in arms, and the magnates no longer can dodge the issue with safety. Turn on the light, and drive the rascals out!"

Not everyone took the issue quite so seriously. In *The Sporting News* for June 10, 1920, "The Gamboleers" and its anonymous author suggested that perhaps there was a double standard operating in this issue:

> Gaze on the wicked gamboleer
>   He is a thing of shame
> He bets a dollar and a half
>   Upon a baseball game;
> They sting him with a fine and heap
>   Disgrace upon his name.
> Gaze on the noble financier
>   Who proudly walks the street;

A pillar of the church is he
    Whom one is proud to meet;
He does not bet on baseball games,
    He bets on corn and wheat.

The hint of populistic irreverence that runs through "The Gamboleers" was not at all unusual, nor was this general attitude toward gambling. In fact gambling and association with gamblers was not unusual among players or owners, and gambling odds were usually quoted in the press before the more important games and before the World Series. However, the official posture was that gambling and baseball simply did not mix and that, in this matter, the basic integrity of the game was at stake. The problem was, of course, that gambling might produce scandal.

In 1919 the American intellectual community was reading *The Education of Henry Adams* and was being told by Adams that the standards and values of the nineteenth century were irrelevant to the realities of the new industrial America. To many, as they viewed the world in 1919, it seemed that Henry Adams was right. They must abandon the old values or even hasten the destruction of those values. To some extent the emergence of the "Lost Generation" was the result. But for others, what was needed was not destruction but rather a vigorous defense and more rigorous practice of the older values, a reaffirmation of them. If things were going wrong, the fault lay not with the values themselves but with the lack of allegiance to them. Conservation, not innovation, was called for; purification, not destruction. The Chicago White Sox provided an example of the collapse of the old standards in their World Series of 1919. When what came to be known as the Black Sox scandal broke, it was the course of purification and reaffirmation that was followed by the baseball establishment.

The Cincinnati Reds had come into the 1919 World Series as definite underdogs, because the White Sox were regarded as one of the great teams of all time. Their only weakness, if any, was in the bullpen, but then bullpens were not as important a factor in 1919 as they are now. It is not surprising then that Chicago was given a strong edge by the leading sportswriters. However, on the eve of the opening game of the series, the gambling odds took a sharp turn in favor of the Reds. This was the first of the postwar, nine-game World Series, and the Reds eventually won it in eight. In analyzing the series, sportswriters generally took the position that the White Sox were the victims of overconfidence. All the breaks had gone against them, and

they had beaten themselves with mental errors, poor hitting, and spotty fielding. A few reporters from Cincinnati and other National League cities saw it as a simple case of the best team having won. That the pregame favorites had lost should not have been startling. It had happened before and would happen again.

But there were persistent rumors: gamblers had reached the players; gamblers had some inside information on the White Sox; the White Sox were fighting among themselves. During the series itself, it was said that gamblers were able to pay players for inside information that would tip the scales of wagering from one team to another. This certainly was possible. If the "lean-faced and long-nosed gamblers" were indeed involved enough for such a practice, the next step might be to offer the players money for something even more serious—rigging the outcome. Therefore, the management must be put on notice to meet the issue head-on. The issue was clear to *The Sporting News*: "to keep baseball clean for Americans—for that kind of American who doesn't organize betting syndicates and make a 'business' of anything there is a chance to filch a dollar out of, however sacred it may be to Americans."

As for the possibility that the series was actually fixed, most people refused to admit it. Certain things were beyond reproach, they felt. The rumors were simply a case of some people, having guessed wrong about the Reds, now being poor losers by yelling "fix." Or perhaps one group of gamblers had put something over on another group. Naturally the whole thing needed to be investigated for the sake of baseball, and certainly the gamblers had to be cleaned out of the game and kept out of the ball parks. But the World Series fixed? Never!

John B. Sheridan of *The Sporting News* found the possibility of fixing any kind of baseball game highly unlikely. For a man to throw a game he would have to be willing to do "terrible things" to his friends, admirers, employers, family, the fans, the good name of America, and the game itself. Such a man would die of "his own self-contempt," Sheridan wrote. The emotional price a player would have to pay was beyond monetary compensation. Sheridan did concede that a player might agree to throw a game, but when he actually got out onto the field, with the crowd cheering him on, with his opponents jeering him, and "with the good name of the National Game and the American people at stake," surely he could not go through with the fix? But sometimes people do what should not be done, so baseball men must be certain that the purity of the game was never in doubt.

Much was at stake here, much more than the profit-loss structure of major-league baseball. With so much at stake, it is not difficult to understand why the full story was so slow in coming out, has not, in fact, probably ever been told. The initial charges of a fix were met with a hostile response. Typical was the reaction of *Baseball Magazine*, which in December 1919 simply dismissed the possibility of a fix out of hand, claiming that it was impossible to fix a baseball game. The following month *Baseball Magazine* attacked Hugh Fullerton, the sportswriter who had first given the fix charges wide circulation.

Regardless of these initial reactions, the charges and rumors would not die. In December 1919 interest in the charges received new life when Ray Schalk, the White Sox catcher, was quoted as saying that when the next season opened seven Sox would be missing from the roster. Sox owner Charles Comiskey, responding to Schalk's comments, said that his own investigation of the fix charges had as yet turned up no evidence but that he and manager Kid Gleason would continue to examine the case, promising that there would be no whitewash. Schalk was criticized in some quarters for talking too much, in others for talking too little and not naming names. The Chicago catcher later denied that he had hinted at anything wrong in the World Series.

The story of the 1919 fix finally came out in the open as a result of an investigation by a Cook County grand jury convened to investigate charges of an attempted fix of a Chicago Cubs–Philadelphia Phillies game during the 1920 season. But by the time of the grand jury's first meeting on September 22, 1920, the scope of the investigation had been widened to include the 1919 World Series.

While some people opposed the investigation of the World Series, *The Sporting News* endorsed it, feeling that it was important to clean up the game by severing all connections between baseball and gamblers and fearing that failure to clean up the game might result in attempts by reform groups to outlaw baseball as they had tried to outlaw horse-racing. "Get the crooks—before they give the reformers a chance to get the game." Clearing the air would ensure that the World Series of 1920 would be decided solely on its merits. The large majority of the players was honest, and the investigative process would serve to restore public confidence in baseball.

On September 27 the first major breakthrough took place, not in Cook County, but in Philadelphia, where James Isaminger wrote a story in the *Philadelphia North American* based on an interview with small-time gambler Bill Maharg. Maharg's charges (as reported in Harold Seymour's *Baseball: The Golden Age*) were that some of the Sox had thrown the first and second games of the 1919 World Series and had been paid $100,000 for their efforts. The next day, Sox pitcher Eddie Cicotte and outfielder Joe Jackson confessed to Charles Comiskey and to the Cook County grand jury that, in fact, they had also thrown two other games. The two men implicated six of their teammates. The story had begun to come out.

Public reaction varied from outrage to disbelief. *The Sporting News* for October 7, 1920, sounded the keynote among the sporting press: over a picture of the eight players implicated was the caption "Fix These Faces in Your Memory," and under the picture was the caption "Eight Men Charged with Selling Out Baseball." The story said, "These are the White Sox players who committed the astounding and contemptible crime of selling out the baseball world...they will be remembered from now on only for the depths of depravity to which they could sink." The men in the picture were Happy Felsch, Chick Gandil, Joe Jackson, Eddie Cicotte, Fred McMullin, Claude Williams, Swede Risberg, and Buck Weaver.

Some sportswriters called for an end to the World Series itself, claiming that it had increased commercialism in the game and thereby invited dishonesty. The "World Championship" could instead be decided by interleague play-offs after midseason. Another writer welcomed this "earthquake" as a means of cleaning up the ship of baseball and ridding it of the "rats and barnacles....We have fallen down, but let us get up and go on with the grand old game. Thank the Lord, and other agencies that we have numbers of American boys to keep the game great and pure."

Other reactions focused on the impact on the kids of America. According to the editors of *Collier's*, the real crime of the Black Sox was not that they had accepted bribes, not that they had thrown games, but that they had destroyed the faith of millions of kids. But, *Collier's* concluded, no gamblers or crooked players could really destroy the great game, because baseball was basically honest. "Baseball dishonest? Then George Washington was a liar and Santa Claus a fake." (In these days of revisionist history, few editors would now dare to use these parallels!)

In the *Chicago Daily News* for September 29, 1920, the fall of Eddie

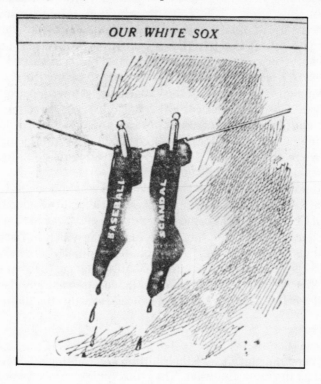

OUR WHITE SOX

Cicotte was similarly treated. In Eddie's hometown neighborhood in Detroit there was a baseball team called the Central Avenue Sox, who had in their possession a certain baseball they valued above all others. They took special care of it, proudly displaying it before their opponents. Eddie Cicotte had given that ball to the Central Avenue Sox; now the boys returned it to Eddie's daughter, Rose. Rose didn't quite understand the intent of the act, but Eddie Cicotte did. It had been the first ball pitched in the World Series of 1919: "Eddie Cicotte pitched it. And yesterday, before the grand jury, Eddie testified that he pitched that ball crooked.... The hero is off his pedestal."

Sports editors of *The News* of New York called for quick action to rid the game of gamblers and thieves, exhorting owners and managers to purge their clubs of every man they were not absolutely certain was "square." This, it was admitted, might cause a few innocents to suffer with the guilty, but that would be better than having even "one rascal in the game." It was clearly no time to be soft: vital issues were at stake; sacrilege had been committed. There were even a few who called for a "pogrom," seeing the fix as yet another sign of the power of the "International Jewish conspiracy." But even *The Sporting News*, which had once referred to the "lean-faced and long-nosed gamblers," was unwilling to go that far, pointing out: "Well, it does look like most of the Attell gang—but then we're all American born, and don't forget that a Sullivan is involved as well as a Rothstein."

And how did the fans feel about it? Their reaction seems to have been mixed. Eliot Asinof reports that a week after the revelations the kids of Chicago were heard to holler derisively, "Play bail." On the other hand, a poll by a Chicago newspaper revealed in December 1920 that a two-to-one majority favored dropping criminal charges against the accused players and reinstating them to the White Sox, since this was only their first offense. In *My Baseball Diary*, James T. Farrell recalls attending a game in Chicago shortly after the scandal broke:

> It was a muggy, sunless day. I went to the park early and watched the players take their hitting and fielding practice. It looked the same as always. They took their turns at the plate.

They had their turns on the field. They seemed calm, no different, no different than they had been on other days before the scandal had broken. The crowd was friendly to them and some cheered. But a subtle gloom hung over the fans. The atmosphere of the park was like the muggy weather. The game began. Cicotte pitched. The suspected players got a hand when they came to bat. The White Sox won easily. Cicotte was master of the Detroit Tigers that day. One could only wish that he had pitched as well in the 1919 Series.

After the game, I went under the stands and stood near the steps leading down from the White Sox clubhouse. A small crowd always collected there to watch the players leave. But on this particular Sunday, there were about 200 to 250 boys waiting. Some of the players left. Lefty Williams, wearing a blue suit and a grey cap, was one, and some of the fans called to him. A few others came down the steps. And then Joe Jackson and Happy Felsch appeared. They were both big men. Jackson was the taller of the two and Felsch the broader. They were sportively dressed in gray silk shirts, white duck trousers and white shoes. They came down the clubhouse steps slowly, their faces masked by impassivity.

A few fans called to them, but they gave no acknowledgment to these greetings. They turned and started to walk away. Spontaneously, the crowd followed in a slow, disorderly manner. I went with the crowd and trailed about five feet behind Jackson and Felsch. They walked somewhat slowly. A fan called out:

"It ain't true, Joe."

The two suspected players did not turn back. They walked on, slowly. The crowd took up this cry and more than once, men and boys called out and repeated:

"It ain't true, Joe."

This call followed Jackson and Felsch as they walked all the way under the stands to the Thirty-fifth Street side of the ball park. They left the park and went for their parked cars in a soccer field behind the right-field bleachers. I waited by the exit of the soccer field. Many others also waited. Soon Felsch and Jackson drove out in their sportive roadsters, through a double file of silent fans.

I went back to the clubhouse. But most of the players had

gone. It was getting dark. A ball park seems very lonely after the crowd has cleared away. Never was a ball park lonelier or more deserted for me than on that September Sunday afternoon. It was almost dark. I went home. I sensed it was true. But I hoped that the players would get out of this and be allowed to go on playing....

My interest in baseball changed after this. For years I had no favorite team. I was growing up, and this marked the end of my days of hero worshipping baseball players. Many fans felt betrayed. I didn't. I felt sorry. I wished it weren't true. I wished the players would have been given another chance.

Many fans did not want to believe that it was true. The line "say it isn't so, Joe" became part of the folk language. The world might not be safe for democracy; maybe the war had been a mistake—a person could live with that—but the world not safe for baseball? Say it isn't so!

The baseball establishment, already in chaos, found it equally difficult to respond. The various factions used the scandal against each other. Those who sought to dethrone Ban Johnson blamed him for having failed to deal effectively with the White Sox the previous fall. They called for new, strong leadership in baseball. Johnson's supporters, in turn, attacked Charles Comiskey for inaction in dealing with his own ball club and claimed that it was only the diligence of Ban Johnson that finally broke the story open. Standing on the sidelines, John Heydler took the holier-than-thou position that his National League was clean, ignoring the fact that the Cook County grand jury had originally been called to investigate the Cubs and the Phillies. The baseball establishment also expressed great surprise and shock when the revelations became public, avowing that the episode was an aberration; actually, it was the culmination of at least twenty years of unattended corruption. Although hypocritical, such a pose by the upper eschelons of baseball was necessary. For years the owners had piously proclaimed the purity of the National Pastime from the housetops, while they casually concealed misconduct. To admit otherwise now might have brought down the entire house of cards on their heads (Seymour, *Baseball: The Golden Age*).

The Black Sox scandal broke just at the close of the 1920 season. The White Sox and the Cleveland Indians were in the midst of a tight pennant race. What if the White Sox won? They were playing without the tainted players, but it still wouldn't seem right. *The Sporting News* suggested that the World Series be canceled in the event of a White Sox pennant, and there were even some facetious prayers to the "God of Baseball" to intervene on behalf of Cleveland. When the Indians clinched the flag it was hailed a triumph for honest baseball.

What is the proper punishment for such a heinous crime as treason? The story of Eddie Cicotte and the Central Avenue Sox suggested one possibility. Jail might be another. But some felt jail was too good for these criminals; in jail they could hide behind the thick walls and avoid facing public scorn. No, jail was too good for them. Out in the world they would "taint the air and thieves [would] scorn them." These were men who had honored a president of the United States by shaking his hand, but now "not a gutter snipe in the slums would admit he knew either one of them. There is your penalty." In this vein *The Sporting News* indicated that forgiveness was out of the question. The Christian virtues of charity and mercy must be set aside in this case. The honesty of the player, the very foundation of baseball, was at stake. "The crime is so grievous and the necessity for strictest integrity so urgent that baseball can not afford to take the chance that a player once crooked would not again yield to temptation...."

In February 1921 there were rumors that the indictments might be set aside, that convictions could not be obtained. Some of the indicted players even said that they would force their way back into baseball through the courts. Such a suggestion was appalling to a large part of the sporting press: of course the players would never be allowed back into the game. *The Sporting News* was shocked that any lawyer would have so little consideration for the National Pastime and public opinion that he might try to force this issue in the courts; even to suggest such a possibility "makes one's hair rise in anger."

The trial began on June 27, 1921. In retrospect it seemed almost like another fix. Harold Seymour describes the strange things which were happening: four prosecuting attorneys switched over to the defense; there was some question as to who was paying the players' legal fees; while on the stand Charles Comiskey was never questioned about the findings of his own investigation. The grand jury files had been tampered with, but this fact was not explored at the trial. The prosecution objected to questions the answers to which should have worked to their advantage. The gamblers originally indicted and mentioned in various grand-jury testimony were never pursued by the prosecutors. In short, "no serious effort was made to uncover the full truth....By containing the mess within limited perimeters and focusing primarily on the ball players, the trial served the interests of both the gamblers and the baseball industry" (Seymour, *Baseball: The Golden Years*). The gamblers were allowed to go free. Baseball was left to deal with the players in its own way. The semblance of housecleaning achieved a satisfactory solution without actually hanging out the dirty laundry in full view.

The importance of appearances in the trial was demonstrated by the reaction in the press to a peripheral issue: a report from the courtroom that Kid Gleason and some of the "Clean Sox" were very friendly with the Black Sox. Some sportswriters were concerned that this might cause fans to doubt the seriousness of the offense. Tom Rice, Brooklyn correspondent for *The Sporting News*, went so far as to call for the expulsion of Gleason and the others from baseball, claiming that these men should be judged by the company they were keeping. Appearance was paramount.

The trial proceeded to its ludicrous conclusion: the seven indicted players were found "not guilty." Judge, jury, defendants, and court spectators were delighted with the decision—the players and the jurors joined in a post-trial celebration at a Chicago restaurant. But the next day came the verdict of Judge Landis, the commissioner of baseball. Landis was not impressed by the "verdict of juries." Players who threw ball games, or who participated in discussions concerning throwing ball games and failed to report such discussions, said Landis, would never again play professional baseball. Nine players were covered by this pronouncement: the seven acquitted by the jury; Fred McMullin, who had not been indicted due to lack of evidence; and Joe Gedeon of the St. Louis Browns, who had attended one of the meetings with the gamblers. There were others, like Charles Comiskey, who had guilty knowledge long before they brought it forward, but Judge Landis ignored them. More astonishing was the failure to expel Giant first baseman Hal Chase, who had been indicted as a prime fixer and who had been cheating in games for years. Years later Landis even gave Chase an official clean bill of health (Seymour, *Baseball: The Golden Age*).

Generally, editorial opinion across the nation supported Judge Landis' action and deplored the verdict of the jury. The *Chicago Daily News* of August 4, 1921, said that the public verdict would not be affected by the verdict of the jury. It was clear, they felt, that a conspiracy had been entered into and that games had been thrown. "Thus a serious blow was corruptedly and shamelessly directed against a popular and wholesome sport. In this case sordid commercialism triumphed over conscience, good faith, elementary decency and manly self-respect." The *Cleveland Plain Dealer* of the same date termed the jury's verdict astonishing, and said that "lovers of the game everywhere" approved of the action taken by Landis, who "could not have decided otherwise without doing irreparable injury to a sport which thousands cherish because it is square" (Asinof, *Eight Men Out*).

Not quite everyone shared in the enthusiasm over the Landis decision. First, the judge, jury, and court spectators certainly fell short of approving the Landis position. Second, a *Chicago Tribune* random sampling of seven men-on-the-street showed that five favored reinstatement of the players, while a petition for the reinstatement of Buck Weaver attracted 14,000 signatures in a single day (Asinof, *Eight Men Out*). Third, William A. Phelon, Cincinnati correspondent of *The Sporting News*, reported that the ball players seemed to favor reinstatement for the Black Sox. Some players even justified the Black Sox action because of the low salaries paid by Charles Comiskey. These few exceptions managed to seep through into a public press that was virtually unanimous against the Black Sox.

The baseball establishment expressed public shock over the verdict of the jury and backed the decision of the new commissioner of baseball without qualification. Ban Johnson said that these men had committed the greatest crime possible against baseball, and the verdict did not alter that fact one bit. Kid Gleason let it be known that if the players were reinstated he would quit the game (Asinof, *Eight Men Out*). All in all, it was an appropriate orgy of righteous indignation, suitable for a proper purification rite.

The Black Sox scandal had other repercussions. The structure of organized baseball had been in chaos. In February 1920 the chairman of the National Commission, Garry Hermann, resigned. The Mays case had taken its toll, and the American League was on the brink of dissolution. A new ruling structure was needed for organized baseball, and the Black Sox scandal sped the arrival of that new form. When it came it was in the shape of a dictatorship and was embodied in the person of Judge Kennesaw Mountain Landis.

For the purpose of ritual purification and reaffirmation of faith the choice of Landis was a master stroke, for it reaffirmed the nineteenth-century verities and rural values. The choice was a message to Henry Adams and the Lost Generation that they were wrong: the world had not changed; the old values were still valid. Morality, truth, justice, American patriotism would carry on. The rural wisdom of the American people would not and could not be corrupted by the new urban-industrial world. There might be threats, but the Judge Landises of this world would prevail. Landis had demonstrated that he was capable of such a task, and his strong stance in the Black Sox matter was a sign that he could do it again.

And what was his past? Who was this man with the peculiar name? J. G. Taylor Spink, publisher of *The Sporting News*, described the man in *Judge Landis and 25 Years of Baseball*. Born in 1866 in Millville, Ohio, he was the son of a Union doctor. The doctor had been wounded at the Battle of Kennesaw Mountain in Georgia and vowed that he would name his next son after the place. The son's life reeked of Algerism. In 1905, at age 38, he was appointed United States district judge for northern Illinois. He first came to national prominence in a 1907 case involving Standard Oil. It was the high point of trust-busting, and Landis, not one to shy away from publicity, fined the company more than $29 million and forced John D.

Rockefeller to come into the courtroom and testify. This decision, like so many in his career, brought publicity—and reversal in a higher court. The reversal, naturally, only served to prove to the judge's proponents that cracker-barrel, horse-sense wisdom was superior to the wisdom of the high courts, which, according to them, were dominated by corruption and/or obscure legalism.

During World War I Landis had had his opportunity to prove that he was an American of an extraordinarily high order. True to the spirit of the times (and with one eye on the grandstand), he hit hard at everything pro-German or having a pro-German scent. Landis even cherished the hope that after the war he might be able to try the Kaiser in his own court. The Kaiser would be charged with the murder of a Chicago resident killed on the Lusitania. Much to his chagrin, Landis was informed by Secretary of State Robert Lansing that under existing treaties the extradition of the Kaiser was not possible.

In another celebrated case, Landis convicted Victor Berger, the Milwaukee socialist congressman, and six other socialists for obstructing the war effort. The biggest case of all came in 1918 when the leader of the International Workers of the World, "Big Bill" Haywood, and 103 other Wobblies appeared before the patriotic judge. They were also convicted of obstruction of the war effort. Once the trial was over Landis is reputed to have referred to the IWW as scum, filth, and slimy rats.

After the war, Landis developed the habit of inquiring into the war record of lawyers who practiced in his court. Those who had been in service were said to get a break over the slackers. The reputation of Kennesaw Mountain Landis was further enhanced when his name appeared on the mailing list for the May Day bombs of 1919. For those who saw things in black and white, here was a true American; he busted trusts; he hated Huns and Bolsheviks; he wanted to put the Kaiser up against the wall; he administered commonsense justice and ignored the convoluted theories of the eastern law professors. If some facet of the American way was in danger, what better man than this to have guarding the door and setting things right? Tristram Coffin has put it another way in The Old Ball Game:

...In the first half of the century America as a whole was closer to its nineteenth-century, rural ways and so more universally willing to accept the necessity of standing at "moral attention." It was not loath to embrace a man who would order the world to do so, especially in the face of "radical" pressures and minority appeasement on the one side, "robber baron" greed on the other. With his country accent, his snow-white hair, string ties, and penchant for cursing, Kennesaw Mountain Landis was a Latter Day Roy Bean. Educated in a somewhat informal manner; short-fused, but a soft touch; a hater of minority groups, socialists, and communists; a VFW-type patriot, he appealed to the conservative, the traditional, the old fashioned, who found him a square bastion against the rioters, city slickers, and pay-off boys of megalopolitan life. And he did take the American law into his own hands, distributing his version of justice in the most ancient of ways.

Landis had other "qualifications" that made him a logical choice for baseball's messiah. He was a fan, frequenting the first-base box seats at Comiskey Park in Chicago. In 1915 he had arbitrated a settlement of the suit involving the Federal League and the other major leagues. At the time of his appointment, November 12, 1920, organized baseball was appealing a $240,000 fine for antitrust violations, and litigation was likely in the Black Sox case. To have a federal judge leading organized baseball at such a time could be fortuitous.

And why did he accept? Undoubtedly, as in all important decisions there must have been many reasons. The explanation given to the public is of greatest interest. Landis explained it this way to Clark Griffith, president and owner of the Washington Nationals (as reprinted in "Judge Landis," *Literary Digest*):

"Grif," he said, "I'm going to tell you just why I took this job. See those kids down there on the street? See that airplane propeller on the wall? Well, that explains my acceptance.

"You see that propeller was on the plane in which my son Maj. Reed Landis, flew while overseas. Reed and I went to one of the world series games in Brooklyn. Outside the gate was a bunch of little kids playing around. Reed turned to me and said: 'Dad, wouldn't it be awful to take baseball away from them?' Well, while you gentlemen were talking to me, I looked up at this propeller and I thought of Reed. Then I thought of his remark in Brooklyn.

"Grif, we've got to keep baseball on a high standard for the sake of the youngsters—that's why I took the job, because I want to help."

Truly a great human being, this white-haired man. The morals and ethics of the youth of America, and therefore America itself, were at stake. There were standards to be maintained, and the judge wanted to help. The *St. Louis Globe-Democrat* was impressed. If the judge could keep baseball on a high ethical plane, he would be doing more for the boys of America than he could ever do on the federal bench, because baseball was crucial to the formation of the moral and sport ethics of the youth of America. This was also important to the country because "the standard of integrity of the boy becomes also his standard as a citizen" (*Literary Digest*). Baseball served as a rallying point for the growth of patriotic sentiment in the youth of America.

Baseball entered the Twenties preparing to defend standards, ethics, morals, patriotism, and the remaining eternal verities under the leadership of a white-haired judge who loved kids. The order in the universe might have become a bit shaky, but, together, the National Game and Kennesaw Mountain Landis would restore and maintain that order. The Scopes "Monkey Trial" at Dayton, Tennessee, had been no aberration. While some people were heading into revolt, and others were happy with the changes, still others were hunkering down, ready to defend the faith.

2

Democracy and Character

> "That's okay, Benny, we got nothing against
> Americans. They invented baseball, didn't
> they?"

CLAIMS and counterclaims have been made for various sports that
one or another is the National Game of the United States. Nonetheless, the consensus is that baseball was the National Pastime during
the years between the two world wars. These years were the Golden
Age of Baseball. Sportswriters, baseball executives, players, and
outside observers, aware of this, sought both to exploit and to
analyze it. An examination of this theme produces a montage of
images, ideals, standards, and values which collectively reveals a
character portrait of what one large group of people—
Americans—thought they were all about.

For the American intellectual community the prewar and postwar
turmoil raised serious questions about the democratic ideal. Some
people fled the country convinced that democracy had failed.
Others, like Walter Lippmann, set out to reexamine democratic
politics and restructure them to suit the new urban-industrial world.
But many believed democracy was the viable ideal at the heart of the
American experience. This was true of the baseball world where
democracy joined sport in mutual reinforcement.

It is not surprising that in the fight for democracy, baseball was thought to have played an important role. Benjamin DeCasseres wrote in the *New York Times* that baseball was the sport of democracies and that the world ought to be made safe for baseball. As long as baseball was popular with the people, the Kaisers and the Trotskys would strike out. General Foch said he won the war by smoking his pipe. The English claimed they won it because of their love of cricket. But DeCasseres said that the country that really won the war was the country that had produced Christy Mathewson, Ty Cobb, and Babe Ruth.

On July 4, 1918, the king and queen of England and other British notables had the great pleasure of witnessing a baseball game in London between teams of players representing the United States Army and Navy. This was, of course, entirely new to them. Members of the aristocracy were particularly puzzled by the practice of protesting a decision of the umpire. After all, everyone knew that the decision of an umpire was final. A British colonel remarked that he was now convinced the Hun couldn't possibly win the war, reasoning that if the Yanks weren't bothered by the overwhelming dignity and autocratic authority of the umpire, they certainly would have no trouble with the Germans.

Peace or war, baseball was the National Pastime of America, the democratic game. It was a game of the people, played by and for them. The materials were inexpensive, and it could be played in sandlot, pasture, or street. It was the game that most nearly typified American institutions and teachings. Baseball was within the reach of all men, satisfying to both spectator and player. *Baseball Magazine* editorialized: "Thomas Jefferson when he wrote the Declaration of Independence made proper provision for baseball when he declared that 'all men are, and of right ought to be, free and equal.' That's what they are at the ball game, banker and bricklayer, lawyer and common laborer."

Writing in *Sporting Life* under the improbable pseudonym of Jim Nasium, Edgar Wolfe examined this relationship very closely. He found baseball to be a democratic game, not restricted to the poor or to blue-collar workers. The middle class was the core of fan support. He estimated that 80 percent of the fans were business officials, office employees, and men of leisure. Only about 20 percent came from the laboring classes. By attracting this growing class of people, while still holding on to the skilled and unskilled workers, baseball served to unite labor and capital in a common interest. By attracting new fans from the offices of big business into the "Benevolent Order of Baseball Bugs," baseball made these people more democratic and therefore better citizens. Interest in baseball introduced a new code of sportsmanship into the business community, making businessmen more appreciative of the "good loser." The rise of the democratic game of baseball modified the American dream. Baseball had created a new democracy of sport in which boys could still grow up to be president of the United States; but if they missed in politics, then maybe they could become the next Babe Ruth.

Every opportunity was seized to demonstrate that baseball and democracy were inseparable. Proof of baseball's democracy was found at the World Series, where 20,000 "plain folk" sat in the bleachers for the low price of $1.10. Baseball had remained within the financial reach of the common man. In 1931 one observer in the *New York Herald Tribune* was struck by the freedom of expression found at baseball games. The fan demanded not only the right to like or dislike his sports entertainment but also the right to express those likes and dislikes with full candor.

As a matter of fact, baseball in the early and mid-Twenties even lacked social prestige because it was *too* democratic: the laborer's son had just as much chance to succeed as the millionaire's son. Sportswriter W. O. McGeehan described another democratic trait: to create idols, place them on pedestals, and watch in joy as they fell from the heights. Baseball fans had a proclivity for this particular aspect of the sport. *Fortune* magazine agreed and pointed out that grandstand heroes died like flies. The fans showered "all their affection on the man of the moment, all their contempt on the man of a moment ago."

The rise of college and professional football in the 1920s led some to conclude that football was replacing baseball as the National Game. To baseball men the suggestion was shocking and provoked indignation. In 1925 *The Sporting News* asserted that football's popularity was only a temporary phenomenon dependent on the popularity of Red Grange. Once Red departed, football would pass back into minor importance. Baseball did not depend on just one man, even a Babe Ruth. Baseball had been the obsession of millions before Ruth and would continue to be long after Ruth departed. It had even been able to survive the scandals of cheating. "Why? Because it is the truly national sport, as much a part of American thought and life as the idea of democracy itself."

Another problem for football was its weak roots. About 50 percent of the attendance at football games was based solely on the tradition of the schools involved. Only about one person in twenty really understood football. But baseball, "the most democratic game in the United States," was known and understood by everyone, all across the country, from the Maine lumberman to the Arizona cowboy. It extended into every hamlet and crossroads, spilling across the borders into Canada, Mexico, and Cuba. Football was attacked for its hypocrisy: it claimed to be amateur while, in fact, college players were being paid by wealthy alumni. The game was excessively rough. Baseball had none of these faults. It was "frankly and cleanly professional," with little or no risk of serious injury. Emphasizing this sharp contrast, *Baseball Magazine* had no doubt which sport was preferred by the American public.

Baseball was democratic because it was the game of the people, but there was some difference of opinion as to precisely which people. It was often hailed as the game of the common man. In 1919 the federal government dropped the war tax on football tickets but not on baseball tickets, eliciting charges of class discrimination. Baseball drew its support from the masses while football drew its support from the rich. The ticket tax was a heavy strain on the baseball fan, especially the man who worked nights and attended three or four games each week. "The fur-coated millionaire who goes to Yale Bowl in his Rolls-Royce and a thermos bottle of hot scotch within reach doesn't have to pay a ten percent tax, but some poor boob who washes dishes in an all-night restaurant has to come across with the tax just the same. Where's the consistency?"

The issue of class discrimination came up again in 1926 with the move in some colleges to drop baseball from their athletic programs because baseball was a professional sport. This struck one anonymous writer in *The Sporting News* as elitism:

> Why is it any more of a crime to capitalize one's athletic ability than it is to capitalize talent for music, for acting, for anything else? The "amateur" idea in sport has its underpinnings in the old tradition that it was ignoble to do anything that brought in an honest dollar. The "gentleman" of the old days would not soil his hands in trade, nor even embark in a profession; he could only live in idleness on money inherited or extracted without effort from his serfs.
>
> And play! Why it was "bolshevism" to suggest that the poor man should be given time to play! And a lot of that idea still prevails among those in our "higher strata of society," so it seems. Recreation is not for the poor man; he ought to be bending his back at labor for the "gentle folks'" profit; play is the right and privilege of "nobility" only.
>
> Is that Americanism?

Clearly it is not. America is a free country where the old notions of recreation have been abandoned, where the workers have leisure time for play. The writer goes on to say:

> And therein lies the salvation of baseball as the instinctive game of the American who could play for play sake, not because it is the "proper thing," as golf or polo or even tennis may be....
>
> They can restrict baseball in the public parks, they can discontinue it as a college game, and they can knock it because it tends to professionalism in athletics, but praise God, as long as America is made up in its youth of lads who are not snobs, who are not aristocrats, who work with their hands, and who can demand their rights to time off for play, then baseball will always be the thing they will turn to as instinctively as a babe turns to its mother's breast.

If baseball had been the sport of the lower classes at first, by the early 1930s the baseball establishment no longer viewed it that way. In 1933 the National League made a movie to stimulate interest among young people. National League president John Heydler

wanted the role of the typical American boy filled by someone from a modest middle-class family, whose father had an industrial background. Johnny Vander Meer, later a star pitcher for the Cincinnati Reds, portrayed that typical American boy. However, working-class identification with baseball remained strong, and as late as 1939 that sensitivity could still be provoked. That year's World Series was carried on radio by the Mutual Network, the highest bidder for broadcast rights, but unfortunately Mutual did not reach all corners of the country as did the CBS and NBC networks. A rash of letters to The Sporting News and editorial comments attacked the handling of the broadcast. Some people claimed that baseball had discriminated against the South; some said the Midwest; some the mountain states. Others saw it as an attack on rural America in general. The most common complaint was that the workingman of America had been sold down the river to the highest bidder. The "poor sucker," who scrimped all week to travel to regular season games, who every year filled the coffers of major-league baseball, got an inadequate radio hook-up for his fidelity. The working man was outraged and would find his revenge, it was said, by staying away from the big-league parks the next year.

Also in 1939, a fan wrote to The Sporting News urging that All-Star balloting be returned to the people. The issue involved democracy. In discussing the democratic nature of the game, this fan claimed that the philosophy of equality was tangibly expressed in the stands, where baseball, as the great leveler, brought together the rich and the poor in a common desire. Equality also permeated the very structure of the game, for no rule restricted players to defense only. Even the pitcher had an equal opportunity to step up to the plate and drive in the winning run.

Opportunity was another word frequently used in discussions of baseball. For many Americans opportunity was implicit in democracy; for some it was the essence of democracy. Associated closely with opportunity was the notion of the self-made man. Both concepts had been facets of the popular culture of the nineteenth century. Both would come under fire in the new urban culture of the twentieth century, but they would not be abandoned. Opportunity and the myth of the self-made man would remain articles of faith for many, forming an important element of the baseball literature of the interwar period.

Opportunity was one of the favorite points of discussion in the baseball press. For John B. Sheridan of *The Sporting News,* the "absolute foundation" of baseball was "Merit." Such things as birth, money, social standing, and political influence were irrelevant in baseball. Thus, baseball shared the "very foundation of American character and of Americanism." It didn't matter who a person knew; he had to have the talent in order to make the team. "Theodore Roosevelt could have anything he wanted in America, save that one of his sons should be a star on a major league baseball team." Whether or not a man succeeded in the majors depended on how hard he worked to improve himself in all facets of the game. This is what made baseball the greatest business and the greatest game in America. Success depended on the individual; opportunity was already there. "If he has the goods no man can hurt him. If he has not no man can help him." Only the reserve clause and an inadequate draft system were acknowledged to inhibit opportunity.

No one questioned the fact of opportunity. George Walberg, young pitcher for the Philadelphia Athletics, exemplified the possibilities for a young man in baseball. In 1921 Walberg had been working the wheat fields of Minnesota. After the harvest he went west to Seattle, where he began to pitch with a semipro team. He had no idea of becoming a big-league pitcher. He did so well in Seattle that in 1922 he was given a tryout with Portland of the Pacific Coast League. Although Walberg's record at Portland was not too impressive, John McGraw, manager of the New York Giants, felt he had possibilities, so McGraw purchased Walberg's contract. After a short stint in New York Walberg was sent back to Portland. Then the A's manager, Connie Mack, picked him up, and by 1923 Walberg was doing some fine work for the A's. Although not yet a star, Walberg had a great future in major-league baseball, according to Mack. "Walberg's case is an illustration of the possibilities in baseball for young fellows who like the game and have an open mind to pick up its fine points."

When opportunity knocked not everyone answered. College boys often failed to take advantage of the opportunities afforded them in major-league baseball. Why? To some sportswriters, it seemed that many of these boys came from wealthy families and felt no need to work hard for a living. They had been pampered and had developed a "temperament the equal of that sported by any little beauty of the musical comedies." When such college boys arrived in the big leagues they discovered they were not as good as they thought. Their egos were crushed. They could not take the razzing of the other players and the harsh methods of the manager. Some quit because they could not face the possibility of being sent to the minor leagues for development of their skills. Many a college player was too concerned with bonus money and high salaries and not concerned enough with the game itself. The exception was the college man who had had to work his way through school. He knew what it meant to earn a dollar. Baseball was no game for softies; there was no substitute for hard work and hard knocks.

Grantland Rice, writing for the North American Newspaper Alliance in 1934, asserted that opportunity had introduced a romantic element into baseball. For instance, there was the boy from the orphanage whose name was carried around the world by baseball. There were "the unknown kids from the farms, the mills and the mines whose names today are in the headlines and whose appearance on the field brings a noisy welcome from 20,000, 40,000 or 50,000 supporters." It was a great game offering unlimited opportunity to the youth of America.

The relationship between baseball and the notions of democracy and opportunity did not die out. By 1940 Dizzy Dean had passed into the Texas League with a sore arm, and Rogers Hornsby was a manager in the same league. Both men were chosen for the Texas League All-Star team in 1940. *The Sporting News* noted that despite the "veneer of cynicism" which had accompanied the changes in society, people could still be enthusiastic about heroes and elevate them to a pedestal. This was the essence of democracy: "No matter how humble a beginning, every youth of the land has a chance to make good and win fame on his own merits, and in no endeavor is there a bigger opportunity than in professional baseball." Dean and

Hornsby had come up from obscurity to become household names in Texas. Now the youth of Texas, Louisiana, and Oklahoma could look to these two men for inspiration. "The path today remains as wide open as it did when the Rajah and Dizzy set forth as young recruits to make their ways in the world. If that doesn't represent true democracy, then there's something wrong with the way things add up." The following year Commissioner Landis proudly pointed out that players in the majors came from all parts of the nation, from all classes, and from nearly every occupation.

"Horatio Algerism" could be found in the grandstand, too. The baseball fan was a true sportsman and disliked the idea of a dynasty; he wanted to see a new champion every year. Boston fans were delighted with the idea that the Cardinals, who had not won a pennant in modern times, might breeze to the championship in 1926. During the season, reported The Sporting News, there were many Boston fans who rooted for the St. Louis Cardinals and were disappointed if the Boston Braves won a game. It sounded "so much like some of the books the men in the bleachers and the grandstands used to read when they were kids, of how the poor little bootblack became the president of the trans-continental railroad."

Team ownership also provided excellent examples of "opportunity," and owners' lives were used to illustrate Algerism. One favorite was the story of Sam Breadon, who started with only a few dollars in his pocket, parlayed them into a successful automobile franchise, and went on to purchase the St. Louis Cardinals. William Kenny, a successful contractor, purchased 2,500 shares of stock in the New York Giants for $750,000. As a boy he had loved baseball, "but he was too poor to get full measure of pleasure out of the game." It had been a rare occasion when Kenny could get together enough money to go to old Brush Park to see the Giants play. Yet he went on to become one of the owners of that same Giant team and was written up in glorious terms in The Sporting News.

The rise of L. Charles Ruch to the presidency of the Philadelphia Phillies offered yet another example of Algerism. At ten he had become a "martyr of indigence, poverty and the fatherless—a bound boy." He worked on a farm for eleven years, receiving only board and clothing. At twenty-one he was free and began doing odd jobs, farming, and wood cutting. After six months he had accumulated $150, enough to go to business college. From there, it was on to bookkeeping and then to advertising, in which he made his fortune. Here it was, another typical American success story of romance and adventure: "Romance that stirred every American youth as he thought of the Lincoln who read by the light of the pine knots in that Kentucky log cabin. Adventure that bore no spear, but wore the armor of a thirst for knowledge...." To some people this must have made strange reading in 1931.

In the land of opportunity and equality, success was possible for all men. Yet it was a competitive order in which these men functioned, and not all would succeed. There were winners and losers in industry, in business, in life—and in baseball. In the latter part of the nineteenth century Herbert Spencer, William Graham Sumner, and other Social Darwinists had explained this to Americans in "scientific" terms. Their views had been popularized in the press and from the pulpit. Social Darwinism had given rugged individualism and the free competitive order the scientific stamp of approval, which helped to complete the apotheosis of these American frontier values. Baseball literature in the interwar period reflected the continued American commitment to these values. Individualism, competition, and associated values were portrayed as the concomitants of success and American ideals.

In baseball, as in so many sports, the competitive factor is self-evident: one team tries to beat another. And in professional sport there could be no good losers. Giants manager John McGraw, held up as an example of a hard loser, epitomized the spirit of major-league baseball. The dominant idea in the National Pastime was to win at any cost.

There was competition in baseball at another level, too. Only a limited number of positions were available to players in the major leagues. T. A. Neilson, writing in the *Windberg* (Pa.) *Era*, found this level of competition was an important reason why baseball was the National Game. Only the players of exceptional ability could remain on top in the major leagues. Neilson saw this as the theory of survival of the fittest in operation. The average young man, striving at all times to give his best in the face of intense competition, helped to maintain the game's appeal and high standard of efficiency.

The fostering of individualism can be seen in many aspects of the game, for the nature of the game itself was an expression of the individualistic spirit. In comparing baseball and football, the editors of The Nation commented: "In baseball all is in the open, every player is obviously an individual, every play stands sharply by itself." But football was a corporate effort, undertaken by a machinelike team of eleven players. The difference was also reflected in the nature and function of the spectators. The football fan was similar to the player on the field. He "sways with the rhythm of the organized cheering"; he was concerned more with the "coherence and solidarity" of the whole than the brilliance of an individual play. This required a "community of sentiment" among football fans which was notably lacking among the "heterogeneous crowds" at major-league baseball games.

In 1927 Eddie Collins, second baseman of the Philadelphia A's, affirmed this view. Collins, who had been a star in both football and baseball, felt that baseball offered many more possibilities for the individual. The success of a football player depended on the play of all his teammates. Those few football stars who achieved fame did so only partly on the basis of their individual brilliance. On the other hand, a star like Ty Cobb would have been outstanding on any baseball club; and Walter Johnson was a consistent winner with a team that was a hopeless tail-ender.

Although individualism was important, there was also a kind of tension between individualism and team play. Opinion was divided as to which was more important in baseball. When Rogers Hornsby replaced Branch Rickey as manager of the St. Louis Cardinals in 1925, the Cardinals responded to the change by beginning to play winning baseball. The Sporting News attributed the shift in Cardinal fortunes to the methods of the new manager, who had "inaugurated a policy of direct application," letting his men "play the games themselves." In contrast Rickey had kept tight control over the actions of his players, not allowing them to think for themselves. In this instance the allowance for individual initiative seemed to pay off.

If success were to be achieved in the individualistic, competitive world of baseball, it would be due to the virtues of the "work ethic"—initiative, hard work, relentless effort, and hustle. These were the marks of a successful player and a successful team. According to H. G. Salsinger, a Detroit sportswriter, the average baseball fan could tolerate a game loss because of an error. However, he would never forgive the ball player who was not giving his best or who gave the appearance of indifference. Lack of effort was "the one unforgiveable sin, the one crime beyond atonement."

The fans appreciated hustle, as was shown by a poem in *The Sporting News*, written by an anonymous St. Louis fan on the death of William "Pickles" Dillhoefer in 1922. Dilly had been a reserve catcher for the Cardinals from 1919 to 1921. He had never hit a home run during his years in the majors, and his lifetime batting average was only .233—not the statistics one would expect of a great hero among the fans. But at least one fan thought otherwise:

> You played each ball game
> With no thought of fame,
> But whole-hearted you played to win;
> And it's a safe bet
> That no fan will forget
> The lad who believed losing a sin.

> Some may want better maskmen
> But, boy, I can ask them
> To show me your peer in one thing;
> Oh, I love one who hustles
> Who laughs as he bustles
> And who pep to all teammates can bring.

> If my own game of life
> Is troubled with strife
> May I play on with your courage and smile;
> Takes a real man to shout,
> "There are only two out,"
> With your spirit I'll make living worth while.

Professional baseball encouraged and engendered many other American characteristics: "instant and automatic action, self-dependence, never-give-up-the-ship, and the passion for victory for victory's sake...." The dominant trait among these was the "passion for winning for mere winning's sake," considered a valuable if not an admirable trait. It also set the American apart from his British cousin. American sportswriters reported the war in glowing, sometimes chauvinistic, terms. "Americans come back with what they go after." It took the Americans only two weeks in the Argonne to take care of the Germans. The British had been trying for four years. The British had failed because "not having had the passion for winning driven into them by professional baseball they muffed the ball when it was hit into their hands."

It is more than coincidence that the baseball saying "The game is never over till the last man is out" has become part of the vernacular. It has joined a long list of copybook maxims dealing with the subject of not quitting. In baseball this comeback quality was greatly admired. For instance, in the 1930 World Series the Philadelphia Athletics won the first two games. The Cardinals came back to win the next two and attracted the attention and admiration of fans throughout the nation. In 1934 Mickey Cochrane, Detroit Tiger catcher and manager, played the World Series with three spike wounds in his legs, fighting back against the Cardinals (according to *The Detroit News*) "with every ounce of strength at his command.... Almost nobody can be against a guy who fights to the last ditch...." In 1940 Babe Ruth made the same point in a *Rotarian* article called "Bat It Out": a good player never quit until he was called out. He ran for first base as if he were in the one-hundred-yard dash, even if he was a sure out. If Henry Ford had not kept going in the face of ridicule, Ruth said, he would never have produced the automobile. "He kept plugging when everybody said his chances of making first base were nil. You can't beat the person who never gives up."

Success was not without its dangers. With success came money, too much of which could lead to soft living. This was a special danger in New York, where success could be frequent and rapid, and the attractions of Gotham were many. When John McGraw's Giants tended to decline before their time, one writer blamed it on the New York atmosphere. There was no place for softness in baseball. A man must show courage, toughness, and the fighting spirit. He must be a man.

There was a fine line between this fighting spirit and unacceptable behavior, however, a line that was often blurred beyond distinction. After a riot by fans in Detroit in 1924, Harry B. Smith of the *San Francisco Chronicle* expressed the opinion that it might be good if some of this rowdy spirit were transferred to the players: "Baseball can't altogether be a namby-pamby sport. It couldn't be and still have secured a strong grip on the populace as is the case." In 1933 president John Heydler issued a statement calling on players in his National League to show more aggressiveness and to avoid fraternizing with opposition players. The *Sporting News* endorsed Heydler's position, pointing out that each baseball game represented a battle similar to that which each fan fought for the necessities and luxuries of life. As the season got under way it became apparent that Heydler was being taken seriously by the players: three players were suspended for fighting and provoking a riot in Washington. Charlie Grimm of the Cubs challenged the Cardinals' Rogers Hornsby to meet him in a dark alley to settle their differences. Dick Bartell of the Phillies was charged with intentionally spiking Dodger Joe Judge. Those who felt baseball had become too "sissified" were delighted. While disclaiming any desire for blood or broken bones, they predicted that the new spirit would pack the stadiums. Yes, baseball was a game for men: "No sissies or pacifists where baseball is played," wrote Paul W. Eaton in his 1929 preseason column.

During the 1934 World Series courage and the fighting spirit seemed to abound. Mickey Cochrane took his Detroit Tigers, only fifth-place finishers the previous season, to win the American League pennant. Cochrane's fighting spirit was an inspiration to his team. Tiger president Frank Navin, in a daring gamble, had paid $100,000 for Cochrane that same year and named him player-manager, although Cochrane had no previous managerial experience. Navin had had to take out a loan to complete the deal for Cochrane. As for the Cardinals, they were led by the Fordham Flash, Frankie Frisch, in his first full year as manager for St. Louis. Past the peak of his playing career, uncertain if he could play every day, Frisch had brought in the pennant in one of the wildest finishes ever recorded in the National League. It seemed that the fates had conspired to bring together two teams of "superb courage" under two "courageous and inspirational leaders." The World Series proved no disappointment. The Cardinals, even though exhausted from the torrid pennant race, won the series in seven games. *The Sporting News* cheered, "It was a great triumph of spirit over body, and brought to a fitting climax as game a fight as baseball has ever witnessed...."

Baseball in the 1930s was no game for the weak and the soft of America. The idea that a player's berth was one of the world's great sinecures was myth. True, the hours were short and the pay good. It was also true that the major leaguer traveled on the best trains and stayed in the best hotels, but when he got out on the diamond with line drives, fast pitches, and foul tips all around, the player needed bravery, an adventurous spirit, and mental and physical courage. There could be injuries, but baseball was still one of the safest sports. Besides, courage and stamina were good qualities to acquire, and in 1939 *The Sporting News* felt it was "better to carry a few scars from the diamond than wounds from battle fields...."

As the National Pastime, baseball dedicated itself to the young men of America, and the connections between baseball and youth were of utmost importance. In 1921 an all-star game was played in Cleveland to raise money for baseball equipment for the poor. Those who played in the game were termed all-stars of the highest order by the sportswriters. "We can envision, too, their names in the Book said to be kept Up Above, with a star for each name and the notation: 'Entered for blessing by Him who said—"Suffer little children to come unto me.""

These religious overtones were not unusual. The baseball establishment accepted the relationship between the American boy and baseball as a kind of sacred trust. Judge Landis, for example, often said in his public speeches: "Nearly every boy builds a shrine to some baseball hero, and before that shrine a candle always burns." A few sportswriters found some problems with this. One suggested that the writers should exercise great care in the business of "grinding out and manufacturing heroes for the small boys of America." These heroes might have feet of clay. But it was also understood that the people wanted heroes, and the average reader of the sports pages was "as sentimental as a seminary girl." A sportswriter could not tell his readers that a certain player did not use his first earnings to buy a house for his mother or that he had lost the money playing craps. Nor could he report that the home team was primarily interested in the pennant because they were already calculating their shares of the World Series receipts. To do so would have defiled the myth and shattered the sacred trust between the boy and his game. Even the standard player's contract (as quoted in an *American Mercury* article by Arthur Mann) included a short tribute to the connection between baseball and the American boy: "If any special responsibility rests upon the ball player it is a responsibility to young America. The boy in the bleachers is in school, even if he doesn't realize it. The heroes of the diamond are his teachers. By them his ideals of sport are powerfully affected. But the influence of the powerful player goes much further than this. The standards which the boy accepts on the bleachers he will carry into life. As the national game is played, so the life of the nation will be lived. Nothing is good enough for baseball that is not good enough for America."

In 1928 a class of schoolboys was asked to write compositions stating their aims in life. One boy said that he wanted to learn to hit home runs like Babe Ruth. This was proof enough for the sportswriters that baseball was not losing its grip on the youth of America. It also indicated that no matter what the boy eventually did in life, "no one can affirm that he did not understand his United States."

The idea of the link was valuable to both the boy and America. Babe Ruth felt that when boys played baseball they sensed that they were learning to play the game of life. Branch Rickey pointed out (in the *Christian Science Monitor Weekly Magazine Section*) that all educational institutions encouraged athletics, knowing it was necessary to keep the boys of America busy. Baseball more than any other sport kept them busy at play. Of course, not all these boys would make it to the major leagues. But to Rickey that was not the point. "Whether they reap the harvest of big-league salaries or merely win their high school letters young America is stronger for having taken an active part in the national pastime."

How did baseball make the youth of America stronger? It was first of all a "character builder," providing a code of conduct as a guide not only to youth but to all Americans. "Character building" was a nebulous term. In 1924 Francis Richter, writing in *The Sporting News*, commented on the infamous Leopold and Loeb case, in which two college students had murdered a young boy. Had Leopold and Loeb been more interested in "clean and manly sport," such a crime would not have been committed, Richter said. Baseball and other sports tended to "correct or alleviate physical defects and mental aberrations in boys and young men until the danger period is past...." Similar evidence was offered by the Catholic chaplain of the Southern Illinois Penitentiary, who wrote *The Sporting News* that each week the prisoners eagerly waited for that paper and that it had a good effect on the inmates. "The wholesome thoughts and true facts of the baseball world, carried in your paper, tend to uplift the minds of our unfortunates here...."

It wasn't just criminals who could experience improved character from contact with baseball. In 1935 the Cardinals held a tryout camp at Bloomington, Illinois. One of the boys who came wrote *The Sporting News* that the 225 young players at the camp were a credit to the "character, health, and morals the king of sports builds in young men." Judge Landis in 1940 found it most remarkable that of those men who had played baseball well, very few had gone to jail or turned out to be crooks.

In the code of conduct for baseball, honesty stood at the top. The Black Sox scandal had been one important violation of that honesty. Near the end of the grand jury proceedings in that affair, a group of Boy Scouts appeared in court. They said that because the Boy Scouts everywhere stood for clean sports and good sportsmanship, and because baseball was the "dearest and nearest sport to the heart of the American boy," they wished to thank Judge McDonald for his efforts to clean up baseball. Judge McDonald's voice shook as he thanked the boys and promised to continue to do his best. In its report to the judge, the grand jury echoed the sentiments of the Boy Scouts, noting that baseball was more than the National Game, it was a national institution playing an important part in the development of American youth. "The national game promotes respect to proper authority, self-confidence, fairmindedness, quick judgment and self-control." In this game which was an index of the national character, "the American principle of merit and fair play must prevail, and it is all important that the game be clean, from the humble player to the highest dignitary."

A vigilant watch was always kept over the integrity of the game. In 1923, when a report circulated that New York's baseball stadiums were to be used to stage boxing matches, baseball's defenders immediately went to the barricades: "Professional baseball at its worst never reached the low level of professional pugilism at its best...." The problem with boxing was that it was too commercialized and had underworld connections. Because boxing matches were often alleged to be fixed, many supporters felt baseball should have no association with it. Apparently the president of the American League agreed, for boxing was banned from all American League parks. Paul Eaton, Washington correspondent of *The Sporting News*, applauded the action as consistent with the maintenance of baseball's integrity and dignity.

The concern over the honesty of the game nearly became an obsession during the Twenties, in part due to a residue of caution from the Black Sox scandal. But it was also due to further problems with gamblers, gambling pools, and less spectacular scandals, which continued to plague baseball during much of the decade. The concern would fade in the Thirties, but it did not entirely disappear even then.

Another character trait fostered by baseball was good sportsmanship. Although this quality was frequently discussed, it was only vaguely defined. It seems to have something to do with honesty and playing fair, but it was also associated with the notion that love of the game superseded all other considerations for both the players and the owners. Although winning was important, at times it might seem that winning was the only thing. In 1920 it was hinted that there was too much emphasis placed on winning, leading to the use of any means possible to gain that objective. Managers blamed the fans for this development; but it was also suggested that the fans had learned this attitude from the players. *The Sporting News*, disturbed by this development, asked, "When will we come to realize that winning

Reprinted, courtesy of the *Chicago Tribune*

the game is not the greatest achievement in baseball, but that a fair and square game, decided on its merits, is the thing?"

One example of a violation of fair play occurred in 1928. The Boston Braves had constructed new bleachers in left and center fields as a home run depository for the newly acquired Rogers Hornsby. These stands were cheaply constructed and unsuitable for the fans, and Jack Ryder of the *Cincinnati Enquirer* called them "one of the cheapest things ever done in the National League...." It was an "unsportsmanlike act" which had nearly ruined one of the best playing fields in the country, and threatened to make baseball a joke in Boston. After this outcry the Braves repented and announced they would move the bleachers back.

In 1919 one of the minor leagues experimented with a profit-sharing plan for their players, but it did not seem to affect their performance. This was no surprise to those who knew baseball. The player was in love with the game, the kind of artistic genius who loved his work for its own sake. Nothing else could prompt him to give his best. Profit-sharing might succeed as a work incentive in other fields, but it neither worked nor was needed in baseball.

In the press much of the talk about sportsmanship focused on the owners. The owner-sportsman image was an ideal in baseball that was often achieved, although many fans thought that the owners were in baseball only for the money. This was true in a few cases, but those men did not last long in baseball. A larger number of owners had invested small fortunes in their teams, often to lose in the race for the pennant. One such owner-sportsman was Charles Ebbets of the Brooklyn Dodgers. On his death in 1925 it was said that his greatest qualities were his intense loyalty to his league and his love of the game.

Probably the most successful owner was Col. Jacob Ruppert of the New York Yankees. In 1925 Joe Vila wrote that many fans were hoping to see the Yankees win another pennant in order to reward the "liberality" of Ruppert. Despite expenses exceeding $400,000 for running the Yankees in 1925, Ruppert was in baseball only for "sport and recreation." As the epitome of an owner-sportsman, Ruppert was portrayed as just a typical fan. Each year he went to Florida for spring training, mingling with the fans and enjoying their company.

"'Say, he's just like one of us,' said a Floridian who had never seen 70,000 fans gathered in Yankee Stadium." The fans never thought of Ruppert as a rich and powerful owner of a massive chain of baseball clubs.

Next in importance to honesty and sportsmanship in the building of the national character was clean living—in the tradition of Frank Merriwell and McGuffey's Reader. For most the clean-living issue was the drinking issue. In 1924 a number of managers completely banned alcoholic beverages, convinced that too many players had gone "in with their spikes high against the Volstedian shins" the previous season and had lessened their effectiveness on the field. Avoidance of excessive drinking was considered a virtue. In 1926 Ralph Davis, Pittsburgh correspondent of The Sporting News, commented on rumors that the Pittsburgh Pirates were heavy drinkers. Davis claimed that the Bucs were "as clean-living a bunch of young Americans as could be collected anywhere" and that the vast majority of them never touched liquor. At the same time, clean living was not to be confused with effeminacy or abstinence. Davis was also quick to point out that the Pirates were not a "namby-pamby lot of athletes."

To the sportswriters and the baseball hierarchy the code of conduct was of primary importance. Profanity, another issue that attracted considerable attention, was often discussed in connection with the new presence of women at ball games, for there was some fear that foul language might keep women away from the games. But no gentleman would use such language in the presence of a lady. As The Sporting News put it: "A ball player with a sister would hang his head in shame if he knew that his sister overhead some of the conversation which he allows himself." And there were plenty of sisters at the ball park. It was asserted that a ball player did not need to use profanity to prove his manhood, and it should be banned on the field and in the clubhouse.

Not only profanity but other forms of abuse and abusive language were considered bad form. In a 1927 editorial titled "Blackguards Always Are Cowards," The Sporting News examined the problem of the bench jockeys, some of whom, under instructions from their managers, were delving into the private lives of opposing pitchers.

The Sporting News recommended that such managers be banned from baseball. Vile slander had no place in the game. Although some claimed that "red blood and profanity must go hand in hand," the greatest players in the history of the game had never needed to use such language on or off the field. Something had to be done to stop these cowards or there might come a time when a man would be unable to sit near the dugout with his wife or daughter.

Personal appearance was also a concern of the player-gentleman. In 1925 American League president Ban Johnson started a cleanup campaign for the players. Although well enough dressed off the field, on the field the player too often wore "clothes that a harvest hand would take to the woods before he would show to his friends...." The issue was still alive in 1931 when *The Sporting News* called for the end of dirty uniforms: "Nothing so disgusts an amusement seeker as untidiness."

Players had a wide variety of other actions considered in bad taste. In the third game of the 1923 World Series, Casey Stengel of the Giants hit a home run. While circling the bases Casey thumbed his nose at the Yankee bench and danced his way into home plate. It was reported that some people were highly offended. Nose thumbing also occurred in 1936 when Wes Ferrell, pitcher for the Boston Red Sox, made the gesture to a group of fans sitting behind the Boston dugout. Boos followed Ferrell's every move for the remainder of the day.

Another sort of poor taste was an issue at the opening of the 1924 season at New York's Polo Grounds. Mayor John Hylan was ready to toss out the first ball when a group of chorus girls crowded around him "in a manner which must have been embarrassing to that honorable individual." Prior to this the girls had "galloped" and "pranced" around the players as they prepared for the game. The fans, who had come to see a ball game, not a chorus line, finally "began to sicken" of this display and bombarded the field with oranges and pop bottles. "It was a cheap and undignified thing to permit and surely did the game no benefit," said *The Sporting News*. Joe Vila called for a return to the dignified ceremonies of opening days past. The "exhibition of flying legs and painted faces was extremely out of place." The Victorian influence would live long in the world of baseball.

However, the fans were also capable of profanity and often used it as abuse. In 1925 Tom Rice reported from Brooklyn that Jacques Fournier, Dodger first baseman, was going to retire unless traded because a group of fans was harassing him with abusive language. The owners were called upon to do something about the "yellow-streaked spectators" and "mongrel minority" that hurled obscenities from the stands knowing that a player could do nothing about it.

On several occasions in the Twenties and Thirties baseball writers found it necessary to comment on the most serious matter of fan conduct, the pop bottle. This, they said, was the dangerous weapon "of the coward who is a unit of the coward mob"; "when in the hand of a lowbrow who would maim and injure promiscuously in a crowd," the bottle became a "dangerous missile." It could do great damage to both players and umpires. The thrower was termed a "liver-hearted sneak" and a "cringing coward." "It is a sad commentary on American sportsmanship to hear that some club owners have found it necessary to prohibit pop being sold from bottles at the parks."

By the mid-Thirties owners were being urged to replace bottles with paper containers. One writer went so far as to blame the entire problem of bottle-throwing on the owners because they had not yet removed the bottles from the parks. He excused the fans, saying they were merely exercising their traditional rights to protest the decisions of the umpire. This shift of blame might reflect a general departure from the ethos of personal responsibility as a response to the complexities of urban society. It may also have stemmed from a greater awareness of mob psychology in the age of Fascist and Nazi gatherings in Rome and Berlin.

Baseball in the Twenties and Thirties reflected the American fan's continued faith in the principles of democracy and opportunity, long a part of the American ethos. It continued to express a belief in individualism and competition. Baseball offered itself as an educator of youth in the proper modes of behavior for the American democratic gentleman. In the midst of turbulence and change it remained unabashedly committed to the older "American way." Major-league baseball was decidedly an urban phenomenon, yet it clung relentlessly to some of the rural values of the nineteenth century. More in tune with McGuffey's *Reader* than David Reisman's *Lonely Crowd*, it retained its title as America's National Pastime.

3

Community and Rural Roots

> Funny thing about both country music and
> baseball with its "village greens": they weren't
> really country, not since they got their new
> names anyway, but urban.

MAJOR-LEAGUE baseball was an urban phenomenon and became a
target for civic pride. Many urbanites were able to find a sense of
community at the ball park. It is also possible that baseball served as
a familiar point of reference to the rural Americans newly arrived in
the city. Baseball could provide these transplanted people with one
of those nebulous, emotional, connecting threads to their rural past.
Tristram Coffin, commenting on this aspect of the National Pastime
in his book, *The Old Ball Game*, felt that a large part of baseball's hold
on its fans stemmed from loyalty to the franchise, which offered
"assurance and stability" to a people caught in a rapidly changing
society. In his opinion no other professional sport "has been able to
'get to' a city the way major league baseball does during a tight
pennant race."

Arnold R. Beisser, a psychologist interested in mass spectator
sports, tends to support this view. In his *Madness in Sports* he sought
to explain the attendance records set by the Los Angeles Dodgers in
their first year in the city, despite a poor win-loss record. Beisser felt
that some of the citizens of Los Angeles needed the Dodgers, needed

something concrete around which they could rally, needed something familiar, yet unique, to provide identity. To some residents, the advent of major-league baseball gave the city more substance. For those who placed importance on baseball, the team provided a clearer picture of the place where they lived. They could now belong to a strong clan without being accused of being a cultist or a fanatic. One could be as avid as he wished over baseball, nothing being more American and less deviant. Others, who had migrated to Los Angeles and were now separated from their families, could find a new "family" in the Dodgers and their fans. Beisser also examined the case history of a resident named Benny, who used baseball as a point of continuity and focus in his life. Benny had come to Los Angeles from St. Louis, but he found himself unable to cope with his new mass environment. Los Angeles was chaos for Benny, and he felt completely lost. But once he got back into his interest in baseball, the necessary order returned to his perception of life and of Los Angeles: The stadium became the center of the city. The freeways were no longer seen as leading in all directions at once. Now they were perceived as an intricate system designed to get Benny to and from the ball games. As the Dodgers improved their play, Benny saw a parallel with his own mental improvement.

Benny's story may reveal a partial explanation of baseball's popularity in the interwar period. Uprooted from his community by economic forces he did not understand, Benny was forced to migrate into the massive confines of Los Angeles. Perhaps many of those who came into the huge cities from rural America underwent a similar experience. For them, baseball may have provided a continuity of experience, as well as a focus and identity, in the unfamiliar, impersonal urban community. As for the immigrant from abroad, baseball might offer him a focus and identity, once he understood the game, and provide a means of demonstrating publicly that he was becoming a true American.

Morris Cohen recognized this quality in baseball when, in a 1919 article for *Dial*, he characterized baseball as a religion. Cohen defined a religious experience as one in which the individual is redeemed from his petty life and finds mystic unity with a larger life. Cohen argued that this was precisely what happens to the baseball fanatic when he watches his favorite team.

In 1929, a fan wrote to The Sporting News complaining that the owners were failing in their duty to promote the game. Fans were beginning to feel that the teams were no longer representing them collectively. The Sporting News agreed and urged the owners to pay closer attention to municipal enthusiasm and local pride—"the basic ingredient of baseball." In 1936 this position was reiterated. The rivalries between the Dodgers and Giants and the Cubs and White Sox, and the 1934 World Series, were all cited as examples of the importance of civic spirit at the major-league level.

Detroit had always been considered the best baseball town in the majors. In 1934 the Tigers had won the American League pennant for the first time since 1909. The next year they won the pennant again and went on to win the World Series. After the close of the 1934 season the Detroit News had printed a front-page editorial discussing the Tiger spirit that had infected the entire city. It was hoped that this spirit could be enlisted in the larger concerns of the community. When the Tigers won the World Series in 1935, there was no containing the people of the Motor City. The Detroit News was pleased with the reaction, noting that only an enthusiastic following deserved a champion. Other cities were encouraged to emulate the Detroit spirit. Mickey Cochrane and the rest of the Tiger organization had worked hard, showing the necessary enthusiasm to attract public favor. The Sporting News claimed that such spirit would have received great community support—win, lose, or draw.

St. Louis was another enthusiastic baseball city. During the 1922 season the Chamber of Commerce and other civic groups passed resolutions encouraging the city's teams in the pennant races. It was not until 1926 that the Cardinals brought St. Louis its first pennant since 1888. The clinching game took place in New York on Friday, September 24. Thousands of St. Louis fans listened to reports of the game blaring from some fifty loudspeakers in the business section of the city. When the game ended, cheers went up from the crowds. "Scenes were enacted in the downtown streets of St. Louis such as had not been seen since Armistice Day." Factory whistles shrilled; cars and trucks blew their horns; drivers backfired their engines. Bands and parades formed spontaneously, and thousands of people surged through the streets tying up traffic. Ticker tape, confetti, and paper were thrown from the windows of office buildings. The celebration went on until well after midnight. This sort of demonstration indicated the great pride the people of St. Louis had in their team. It also provided a contrast with New York, where too many pennants were leading to boredom. And if the celebration was great after that pennant clincher, it was even greater after the World Series triumph over the dreaded Yankees. The city exploded with the game-ending out. St. Louis became one large "roaring sound." The players were hailed as the heroes of the year in the *Post-Dispatch:* "The great Caesar, home from the wars, could have commanded no greater tumult from Rome."

The community spirit of Brooklyn for the Dodgers was equally impressive. Unlike Giant and Yankee fans, these New Yorkers never got bored with too many pennants. The interwar years constituted a twenty-one-year dry spell for Brooklyn fans, with a pennant won in 1920 and not again until 1941. Despite the long drought, the fans of Brooklyn were legendary in their support for the Dodgers. Without pennants to worry about, they concentrated their attention on the defeat of the Giants. One great moment for Brooklyn fans came in 1934. During the previous off-season, Giant manager Bill Terry had been quoted as asking, "Is Brooklyn still in the league?" Dodger fans smarted from the remark all season long. Then, on the last weekend of the season, Dodger fans had their revenge. The Giants and Dodgers were playing at the Polo Grounds, and the Giants were locked in a fight for the pennant with the Cardinals. Dodger fans arrived at the Polo Grounds carrying signs reading, "Yep, Brooklyn still is in the league." They shouted, screamed, and hooted their way through the game. And when it was all over "they carried their heroes off the field in the gloaming with the Giants out of the race, out of the series, out of everything but confusion."

But a victory over the Giants was likely to provoke hysteria in Brooklyn at any time, not always in an acceptable manner. In 1938, after ten straight losses to the Giants, the Dodgers finally beat them.

Robert Joyce, a Brooklyn fan, went off to his favorite bar to celebrate, but he grew angry when the other patrons failed to show the proper enthusiasm for his beloved Dodgers. He left the bar and returned later with a pistol, seeking revenge. He killed one man and wounded another. While admitting the incident was tragic, *The Sporting News*, in an editorial titled, "Brooklyn Cowboy Runs Amuck," took most interest in the event as proof of the fact that Brooklyn was the "nation's baseball hotspot." Brooklyn baseball was more than a game and summer amusement; it was a "religion, a cause, a mania and a disease."

If this sort of commitment was given to teams in losing years, when the Dodgers raced to the pennant the reaction was limited only by the bounds of human imagination. The celebration following the pennant-clinching game of 1941 drew upwards of one million people into the streets of Brooklyn, and the parade and speeches approached riot conditions. During the pennant race that year, Dan Parker of the *New York Daily Mirror* wrote a poem, later put to music by Bud Green and Ted Berkman, that captured some of the flavor of Dodgerism. It is reprinted from Frank Graham's *The Brooklyn Dodgers*.

> Murgatroyd Darcy, a broad from Canarsie
> Went 'round with a fellow named Rodge.
> At dancing a rumba or jitterbug numbah
> You couldn't beat Rodge—'Twas his dodge.
> The pair danced together throughout the cold weather
> But when the trees blossomed again
> Miss Murgatroyd Darcy, the belle of Canarsie
> To Rodgers would sing this refrain:
>
> Leave us go root for the Dodgers, Rodgers,
> They're playing ball under the lights.
> Leave us cut out all the juke jernts, Rodgers,
> Where we've been wastin' our nights
> Dancin' the shag or the rumba is silly
> When we can be rooting for Adolf Camilli
> So leave us go root for the Dodgers, Rodgers,
> Them Dodgers is my gallant knights.

Brooklyn did not have a monopoly on fanaticism, bizarre incidents, and faithful fans. When, in 1938 in Cincinnati, a woman committed suicide, her farewell note provided for the distribution of her tickets to the All-Star game, which she had ordered but not yet received. Cincinnati like other cities had its symbolic faithful fan who became a legend around the city and the league. In the early Twenties that position was filled by a man known as "Al the Milkman." Al was a bleacherite and had his own seat, reserved for him by custom. He became well known for his practice of presenting floral pieces to Reds who hit home runs.

There was, then, a kind of community spirit that grew up around baseball as fans identified closely with their local teams. However, the size of that community of the faithful might shrink when the team was losing. In addition, an awareness grew of the economic value of a winning team in a major-league city, for it provided the city with free publicity around the league and around the nation and attracted visitors, especially at World Series time.

Even in its urban setting baseball tended to stress its rural origins and attachments. In doing so, baseball tied itself to one of the most enduring forces in American culture. Agrarianism has been powerful in American history: The small landowning farmer was the backbone of Jeffersonian politics, bearing the burden and the virtues of American democracy. The log-cabin image became a necessity for the production of presidential timber. The Transcendentalists removed themselves to Brook Farm to absorb the purity of being close to the soil. Near the end of the nineteenth century, the Populists and William Jennings Bryan could still speak of the farm as the linchpin of American culture. Frederick Jackson Turner spawned an entire generation of historians who sought the basis of American culture on the frontier and, of course, found it. Teddy Roosevelt preached the manly virtues of roughing it, and Charles Lindbergh was praised as a simple farm boy from Minnesota. And more recently there is the improbable but pervasive spectacle of Americans speeding down the interstates in their recreational vehicles, seeking to commune with nature and return to the soil—all in air-conditioned comfort.

The processes of industrialization and urbanization have challenged the validity of the agrarian myth in the twentieth century. Nonetheless, for many people these same processes have only confirmed the verity of the myth. There emerged from the challenge a series of battles between the urban-industrial and the rural-agrarian points of view. These battles took many forms: a straightforward city versus the country, old versus new, West versus East, or, as in the case of religion, modernist versus fundamentalist. In any form it provoked lively debate. The classic confrontation in the Twenties was the Scopes Trial.

As observed earlier, baseball in the Twenties and Thirties reflected a commitment to its rural origins and the tensions of the urban-rural conflict. There was no doubt that many in baseball firmly believed in agrarian principles. In a 1924 editorial titled, "Pitchers and Geography," *The Sporting News* paid tribute to the importance of the rural factor in baseball, noting that the greatest pitchers of an earlier day had come from Ohio, Indiana, and western Pennsylvania. The greatest pitchers of the Twenties were Walter Johnson from Kansas, Grover Cleveland Alexander from Nebraska, and Dazzy Vance from Iowa. Very few of the best pitchers had come from the coastal regions of the United States. Was it perhaps the atmosphere or the environment of the interior that made the arms nurtured there mightier than those of the coast? "Perhaps it is the heritage of the pioneer who swung the axe and left the steel and brawn of his arms to the sons who followed." Although poor genetics, this is superb agrarianism.

The farm origins of major-league players were a source of pride to many sportswriters. In 1925, in *The Country Gentleman*, Robert Reed reported that one-third to one-half of all players in the majors were from farms. He pointed out that Walter Johnson still owned a farm; Babe Ruth, although not born or raised on a farm, still went to his farm every chance he got. The farm boy had made a place for himself in major-league baseball. Naturally, he played the game hard and clean. In another issue of the same journal, Cullen Cain related a story about Giant pitcher Jesse Barnes, who had developed a sore arm during spring training, forcing him to return home to Kansas.

His arm had gone numb, but "the balm in the breezes that blow across Kansas, and the wholesome help of hard work on the farm, soon cured Jesse's lame arm...."

It seemed to John B. Sheridan that practically all the great players except Ruth and Frisch had come from the small towns or the country, giving as the reason "hard working forebears, fresh air, and hard work...." Bob Dundon of the *Louisville Herald* had another explanation for the large number of players from the farms: "A boy who is fortunate enough to have been born in the country, early in life learns the lessons of self-reliance, which are almost invaluable to him in after years." Ty Cobb, though, claimed that any boy from the country who had health, brains, and ambition had to succeed in the city. He simply could not afford to go back home a total loss.

When *The Sporting News* discussed the American boy and baseball, it wasn't talking about just any boy, but a particular boy from the small towns and hamlets of America. There was more town baseball being played in 1927 than at any time in the previous ten years. This was good, not only for those playing the game, but good for baseball itself, for it was the town teams that were building the foundation of organized baseball. These towns and hamlets, also referred to as "our real United States," were more important to baseball than all the big-league owners with their huge structures and high-salaried players. Presumably, this "real" United States was in contrast to some "unreal" United States, an expression of the dichotomy between the natural and the artificial in society, with the implication that the former was superior.

Although discussed less in the baseball literature of the Thirties, the primary value of the rural life was still occasionally touted. Following the 1933 season *The Sporting News* discussed the celebrations being held in towns across the country as the home folks welcomed back their baseball heroes, asserting that such demonstrations were worthwhile and helpful to baseball because they represented the "genuine admiration and esteem of people who are really worthwhile...." These demonstrations also proved that "after all, Americans still are just folks and good neighbors....Cynicism doesn't thrive well in such an atmosphere and anything that chokes [cynicism's] growth is a good thing." Cynicism, the editors felt, could never grow in rural America among such a group of people who were both "real" and "really worthwhile."

That players were eager to return home at the end of the season was one reason why baseball was called the National Game. "If country boys went to the majors, became 'citified,' and got 'Uppity' with their home folks, or failed to come home at all, baseball couldn't long be called the national sport." In addition, these welcome-home celebrations were helping to further national unity. They were a boon to neighborliness, the bulwark of the nation. These rural, small-town virtues had special significance in 1941 as the nation prepared to undergo yet another test for democracy.

Let us not think that there was only praise for the country-boy ball player. He might also be ridiculed as a rube, as in the stories by Ring Lardner. In some aspects the country boy might be at a disadvantage with his urban cousin; he was often especially susceptible to the side effects that sometimes accompanied a sudden rise to prominence. The city-bred boy already had much of the naiveté knocked out of him by urban life. In his sophistication, he knew that the world of amusement was fickle—the man up today might be down tomorrow. But the country boy was apt to feel that when he was up, he was sitting at the center of the universe. When down he was apt to be "sourly vindictive."

College boys were generally considered by the sportswriters the moral equivalent of the city boy. In 1924 resentment was expressed over the fact that college boys were getting bonuses and other special privileges in their major-league contracts, and while this may have been good bait to sign the college player, it was poor policy for baseball in general. The same things ought to be offered to the boy from the farm, the writer felt. "There is no privileged class in baseball.... It's the best old blue overalls game ever invented." In a 1933 comparison between college player and country boy, John Kieran saw the country boy as more prudent with his money. Many of the college boys with big contracts tended to live big, go to the best restaurants, drive sports cars, stay at the best hotels, and visit the race-track. The player from the country remained uncorrupt and true to the world of Poor Richard and Calvin Coolidge.

Rural resentment of the city appeared in a letter to *The Sporting News* in 1936. A reader from Wynne, Arkansas, wrote to object to an editorial on the Philadelphia Athletics training camp in which the A's were referred to as an aggregation of WPA workers, sandlotters, and throwers, gathered from various small towns and RFD routes across the nation. The fan considered this insulting and said it revealed the ignorance of the editor, who, if he knew anything about baseball, should know that most of the good players came from small towns. The fan went on: "No one, reading [the editorial], can fail to see that you consider yourself a big city guy, and are under the impression that all the good players hail from New York or St. Louis, else they would be failures...."

There were a few signs that urbanites still had a touch of rural simplicity. In September 1933, 10,000 people turned out at the train station to welcome home from a road trip the New York Giants, who were in the midst of a pennant race. Such an occasion transformed the city into a small town, showing that New York wasn't really as cosmopolitan as its boast; for it was not immune to sentiment. Underneath his veneer, the New Yorker was very much like his country cousin, "proving that, after all, Gotham is only a great big village...."

On the other hand, the city did seem to be producing a different type of man. Wee Willie Keeler, the man who said "hit 'em where they ain't," was cited as a typical New York product. Unlike farm-reared Walter Johnson or Grover Cleveland Alexander, Keeler lacked size. But what he lacked in physique, he made up in "sheer grit," enabling him to be a winner like New York youngsters in other occupations.

The baseball press exhibited a certain amount of xenophobia. The city was portrayed by some writers as an alien element in American culture because it housed a large non-Anglo-Saxon immigrant population. Some people in baseball viewed this as a problem with serious implications and felt that many in this alien city population would not adapt well to baseball. The newcomers needed to be taught that sport was not "something for sale." They must learn to understand the "Anglo-Saxon idea of sport." They were accused of having the "notion that money is the basis of all games rather than play." Baseball, the sportswriters averred, could play an important part in the Americanization of the immigrants, since it was the purveyor of democracy. Therefore, baseball's efforts to reach the young city boys were considered very important, and Ban Johnson was highly praised when he instituted a baseball day for boys in all American League parks.

Anti-urbanism in baseball generally focused on New York City. At times, resentment by the pure innocents of the Midwest encompassed the entire "effete" East. These feelings were strongest in the Twenties. By the late Thirties, the call to "break up the Yankees" was only vaguely related to anti-urbanism. In the post–World War I era, the Carl Mays case sounded an early alarm: The attempt by the Yankees to overrule the suspension of Mays by Ban Johnson was seen as an ominous sign. For years, this trend of thought went on, the National League had been dominated by the New York Giants because the league offices were in New York City. The American League had been free of this problem because their offices were in Chicago. However, with the arrival of Sunday baseball in New York, the resulting increase in economic power might lead to New York dominance of the American League, too, which could have dangerous consequences. The public would come to resent "one-town domination," and owners of other clubs would be discouraged in the face of the dominance of "unlimited bank rolls."

It was also reported that New York and the National League favored Sen. James J. Walker as the new national commissioner of baseball in 1920, while out West, Judge Landis was the favorite. Oscar C. Reichow, Chicago correspondent for *The Sporting News*, believed that Landis would be the best man. "Of course, it may be hard to make them believe that in New York, where they think baseball is made, molded and governed, forgetting that Chicago is on the map." New Yorkers were obsessed with this image. This led New

Yorkers to believe that all New York had to do was pick the players it wanted, and the players would come to them automatically. Reichow said that baseball had already been ruined in Boston by the Mays and Ruth deals, and it seemed "to be the impression in the East that the leagues cannot exist unless New York teams are leaders in the scrap for the championships."

The 1919 pennant race between the New York Giants and the Cincinnati Reds was interpreted by one *New York Times* writer as an example of the East-West antagonism (reprinted from *Literary Digest*): "The Giants, to the embittered Buckeye fan, came to personify the malignant destiny which thwarted all the efforts of midwestern virtue. And so the struggle which is now at its height has a quite different meaning in Cincinnati from that which is given to it in New York. To the Giants this is a pennant race like any other; they may win, they may lose; it is all in a day's work, and they are calloused to victory no less than to defeat. But to Cincinnati it is the wiping out of ancient wrong, the correction of old injustice, the final vindication of the principles of eternal truth. The Giants can expect no mercy from those who are merely demonstrating the ultimate triumph of right over the forces of evil."

Another eastern writer, James Isaminger, found that people in the Midwest responded more enthusiastically to a pennant winner. In New York, the World Series sometimes seemed to get lost in the greatness of the city. But out West it was different: In 1919 in Cincinnati and in 1920 in Cleveland, every playing day of the World Series was a holiday. "The old-fashioned fan who is rampant and roistering, steeped in the old-fashioned faith," could be found in large numbers. Baseball talk filled the air, the hotels were jammed, and World Series prices prevailed.

In an August series in 1921, when the Cincinnati Reds beat the New York Giants, damaging Giant pennant hopes, W. A. Phelon, Cincinnati correspondent of *The Sporting News*, predicted that there would be "little weeping or wailing outside of Manhattan." The Giants were not going to be allowed to buy their way into a pennant. Too many players, becoming dissatisfied, had developed a longing for the golden wealth of New York. Cincinnati had done its part. But the Giants did go on to win the 1921 pennant in the National League, and the Yankees did the same in the American League. Out West this turn of events drew critical comment. *The Sporting News* reported that the fans were bored by an all–New York World Series. The game of baseball was being hurt by the lack of interest, the editors declared. New York pennant winners might be necessary to keep interest in the game alive in New York, but elsewhere it served as a deterrent to baseball interest generally. "Baseball is the national game, not just a diversion for Manhattanites. An 'all New York' Series proves it."

When the Giants and Yankees won their third straight pennants in 1923, the ill turn of events was called a tribute to the "potency of the New York check book." The public was growing weary of New York victories and disgusted with the futile efforts to combat the New York money power. One writer predicted that the 1923 World Series would be a city series, of only "academic interest" to the remainder of the country.

By the late Twenties feelings had not changed. In 1928, when it appeared that the Cardinals and Yankees would repeat the World Series of 1926, Ernest Lanigan, writing in *The Sporting News*, looked forward to such a prospect. He felt that the Cardinals would be favored to win over "America's highest-priced ball club of any time and a club about which a lot of bunk has been written as being the greatest ball club of all time." The Cardinals were favored, not by the experts, but by the fans. The cash customers preferred Bottomley and Frisch to "George Herman Ruth and the other literary lights of the New York American League Club."

Despite this hostility, there could even be disappointment when a New York team failed to make it to the World Series. But this was consistent. For instance, Detroit Tiger fans were openly disappointed when the Cardinals beat out the Giants in the last days of the 1934 season. New York sportswriter Joe Williams reported that the people of Detroit would have considered it a much greater civic triumph if they could beat a New York team in the World Series.

"This of course stems from the familiar psychology of embarrassing the city slicker." It couldn't be as much fun beating the Cardinals, who represented another city of the Midwest—"devoid of wickedness, smugness and brassy sophistication...." It is interesting that city slickers apparently lived only in New York, not in Detroit and St. Louis. Presumably, these cities were populated entirely by rubes.

New York smugness was not an unusual commodity. Many New Yorkers were firmly convinced that the survival of major-league baseball depended on the success of New York teams. The notion that Western civilization ceased at the Hudson River also occasionally surfaced. In 1939 Eddie Brannick, secretary of the New York Giants, commented on the new head man of the Dodgers, Larry MacPhail, who had come to Brooklyn from Cincinnati. He was revolutionizing baseball in New York as he had done in Ohio. The other New York area baseball executives were concerned. Brannick said that someone ought to tip off MacPhail, telling him that he was now far from the Cincinnati frontier and in the East, "where they

Reprinted from the *New York Post*

have hot and cold water, libraries and colleges like Yale, Harvard and Princeton." Brannick himself had been born in the midst of the sophistication of the Hell's Kitchen section of New York City.

Anti-eastern and anti–New York comment could arise on most any occasion. In 1929 the Arizona State League was in financial trouble, and there was some concern that it might not survive for another season. The Sporting News considered it important to baseball that this league succeed because many of the younger players in baseball were coming from the West. "The trouble in the East is that the young men learn to sign contracts before they learn how to play baseball."

The following year, when Connie Mack was given the Edward Bok Award for his contribution to the city of Philadelphia, some New York writers felt that something as insignificant as baseball should not be honored in such a manner. The counterattack in The Sporting News against this display of New York chauvinism said it was better to give awards for something close to the hearts of the average American, like baseball, than to pass them out for "the discovery of the demimetazoon, the kangaroolikebacillus, or what not." Let New York ridicule others, but it would have to wallow in "its night clubs, operated by gunmen and their lady friends." New Yorkers could get no more out of life than the people of Philadelphia.

In the addition to the sense of community and the urban-rural conflict, there are other themes that run through the baseball litera-ture between the wars that reflect other American traits and help explain why baseball is called the National Pastime. Traditionally, Americans showed a decided preference for the man of action over the man of thought, as reflected in the personalities of folk heroes, the rhetoric of political campaigns, and, most recently, in the writ-ings of the American historian Daniel Boorstin. In 1921 John B. Sheridan recognized this American penchant for action in baseball. His only question was whether baseball was responsible for the "quick, nervous, vigorous and decisive action of Americans" or whether baseball drew these characteristics from the Americans who played the game.

This conflict between thought and action can be seen in the

comment on the replacement of Branch Rickey by Rogers Hornsby as manager of the St. Louis Cardinals in 1925. Rickey was greatly admired as a man who had made many innovations in baseball. He was both praised and roundly criticized for them, and he was considered by some to be the leading theorist of the game, as well as a consummate tactician. But in the opinion of many, Rickey thought too much. Theorems and blackboard drills were not the way to win ball games. It took "straightaway ball playing" under the leadership of a practical man like Rogers Hornsby. "He convinced the team that they were capable of winning the pennant and they went out and did it." The man of action was superior to the man of thought, in the eyes of many Americans.

American optimism was reflected in baseball with the notion that the game was never over until the last man was out. It was also reflected in the spring ritual of renewal. At season's end it was possible to sit down and realistically analyze the shortcomings of a favorite team, but when spring rolled around all realism was forgotten. Everyone started the new season convinced that his favorite team would be a winner. This optimism was appropriate for the National Game, in contrast to the cynicism of Europe and the fatalism of the Orient. It was even seen to parallel the cycle of nature, with the "dark, brooding side of things" giving way to the bright optimism as the "knockers become sweet boosters." *The Sporting News* drew an analogy between the cycles of nature and the fortunes of the players: "Spring is a season of faith for the recruit, hope for the veteran and charity toward both by the rest of us. A lot of dead timber is cut away during the winter months, but some of it is permitted to remain for spring training in the trust that when the sap begins to rise, rejuvenation will come with [it]. Sometimes it does; tragically enough, too frequently [it] doesn't. That is where the young blood gets its chance. Filled with energy, strength and courage, the recruit of today fares forth to display his wares, confident that he will be the star of tomorrow." This sort of rhythmic cycle was present in the baseball writing of the interwar years, and to a lesser extent it can be found today. Each spring even the writers covering the worst teams generated some hope, sometimes sustaining it into the early days of the season. Often some poor team might have a brief spurt in the spring and win maybe eight of ten games, which set off even greater optimism. But slowly, as the weeks and months passed, disillusionment set in, first for the worst teams, then, eventually, it came for all but the pennant winners. Resignation to defeat came in the fall as the last hopes of the contenders faded. Some had already been overcome in the heat of August, a month of legendary proportions in baseball, which only the most fit survive. Finally, the colorful spectacle of the World Series arrived in early October. In the winter, the game moved off the field to the warmth of the hot-stove league. Just as there was a kind of flow to every baseball game, there was this flow for an entire season coinciding with the cycle of nature. In the process the periodic renewal, with a flush of hope and optimism, with its optimism and renewal, suggested the particularly American approach to time and history. For Americans the only time of importance is the present and future, where they must live. There is no need to look back. The past must not and will not burden the American. Its only useful purpose is to forewarn by example against present and future mistakes. The present and future will be, must be, better. This has been the promise of all of Western history in the last three centuries. The cry of "Wait till next year" and the irrationality of spring training optimism both serve to reaffirm the basic truth at the heart of America's outlook on life. How important these ideas actually were to baseball's popularity is uncertain, but they did not go unnoticed by the sportswriters of the Twenties and Thirties.

The spirit of America's devotion to nationalism and patriotism could be found in baseball, the National Game. Baseball was valuable to the nation because it taught Americans to think quickly; to react instantly to the unexpected; and "to meet the unanticipated and surprising with assurance, courage and effect." The American boy should understand two things by the time he reached the age of eighteen: the meaning of the Constitution and the meaning of playing baseball. If the boy grasped both of these, he "is sure to be a true American." If a boy played a good game of baseball during the day, "he can safely be 'placed upon guard tonight.'"

Baseball and Americanism belonged together. The National American Legion Baseball Championship in 1929 prompted *The Sporting News* to comment on this connection. World War I had brought baseball considerable growth, for wherever the flag went, baseball followed with the soldiers. The moral was clear: without the "fight for the safety of the world and for civilization," there would be no American Legion. Without the American Legion there would be no baseball championship for boys. "They are good comrades under the same tent."

The annual opening of the baseball season brought forth renewed patriotic spirit. It was the custom on opening day to raise the flag and play "The Star-Spangled Banner." In Washington it was done in the presence of the president of the United States, while civic dignitaries appeared in the other cities. It was seen as wholly fitting that the National Game should help in the renewal of patriotism in this manner, "for, unquestionably, there are few witnessing the ceremony who do not feel a little throb in the heart and a new sense of duty toward their country...." (Daily ceremonies with flag and anthem did not come until there were adequate loudspeaker systems and war fervor in the country.)

As good Americans, all baseball people were careful with the flag of the United States. It was never improperly treated by them. This mood explains why it was particularly appalling when in 1930 a boxer entered the ring draped in the flag. To no one's surprise, he was disqualified for not fighting fairly. *The Sporting News* was indignant: "Many cheap things have been done with the United States flag in New York City, and in other cities, but we do not think a more gross insult ever was paid to it than in this instance, and the spectators thought so, too." This, of course, could never happen at a baseball game.

If baseball was the National Pastime, it ought to attract the attention of the president, and it did.* He threw out the first ceremonial ball of the season. Some presidents saw political capital in baseball and associated themselves with the game on numerous other occasions. This made good copy for the sportswriters and offered posi-

---

* For archival references to papers of the presidents, see the manuscript section of the Bibliography.

tive proof that baseball was the National Game. It seems appropriate that the most avid presidential baseball fan was one of the blandest, most "average" man ever to occupy the White House. When Warren G. Harding campaigned from his front porch during the 1920 presidential election, he was visited by the Chicago Cubs, who had come to Marion, Ohio, to play an exhibition game for the candidate. Harding spoke to the players and used baseball imagery in the way that more recent presidents have borrowed from the football lexicon. For those seeking the meaning of "normalcy," the text follows:

Cubs:

I pay to you my tribute to baseball, because I like the game, just like every other American. It has been in the blood for over a half century, and it has helped us as a people. Of course, there has been a vast improvement since the early game, but I am sure it is not reactionary to remind you that you still try to hit them out and the big thing is to reach the home plate. These are progressive ideas, but it rejoices the average crowd of rooters to note an old-fashioned Tinker-to-Evers-to-Chance.

I like the tension of a tight game, I like to see the balls go over the plate, and see decisions follow. I admire the skill of the pitcher, but I like to see the ball hit. I like the rooters. It is great to be a rooter. It is fine to see him recognizing great play, but I like his partisanship, his interest, and he works as hard as the players. That is the explanation of baseball popularity. We are all partisans of some team. I am sure I rejoiced as much as Garry Herman when the Reds copped last year. It adds to the absorbing spirit to be an enthusiastic partisan. I never saw a game without taking sides, and never want to see one. There is the soul of the game. I feel the same way in big national matters. I like to think of America First. I want our country to float the championship pennant in the contest of human achievement.

You can't win a ball game with a one-man team. Games are won by good pitching, good catching, good fielding, good defense and good offense, hitting them out and team work. I like a pitcher who puts the ball over and trusts his fielders to play their stations, I like a team that knows its signals, and I salute the player who ignores the individual record and goes out to win the game.

No one man can win a pennant. It can't be done in baseball or in the conduct of government. From either viewpoint the game is too big and too fast, and too many rooters concerned.

Maybe it is old-fashioned, but I am for team play. This harmony of endeavor, where every man plays his part, no matter who is starring, is what wins in baseball and will win victories for these United States.

I am opposing the one-man play for the nation. Too much fanning out, too much unpreparedness, for war or for peace. Nobody has confidence in a ball team which is untrained. National unpreparedness for war cost us many precious lives and endless billions in waste, and unpreparedness for peace is costing billions more and holding us in anxiety and uncertainty.

It is my observation that the National team, now playing for the United States, played loosely and muffed disappointingly in our domestic affairs, and then struck out at Paris. No one can dispute—the American team played badly when it got on a foreign field.

As a spokesman for the Republican Party I am urging team play in government, on the home grounds, with all the home fans behind us, and team play when we represent America in the all-the-world series. There are too many men batting above three hundred to rely on one hitter.

And I am advocating something more—play according to the rules. It is the only fair way, because the rules apply to all players precisely alike. The rules in the supreme American game are in the federal constitution, and the umpire is the American people. Stick to the rules, hold fast to the constitution, and we can be sure we are right.

There was a meeting of league officials where they sought to change the rules. In the parlance of the game, the contending teams tried a squeeze play, and expected to score—six to one against the United States. But the American Senate was ready with the ball at the plate, and we are still flying our pennant which we won at home and hold respected throughout the world.

Hail to the team play of America! Hail to a hundred millions of American rooters, the citizenship of the republic, expect Uncle Sam to put them over or bat them out as the situation

requires, and count upon team play in government, team play
in citizenship and everybody interested in America first.

Harding was elected president. In 1921 he attended opening day
ceremonies and threw out the first ball. This was gratifying to the
National Game, in the midst of the Black Sox controversy. One
sportswriter felt that if there was any doubt about the honesty of
baseball, the president would not have attended. The National Game
was vindicated. By 1922 Harding was being referred to as "president
of the fans." It was reported that Harding was a "regular rooter" who
always kept a complete scorecard and knew the "inside stuff" of
baseball.

When Warren Harding died in office in 1923, the baseball press
reacted strongly. Not only had the nation lost its chief executive, but
baseball had lost its number one fan. Games were canceled in observation of a national day of mourning. It was revealed that Ty Cobb
and Harding were mutual admirers. One of Cobb's most treasured
possessions was an autographed picture of the president.
Sportswriter James C. Isaminger reminded the fans that Harding's
love of the game was not just a pose: he was a "real, simon pure fan
and never could see enough games." He always kept up with the
baseball news. Tom Rice called him the "first thirty-third degree,
dyed-in-the-wool fan that ever sat in the White House." If Harding
went out to the ball park and saw the Washington team lose, he did
not enjoy his supper. If on the other hand they won, Harding returned to the White House feeling that it was a pretty good world and
everything would work out in Europe. Harding was deeply affected
by baseball. It provided him an escape from the great burdens of the
presidency. Francis Richter noted that Harding belonged to the
baseball fans of America, the plain people from whom he had come,
and from whom he inherited his love of the game. He was free from
snobbery and "truly loved the National Game of the American
people, just as he loved and revered all things American."

Although every modern president has had the opportunity to throw
out the first ball of the season, few have had the privilege of seeing

Washington, D.C., as the home team in a World Series. Calvin Coolidge was one of the few. In 1924, when Washington won the American League pennant, the president was inundated with requests for tickets to the series. He also received political advice from around the country, recommending that it would be wise for him to go to the World Series, as it would offer him good exposure in an election year. He did attend three games. At the end of the series Coolidge issued a statement expressing his pleasure at the outcome. Although admitting he was not a baseball historian, he said that he could not recall a more exciting World Series. He was delighted that Walter Johnson had been the winning pitcher in the final game. Coolidge also paid tribute to the "high degree of skill" and "high-class sportsmanship" which would increase respect for and confidence in the National Game. "It would be difficult to conceive a finer example of true sport."

A number of fans wrote to thank the president for his interest in baseball. Harry Clatfelter of Peoria said that he thanked God for a president who was "human enough to chuck the whole United States inside his roll top and slam the lid down while he goes out to see his hometown team play a World Series ball game." *The Sporting News* expressed its delight in an editorial titled "To the President." They thanked Coolidge for attending the games, and saw this as a vote of confidence for baseball. *The Sporting News* was also impressed with Mrs. Coolidge, "about the most ardent 'rooter' for a home team that ever coaxed a home run over the plate."

Herbert Hoover was also an avid baseball fan. In 1929, attending opening day in the rain and cold, Hoover remained the entire game, which drew favorable comment from the fans and writers. It was reported that the First Lady sought relief from the weather by eating peanuts. Hoover attended other openings and several World Series games during his administration. As the depression deepened, his name was mentioned in connection with baseball with less prominence and less ballyhoo. In fact, Hoover was the recipient of a lusty Bronx cheer on one of his appearances. Apparently baseball did not appreciate the kind of exposure that an unpopular chief executive could offer.

The days of the depression were not good ones for the nation or for the National Pastime. When Franklin Roosevelt assumed the presidency in 1933, he was welcomed by the nation and by baseball. He, like his predecessors, was a baseball fan. In accepting the invitation to attend the opening of the 1933 season, Roosevelt said that baseball had done much to keep up the spirit of the people during the dark days of the economic crisis. *The Sporting News* was grateful for his acknowledgment and praised the president for his "prompt and courageous efforts...to restore public confidence and to rehabilitate the nation." By "driving home the runs when they are most needed," Roosevelt was assuring a brighter future for baseball—and America.

Shortly after his inauguration, Roosevelt used baseball terminology to make a point in one of his radio messages. He said that he didn't expect to get a hit every time at bat. However, he would seek the highest possible batting average for himself and for the team. By his choice of words the president struck a responsive chord with followers of the National Pastime. *The Sporting News* pointed out that the subordination of self to team play had won many pennants, even for teams that looked inferior on paper. It was a good lesson for America: "A nation, schooled in baseball, should find it easy to play ball with President Roosevelt and join him in united team-play to beat the common enemy."

Following his appearance at opening day in 1934, enthusiasm for FDR remained high. He proved that he was a true fan by remaining at the game when a storm threatened. It seemed to many fans that the country was lucky to have Franklin Roosevelt in the White House, and baseball was lucky that he was such a good fan. His presence at opening day also proved that at the ball park "the whole world is kin and that there the cares and worries of even the most heavily burdened can be forgotten...." It was good to know that the man who was steering the nation through perilous times could share the joys and sorrows of the average fan.

During his several terms in office, Roosevelt was involved in baseball in many ways. In 1935 he turned on the lights for the first night game ever played in the major leagues. Throughout the second half of the Thirties and into the early Forties, he sent messages of praise for baseball to the Baseball Writer's Association Dinner in New York. He also sent a message for the Centennial

Celebration of Baseball at Cooperstown, New York, in 1939; a message to Walter Johnson on the occasion of a dinner honoring Johnson in 1937; and several messages to Connie Mack on the landmarks in Mack's career.

Baseball was indeed the National Pastime of the United States of America. It was important enough to occupy the time of the White House and democratic enough to list the president and the ditchdigger among its fans.

4

Superstar

Can't even be sure about the simple *facts*. Some
writers even argue that Rutherford and Casey
never existed—nothing more than another of
the ancient myths of the sun symbolized as a
victim slaughtered by the monster or force of
darkness.

THE Sultan of Swat. The King of Slam. The Baron of Bam. The Great
Bambino. The Babe. All of these endearments and more were used
for one man: George Herman Ruth, the single most dominant figure
in the history of sport in America. His legend has endured and
haunted those who challenge the statistics. In a sense Ruth
transcends time and place. There have undoubtedly been greater
athletes, perhaps even superior baseball players, but there may never
be another Babe Ruth. Not only was Babe Ruth a classic hero, he was
and is a symbol of his times.

The United States in the 1920s was a society in transition and
therefore in tension. In a relatively short time, the United States had
passed from a largely rural-agricultural world to one that was
urban-industrial. Not only had the nation as a whole made this
transition demographically, but many individuals made the same
transition in very personal terms, and such change required considerable adjustment in life-styles and value systems. Rugged indi-

73

vidualism had been well suited to the frontier and the insulated life of rural America, but it was dysfunctional in a complex urban setting. Some people responded by clinging tenaciously to the past, proclaiming the older values and virtues from the housetops. The baseball world reacted this way. Others lashed out; for instance, there were fundamentalist wars within religion and science. But perhaps an even more common reaction was to try to have it both ways; make the fewest adjustments and accommodations possible, while reassuring oneself that things really hadn't changed all that much. Celebrate those older values, encapsulate them in some symbol or institution, reaffirm them vicariously. Deify the rugged individual in a mass ritual set on a stretch of grass in the middle of a concrete-and-asphalt urban center. Personify all of these feelings in a larger-than-life figure, and what begins to appear is the outline of "The Great Babe Ruth."

Born February 6, 1895, in Baltimore, Maryland, he inherited the name of his German father, George Herman Ruth. His mother, Kate, was of Irish descent. The Ruths were saloon keepers on the Baltimore waterfront. Babe Ruth had a brother, John, and a sister, Mayme. In the first line of his autobiography Ruth says simply, "I was a bad kid"—he was seven when he first entered St. Mary's Industrial School. Between 1902 and 1914 Ruth was in and out of St. Mary's several times. His last exit was on February 27, 1914, when he left to join the old Baltimore Orioles of the International League as a young and promising pitcher. St. Mary's had among its residents a number of orphans; perhaps this explains the legend that Ruth himself was an orphan. Or perhaps people, having read enough Horatio Alger, therefore felt that Ruth ought to be an orphan and so made him one. In 1934 Ruth's sister expressed her irritation over the orphan legend, pointing out that actually Babe had been put in St. Mary's because he had the bad habit of "playing hooky." But the legend would not die, and even as recently as 1973 an NBC newsman referred to the Bambino as an orphan. This illustrates one great difficulty in dealing with Babe Ruth, the problem of separating legend from fact. It is best to follow the rule outlined by Roger Kahn in his *Esquire* article, "The Real Babe Ruth": the stories of Ruth on the baseball field are true, or nearly true; however, truth fades fast when the stories move off the field.

On the field it was the home run that was Babe Ruth's trademark. The statistics are impressive: 714 career home runs, 60 in one season and 59 in another. The home run made Babe Ruth and Babe Ruth made the home run. In 1918 Babe Ruth led the major leagues with 11 home runs. In 1919, while performing both as a pitcher and as an

outfielder, he set a new all-time single season mark, 29, exceeding the old mark of 27 established by Ned Williamson of the 1884 Chicago White Stockings. (Although Williamson had played in only 107 games, and Ruth in 130, no one proposed putting an asterisk beside Ruth's name in the record book as happened when Roger Maris hit his 61 home runs, breaking Ruth's record.)

By that 1919 season the Ruth mystique was already beginning to materialize. On Labor Day, before 29,000 fans, Ruth hit his twenty-fourth homer of the season in the second game of a doubleheader, after pitching and batting the Red Sox to victory in the first game. When the homer came, the crowd roared its approval for some ten minutes and threw their straw hats all over the field. When Ruth returned to the outfield for the next inning, he was greeted by another five-minute ovation. At the conclusion of the game thousands of fans rushed onto the field and carried Ruth to the dugout on their shoulders. His career home run total at that point was 49. In 1920, his first year in New York, he again led the league in homers, this time with 54. In 1921 it was 59. By then he was a national idol. Frank Lane of *Baseball Magazine*, seeking to explain Ruth's enormous popularity, said that Ruth had taken the most popular part of the game and made it his own. "He did, with the home run, things that were incredible and that seemed impossible, in fact, were impossible to everyone else." He outdistanced the entire field; no one else even came close. It was soon accepted as gospel that no one would ever surpass the 1921 total of 59, except perhaps Ruth himself—which he did in 1927 when he hit 60.

By 1927 baseball was a new game. Home run statistics had increased geometrically, but Ruth still towered over the pack. In the American League, Gehrig was second with 47 and Lazzeri a distant third with only 18. The best the National League could produce was 30 by Hack Wilson of Chicago and Cy Williams of Philadelphia. From 1918 to 1931 Ruth led the majors in home runs in all but three seasons: 1922 and 1925 (when he was suspended for part of the season and suffered from injuries) and in 1930 (when he led the American League with 49 but was outdistanced for the major-league title by Hack Wilson's 56). It is not surprising that by 1927 *The

Sporting News called him a superman. "His class is his own, and it begins with Babe and ends with Babe." But bare statistics only begin to tell the story.

Although the sportswriters of his day did not seem as obsessed with counting Ruth's home runs as others would be as soon as someone began to assault his records, they did take special note of certain milestones. Home run number 500 came late in the 1929 season and prompted editorial comment from the *New York Evening World*, who placed the run in a category with the skyscraper, the automobile, and the great universities as a symbol of American greatness. The *Evening World* said that Ruth's picture should be taken with Thomas Edison, Harvey Firestone, Charles A. Lindbergh, and Henry Ford, illustrious company for Ruth—a self-made man among self-made men whose worth could be measured in practical terms. The *Evening World* saw Yankee Stadium as a monument to Ruth's achievements. The stadium had the "austere dignity" of a bank and for the same reason: "Money speaks there in the low, modulated voice that is more eloquent than the shouts of a mob storming the Bastille." Yankee Stadium a bank, built by the home runs of Babe Ruth! What higher compliment could be offered to the Babe in the United States of the late Twenties? As the *Evening World* said, "This is no mere record about to be marked up in perishable chalk. It is the middle of an epoch."

Not only had Babe's home runs built Yankee Stadium, they also attracted fans to ball parks all around the American League. Sportswriter Fred Lieb recalled a weekend series in St. Louis during Ruth's first or second year with the Yankees. When Lieb and the Yankees arrived at the Chase Hotel, Lieb noticed "three guys dressed in cowboy suits" looking like they had just stepped out of a "circus or Buffalo Bill show." These three men were from Wyoming and had spent three days on horseback and two days on the train just to see Babe Ruth hit a home run. Ruth obliged by hitting one in the Saturday game.* This rather extreme case serves to illustrate Ruth's power as a drawing card.

*This and other Lieb quotations in this chapter are from Frederick Lieb 1972: personal communication.

It was not just the numbers of runs that were impressive, it was also his powerful swing and the great distances he hit the ball. Fans were almost as pleased to see him strike out as hit a home run. What added much of the legendary and heroic proportions was Ruth's ability to hit home runs for special occasions and with a special flare. The most famous was the so-called designated home run in the 1932 World Series, surrounding which there was a good deal of con-

Reprinted, courtesy of the *Chicago Tribune*

troversy. Some claim it never happened. Others claim Ruth was simply pointing at Charlie Root, the Cubs pitcher, and not at the outfield grandstand. (Tris Coffin, in *The Old Ball Game*, says Root himself later offered such an explanation.) This particular World Series had been a lively one. Former Yankee Mark Koenig had joined the Cubs about midseason, had been instrumental in the Cubs' pennant drive, but he had been voted only a half share of World Series money by the Cub players. The Yankees, especially Ruth, had been riding the Cubs since the start of the series for being cheap in the Koenig matter; the Cubs returned the compliments in kind. When the Yankees arrived in Chicago prior to the third game of the series, they were greeted by a group of Cub fans, mostly female, who spit on them, and Ruth and his wife had borne the brunt of the abuse. It was not surprising, then, that when Ruth stepped to the plate in the fifth inning of the third game, with one out and the score tied, the Cub bench began to taunt him.

But it seems decidedly unhealthy for any one to taunt the great man Ruth too much and very soon the crowd was to learn its lesson. A single lemon rolled out to the plate as Ruth came up in the fifth and in no mistaken motions the Babe notified the crowd that the nature of his retaliation would be a wallop right out the confines of the park.

Root pitched two balls and two strikes, while Ruth signaled with his fingers after each pitch to let the spectators know exactly how the situation stood. Then the mightiest blow of all fell.

It was a tremendous smash that bore straight down the center of the field in an enormous arc, came down alongside the flagpole and disappeared behind the corner formed by the scoreboard and the end of the right field bleachers.

It was Ruth's fifteenth home run in world's series competition and easily one of his most gorgeous. The crowd, suddenly unmindful of everything save that it had just witnessed an epic feat, hailed the Babe with a salvo of applause.

Other accounts by New York writers agree in substance with this one by John Drebinger of the *New York Times* (October 2, 1932). Fred Lieb remembered it about the same way, adding that he had dinner with Lou Gehrig after the game. Although Gehrig had himself hit two home runs in the game, all he could talk about was Ruth's designated home run, saying, "Look at the gall of that big monkey, gettin' away with that." Lieb also recalled that Joe Williams questioned Ruth after the game. The Babe confirmed his actions and intent. When Williams asked what he would have done had he failed, Ruth replied that he supposed he would look like a fool; but then the thought of failure, confessed the Babe, had never crossed his mind. He knew he was good, said Lieb. "He used to have a vulgar expression: 'I can knock the cock off any ball that's ever pitched.'" Such a man just might have had the gall to pull a designated home run in a World Series. Whatever the truth of the matter, most people came to believe that it indeed had happened, and the next generation actually did see it, courtesy of Hollywood. This was, after all, the stuff that heroes and supermen were made of—defying odds and probabilities, challenging common sense—the transcendent individual.

In addition to that designated home run, Babe Ruth had hit other homers for special occasions. In 1923 a crowd officially reported to be 74,200, dotted with dignitaries from the world of baseball and the world of politics, with a smattering of generals and colonels, gathered to dedicate Yankee Stadium, the latest wonder of the world. It was the largest crowd ever to see a baseball game. John Philip Sousa led the Seventh Regiment Band in the "Star-Spangled Banner," among other impressive pre-game ceremonies. But it was Babe Ruth who performed the "real baptism" for Yankee Stadium: in the third inning, with two men on base, he hit a ball into the right-field bleachers, an area designed expressly as a depository for his homers. The New York Times reported: "As Ruth circled the bases he received probably the greatest ovation of his career. The biggest crowd in baseball history rose to its feet and let loose the biggest shout in baseball history."

About a week later President Harding visited the new stadium, and again Ruth responded with a home run. The Times gleefully said, "If it had been Europe instead of the United States you might have thought that the Ruthian drive was by royal command. It seemed like a prearranged part of the program.... The President wanted to see Ruth hit a home run, and Ruth hit one." Could a man really hit a home run at will?

Babe Ruth hit a home run his first time at bat on the opening day of the season in 1929. As he circled the bases in Yankee Stadium his bride of two days, Claire, sat watching with pride—the writers assumed that he had hit one for "the little woman."

In 1933 major-league baseball inaugurated the All-Star game. On July 6, 49,000 fans packed Comiskey Field in Chicago, and millions listened to the game over radio. It was the first time so much baseball talent had been gathered in one place for a game. In what was dubbed the "Game of the Century," the Baseball Player of the Century would once again dominate. Not only did Babe Ruth hit the first home run ever in All-Star competition, but it proved to be the margin of victory for the American League as they defeated the Nationals 4 to 2. *The Sporting News* found it only fitting that the man who had been occupying the limelight so long should monoplize attention in the inaugural All-Star contest.

There are also numerous stories about Ruthian home runs hit for sick boys whom the Babe had visited in hospitals. The veracity of such stories is questionable, but they fit well with the notion that Ruth could hit homers at will, and they further compound the Ruthian legend. A further refinement of the legend is provided by stories of Ruth's ability to overcome physical handicaps to hit home runs. On July 2, 1930, Ruth tore off the nail on the second finger of his left hand. Although team doctors said that Ruth would be out of action for some time, the next day Ruth was back throwing and batting with his finger bandaged. Two days later he hit his thirty-second home run of the season. For *The Sporting News* this was page one material, worthy of a picture and the caption "Babe Ruth Shows His Courage."

More common were stories of physical handicaps that stemmed from Ruth's drinking abilities and notorious night life. Sam Breadon, Cardinal owner, frequently told this story about how a man came to his office before one of the World Series games in St. Louis. As Fred Lieb remembered it, the Cardinals were playing the Yankees. The man told Breadon that there was no need to worry about Babe Ruth as a factor in the game that day because, claimed the man, Ruth had spent the previous night with five different women. Ruth proceeded to hit three home runs that day, which prompted Breadon to say, "that son-of-a-bitch, never give me any news like that again. 'Don't worry,' he says. 'This man is just super-human.' "

As time passed the home runs accumulated, finally stopping in 1935 when Ruth retired after a short stay with the Boston Braves. The last home run Ruth hit was on May 25, 1935, when he hit three in one day. It was appropriate that he should end his home run bonanza in this fashion, with numbers 712, 713, and 714 coming in one game. Nor did it hurt the myth-making process that the last home run was one of the longer of his career. The Associated Press report, printed without special fanfare in the *New York Times*, showed that Ruth hit three home runs and collected one single, going four-for-four at bat that day. He drove in six runs as the Braves lost to the Pittsburgh Pirates 11 to 7. Ruth's first homer of the day came off Red Lucas and the last two came off Guy Bush, who, ironically, had been one of those Cubs who had razzed Ruth the day of the designated home run in 1932. Home run number 714 was described by the AP writer as "a prodigious clout that carried clear over the rightfield grandstand, bounded into the street and rolled into Schenley Park. Baseball men said it was the longest drive ever made at Forbes Field." Ruth's home runs, famed not just for their numbers but for their distance and height, contributed the term "Ruthian clout" to the lexicon of baseball.

In addition to Babe Ruth the home run king, there was also Babe Ruth the symbol, or, more correctly, the multitude of symbols. He was a man of enormous physical power, seen as both saving and transforming baseball; a man of incredible appetites; a man of kindness. He loved kids and kids loved him. He was in fact a kid himself: the child-man playing a children's game and getting paid enormous sums of money. He frolicked like a child and defied the rules of the baseball establishment like a perpetual adolescent. He stood above the crowd both on and off the field, a dominant figure wherever he went. He was a celebrated and endangered species in the emerging corporate America.

In the Babe's first season in New York, Yankee manager Miller

Huggins dubbed Ruth the greatest drawing card of all time, and sought to explain it by comparing Ruth to Ty Cobb. He said that Cobb had been the greatest player of all time but that Cobb's appeal was only to those who understood the inner workings of baseball. To the student of the game, Cobb was a marvel. But Babe Ruth's appeal was universal: the public loved a big fellow who carried a wallop, and no one busted the ball like Ruth. Huggins pointed out that on the road even opposing fans booed when Ruth was intentionally walked. In Chicago, in the midst of a pennant race with the Yankees, White Sox fans booed the intentional pass to the Babe, even when the strategy might have won the game for their own team.

When baseball passed through the Black Sox scandal late in Ruth's first New York season without any adverse effects, many credited Ruth with having saved the game. Sportswriter Walter Camp claimed that the Babe "literally pounded baseball back to life." Ruth was possessed of genius, and each time he hit a home run "his face resembled nothing quite so much as a beaming sunrise." If Ruth struck out, this too was spectacular, as "he fanned the air with such mighty sincerity" that the fans in the stands were delighted. But there was more to Ruth than just the home run and the strikeout. He was the complete ball player: "Today he ranges over the right-field territory like a shaggy buffalo endowed with legs of an antelope; he throws to the bases with bullet-like speed and accuracy; he slides on a close play with all the abandon of an express train trying to make up lost time, and at bat he crashes his terrific home run to right field, crosses a wary infield with a delicate bunt, or shortens his grip on his bat and pokes singles and doubles to any field." Not only was this great praise for Ruth, but the blend of metaphors and symbols is of some interest. The buffalo, the antelope, and the express train offer a mix of rural and industrial symbols. This may be indicative of the need for a society in transition to celebrate both the old and the new, the rural and the industrial—having it both ways by combining the symbols in one hero.

Camp's assessment of Ruth as the complete ball player came in the midst of the 1923 season, the year that the Babe was unanimously named the most valuable player in the American League. *The Sporting News*, commenting on the choice, claimed that Ruth was the "greatest ever" and predicted that "his name and deeds will echo through the ages...." Early in his career Ruth was claimed an immortal. Over and over again he was labeled the greatest player of all time. In 1930 the *New York World* noted that only Cobb might be compared with Ruth, "yet it is a question whether Cobb in his best days was the equal of this great machine." To many, Ruth transcended the human. Roger Kahn reports that Ruth's teammate and close friend, Joe Dugan, reflecting on Ruth's greatness and life-style, felt that the Bambino wasn't human but animal. On further reflection Dugan concluded, "There never was anyone like him. He was a god." Dugan may have been exaggerating, but according to Fred Lieb some of the fans seemed to share Dugan's view. They would try to touch Ruth and, when they did, seemed to feel they had been given something. It was "like the woman who touched Jesus and was healed."

Lieb also added another tale to the Ruth mystique. During a spring exhibition game against the Reds in Tampa, an automobile parked outside the right-field foul line attracted some attention. On a tip from Leo Durocher, Lieb's wife went out to talk to the driver, who told her about his son. The boy in the back seat, who had been suffering from some sort of paralysis for about three years, had been unable to lift himself up for some time. He was a terrific Ruth fan, papering the walls of his room with pictures of the Babe. The boy's father told Mrs. Lieb what had happened at the ball park: Babe Ruth had passed the car and waved at the boy, saying, "Hello, kid." The boy responded by lifting himself up. The tears rolling down his cheeks, the father told Mrs. Lieb, "My boy stood up! My boy stood up! The first time in three years and that Ruth did it!" Mrs. Lieb did not get the man's name, and the story was never followed up, but according to Fred Lieb the story was not only true but illustrated Ruth's power over kids.

Baseball writers believed that there was a special relationship between baseball and the youth of America. As the leading figure in baseball, Babe Ruth therefore had to demonstrate this relationship. In fact, the baseball-youth connection was never better exploited than when it was personified in Babe Ruth. This is not to say that the affection the Babe had for kids and the special relationship between him and the boys were merely creations of baseball public relations. Certainly the boys of America greatly admired, even idolized, the mighty Bambino, and it was also true that Ruth liked children, but, as Roger Kahn put it, "his life was not a priestly dedication to healing sick boys." This side of Babe Ruth's life served to illuminate the baseball-youth relationship, but it also softened some of the more harsh and power-laden elements in the Ruthian image. It helped to keep the superman human.

Near the end of the 1920 season, under the auspices of Babe Ruth, the St. Mary's Industrial School accompanied the Yankees on their last western road trip, the band giving concerts in the evenings at the ball parks with the Babe as featured speaker. The trip successfully raised money for the school, and "thousands of baseball fans came to know Babe Ruth other than as a great ball player. They discovered him to be a human being like themselves, of likeable personality and of good common sense." In addition it demonstrated that Ruth was not the kind of man who let success go to his head. He remembered his past.

The first instance of what might be called the exploitation of the Ruth-youth relationship came in 1922. It had been a difficult year for the Sultan of Swat. Opening the season under suspension for defiance of Commissioner Landis' ruling against barnstorming, he never really hit his stride, failing to live up to the promise of greatness displayed in 1921. After the season ended, a dinner was staged for the sportswriters at which Ruth announced that he was a changed man; he was turning over a new leaf. Near the end of the evening came the touching climax. Sen. Jimmy Walker, Democratic leader of the New York state senate, gave a short speech, making reference to how dear the Babe was to the hearts of young America. The speech brought tears to Ruth's eyes. "If I fall down, every kid ought to be ashamed of me," said Ruth. "I'll be darned if I don't hope he does. But I won't fall." And he didn't.

As the 1923 season opened, speculation centered on Ruth's ability to make a comeback. He seemed to be having a slow start in spring training, but a story out of Vicksburg, Mississippi, was very heartening to *The Sporting News*. Hearing about a seven-year-old invalid boy who wanted to get out to the ball park to see Ruth, the Babe drove out to spend "an hour of 'just kids' in communion." The sportswriters felt that Ruth had been trying too hard in spring training and paying too much attention to his critics. He needed to become his "natural self," and *The Sporting News* felt that an hour with a kid would help him return to normal. After all, he was just a big kid himself.

The passage of time brought the appearance of this sort of story more frequently. In 1926 Ruth was lending his time and talents to the American League's efforts to promote baseball among boys. He had appeared in Chicago as Santa Claus for a group of crippled children and had been part of Boy Scouts' Day in Philadelphia. In 1928 Ruth and Gehrig went on a barnstorming tour at the close of the season, spending part of each day in entertaining children, including those in hospitals. To many, his "natural love for children" was Ruth's finest quality. With Ruth out among the kids the future of baseball was secure. "What would be the decision of the average boy," asked Charles Doyle of the *Pittsburgh Sun-Telegraph*, "if he could choose between caddying for Walter Hagen or sitting on the bench with Babe Ruth?"

When in 1929 Ruth spoke to a group of schoolboys at a rally sponsored by the *New York Telegram*, the Babe came out against the use of bad language by the fans in the stands because of its bad effects on children. Some wondered "when cuss words became so distasteful to him...," but this turnabout only proved how big a man he really was and how much he really cared for those kids out in the bleachers. "They are his real friends."

As Ruth's career came closer to its end, there was a good deal of speculation as to his future. Many writers felt it imperative that the Babe retain some sort of connection with baseball. In a syndicated column appearing in *The Sporting News* early in 1933, Bob Zuppke, University of Illinois football coach, suggested that after Ruth's retirement he should be sent around the country to speak to grade-school children. According to Zuppke, Ruth was the idol of boys everywhere and a symbol of strength and physical fitness. Also, young people wanted heroes that were men of action. Ruth had a "marvelous physical and mental combination" which all "right-minded" boys tried to emulate. Zuppke concluded that it was better to have the boys out "pretending to be Babe Ruths on the sandlots rather than gangsters and stick-up men."

When his career on the field ended, Ruth did maintain his connections with young America. In a 1940 article in *Rotarian* he offered some training rules for boys (which, of course, he himself had never followed). These were a good statement of the do's and don't's of life for aspiring middle-class Americans in search of bourgeois respectability:

> Early to bed and early to rise with at least eight hours' sleep every night.
> No tobacco until you're 21, then decide for yourself.
> Too much athletics is just as bad as too much study. Do all things in moderation.
> You need perfect eyesight to be a ball player and good eyes in almost anything you do. Don't strain your eyes.
> Obey your parents, teachers, coach. To find fault with decisions means the woodshed or the bench.
> Learn to take it with a grin. It's not easy, but if you can do it, the world is yours.

The great appeal of Babe Ruth was not limited to children. It was more than just kids that filled Yankee Stadium and other ball parks across the nation. The baseball literature of the period abounds with descriptions and analyses of this appeal. After the 1928 World Series ended in St. Louis, the Yankees headed victoriously for New York aboard a train. At every stop along the way large crowds had gathered, and at every stop the chant was the same, "We want Ruth." The Babe came out, shook hands, signed autographs, and gave a short speech. This scene was repeated in small towns all along the route, well into the night and early morning hours. As Joe Williams of the *New York Telegram* noted, "In New York he may be a great ball player, but outside New York he is a god."

Ruth's popularity was due to more than just home runs. Ruth had a warm human element that appealed to the public. He had totally mastered his business. In another analysis offered by the *Honolulu Advertiser* in an editorial marking Ruth's first visit to the islands in 1933, the editors said that Ruth represented a particular aspect of the American dream. He had started in humble circumstances. Overcoming obstacles with a willingness to work and supreme self-confidence, he had gained fame and fortune. Yet he had remained modest and retained his unassuming manner. In both his public and private life Ruth was a symbol of the best in sports. "He is the spirit of American sports in person, playing hard at all times and coming through with the needed wallop when all is apparently lost."

Similar sentiments were expressed by William Pukner of Guttenberg, New York, in his 1932 award-winning essay on his favorite player. To Pukner, Ruth was a hero because of his accomplishments on the field and because of his "splendid traits" which were the elements for a story of inspiration. It was mastery of self that Pukner saw as Ruth's most "creditable accomplishment." It was a "demonstration of courageous manhood." Ruth had risen quickly to great heights in baseball, but he could not handle it and suffered an "ignominious and humiliating" fall. But he came back, surpassing his former greatness and reaching still greater heights, thereby becoming a "shining idol for young and old alike."

The reference to Ruth's fall points to another ingredient in the Ruth legend. Harold Seymour noted recently that Ruth hardly qualified for a job with the Big Brothers of America. "If he had, he would not have excited the perfervid acclaim that he did. The route to the common man's heart is paved with ribaldry and excess," and there was plenty of both in the life of the Bambino. Food, drink, and sex were the basic areas of excess although the third was not as publicly acclaimed as the first two.

Early in his career Ruth acquired his reputation as a man of large appetites. Noting that Ruth had a "Rabelaisian nature," John B. Sheridan of *The Sporting News* saw in Ruth the prototype of the baseball man, who ate, smoked, caroused, and hit the ball enormously. Sheridan advised Lou Gehrig that if he wanted to earn as much money as the Babe, he would have to develop the same reputation as Ruth in eating, drinking, gambling, and "lovin' 'em and

leavin' 'em." This was one of the rare instances that public mention
was made of Ruth's taste for women.

Instead, the contemporary literature stressed his gastronomic
excesses. In 1924 a rumor that one of Ruth's ribs was broken turned
out to be that he was suffering from acute indigestion from eating ten
to fifteen hot dogs at a single session. Such stories were legion. The
popular folk myth includes stories about him sitting on the Yankee
bench and eating hot dogs and guzzling soft drinks during a game.
Ty Cobb (in *My Life in Baseball*) recalled that everyone in the league
hoped that Ruth "would eat and drink himself into a stupor and be
unable to get the bat around his stomach." Cobb added that it was a
false hope. "I've seen him at midnight, propped up in bed, order six
huge club sandwiches and put them away, along with a platter of
pig's knuckles, and a pitcher of beer. And all the time, he'd be
smoking big black cigars." Roger Kahn has it that at Ruth's funeral,
Joe Dugan, complaining of the heat, said that he would give his right
arm for a cold beer. Waite Hoyt, former Yankee pitcher, turned to him
and said, "So would the Babe."

The most famous of the overeating, overdrinking incidents was
the so-called stomach-ache-heard-'round-the-world. Near the end of
spring training in 1925 the Yankees were headed north, and Ruth's
collapse coming off the train in Asheville, North Carolina, created
quite a sensation. In some British papers his death was reported, and
rumors to that effect circulated in the United States. He was brought
to New York, where it was reported he underwent abdominal surgery
for an intestinal abscess. The Yankee management explained that
Ruth had been suffering from a case of massive indigestion. All of
this undoubtedly contributed to his reputation as a man of large
appetites. However, there have been recent suggestions that his
problems in 1925 were more related to his sexual appetite than to his
penchant for hot dogs. If this were true, it certainly was not reported
in the press. According to Fred Lieb, he and his colleagues tended to
cover up this side of Ruth's life. Lieb compared Ruth to Joe Namath
in this respect. Kahn and Seymour had similar tales. Seymour also
noted that the term "sultan" could be applied on or off the field; Ruth
was known to have "dallied with women all over the circuit and also

patronized the brothels." It should be added that Ruth was not the only playboy on the Yankee team or in baseball. And Ruth was never seen to be even the least bit shaky during a game.

In addition to fast women, Ruth also liked fast cars. On numerous occasions he received citations for speeding; in July 1920 he was in a serious accident, at two o'clock in the morning, that created a great stir in New York. Ruth was not hurt, but many New Yorkers stayed home from work the following morning and gathered around the news bulletin boards in order to get the details. By early afternoon, when Ruth's condition was known, the city was able to return to normal.

The Babe also played fast and loose with his money. During the off-season of 1920–21 he made a trip to Cuba, where he lost a reported $35,000 on the horses. He returned to the United States broke, despite having received $1,000 a game while in Cuba. About the same time he lost another $35,000 investing in a movie, in which he was to have starred. On occasion, he was reprimanded in print for this sort of irresponsibility, but it was usually excused as Ruth's innocence. One writer noted in *The Sporting News* that it was "the old story about giants with the brains of a boy." Besides, the public loved it.

Like that of so many other players of his time, Babe Ruth's vocabulary suffered from his lack of education and was made up largely of the lingo of the locker room. According to Fred Lieb, Ruth's language was heavily laced with profanities, the Babe was able to squeeze four profanities into a six-word sentence. The general crudity was seldom put into print. One small-town writer, apparently unschooled in rewrite, did capture the essence of Ruthian prose in his interview with the Babe shortly after his return from Cuba in early 1921. When asked about his trip, Ruth said, "Them greasers are punk players. Only a few of them are any good. This guy they calls after me because he made a few homers is as black as a ton-and-a-half of coal in a dark cellar."

The Bambino was a colorful character in an age that seemed to put a premium on that undefinable quality. This and his success endeared him to the baseball public. One writer quoted by *Literary Digest* called him a "new Paul Bunyan," "a lovable vagabond," and an "urchin." He was reckless and had "Gargantuan appetites." "He has all of our faults, and in spite of them all the material success we should like to have." This may have been the key to his popularity.

In the emerging urban-industrial society, Babe Ruth stood out. He refused to be reshaped and become one of the faceless urban mass or made over into a company man. To a people heading into the corporate anonymity of the twentieth century he was a screaming symbol, saying "I won't go"—to some, the last gasp of the rugged individual. Not only did he perform skillfully with bat and ball and live the wild life of many people's fantasies, but, above all, he defied the establishment. He flaunted authority and thumbed his nose at the boss and at the rules, and still he succeeded. He withstood the pressures pushing modern man to conformity and anonymity. It is virtually impossible to imagine a Ruth in post–World War II baseball.

Early in his career Ruth gave signs that he would be difficult to handle. Although it was primarily finances that led Boston Red Sox owner Harry Frazee to sell Ruth to the Yankees, there were some indications that the question of discipline may have played at least a minor role. Stories circulated that Ruth was insubordinate, a man who didn't know the meaning of training rules, whose conduct was producing dissension in the Boston club. Some people felt that Ruth thought himself bigger than the Boston Red Sox and bigger than the game of baseball. This may just have been the Boston management's way of rationalizing the sale of Ruth to the Yankees.

It did not take the Babe long after joining the Yankees to demonstrate his uncontrollability. During the 1921 World Series, Ruth had been unable to play in some games because of an injury. When one writer suggested in print that Ruth was not badly hurt, the Babe stormed up to the press box before one of the games and publicly challenged him. Following the 1921 World Series, Ruth and two other Yankee players went on a barnstorming tour, defying Judge Landis' ruling that participants in the World Series could not barnstorm. Ruth ignored both the commissioner and the Yankee front office, maintaining that the ruling was unfair and that he had contractual obligations to fulfill. The result was suspension for the opening of the 1922 season. The suspension kept Ruth out of the Yankee lineup until May 20. During the winter and spring considerable criticism of Landis appeared in print. Clark Griffith, among others, pointed out that the suspension was hurting the Yankees and the rest of the American League clubs more than it hurt Ruth. It was estimated that the Yankees alone would lose $144,000 in gate receipts at home and on the road. In addition the suspension would have a direct bearing on the pennant race of 1922. Landis stood his ground in the face of this and other public pressure.

It must have given Ruth's ego a great boost to see this pressure applied on Landis, and he must have been even more pleased when Yankee Stadium was sold out for his May 20 return to the lineup. It was estimated that 100,000 tickets could have been sold. The New York police had to be brought out to control the crowd. The only disappointment was that Ruth could not deliver one of his patented home runs for special occasions.

Ruth had difficulties in 1922 and never really got into the groove. He was frustrated and showed it. A week or so after his return to the lineup, the fans began to taunt him. During a game in Yankee Stadium he tried to stretch a single into a double and was called out as he slid into second base. Angry, Ruth jumped up and threw dirt in the umpire's face. Needless to say, he was ejected from the game. As he returned to the dugout the fans booed, and one fan near the dugout caught Ruth's attention, probably with a string of obscenities although press reports said that the man called Ruth a "big bum." Ruth climbed over the dugout and set out after the man, who wisely found the nearest exit. The boos increased, and Ruth challenged the entire crowd to a fight. There were no takers. Ruth drew another suspension for these antics. Joe Vila charged that Ruth was spending too much time at the racetrack and had refused to take morning batting practice while suspended. Ruth was clearly out of shape, with a bad eye and an expanded waistline.

One of the redeeming features of bad conduct is that it allows for conversion, reform, and the great comeback. Following his poor season and dismal World Series in 1922, Ruth came under considerable criticism from the press. His press agent announced that the Babe (who was now being referred to as the Swatless Sultan) would not be barnstorming. He would also turn down all vaudeville offers, because the footlights bothered his eyesight and inhibited his home-run abilities. Instead, Babe would head to his new Massachusetts farm, where he would rest during the winter months. During the winter, pictures appeared in the nation's sports pages showing Ruth in communion with nature, getting back to the simple life and staying in shape by chopping wood. What better way to reform the man corrupted by the wiles of the city than for him to return to the simplicity of rural America? And the whole process began with the dinner in New York at which Ruth had been so deeply moved by the words of Senator Walker. The "cure" worked, and Ruth returned to be named the MVP of 1923.

But the Bambino had not permanently changed. The next major blowup came late in the 1925 season. The Yankees were not having a good season. During a western road trip manager Huggins finally cracked down on the Babe, suspending him and fining him $5,000. Ruth was outraged. He denied that he had been drinking excessively or was guilty of any other misconduct. He claimed instead that Huggins was just looking for an excuse for the poor showing of the Yankees. Ruth laid the blame for the Yankee failure at the feet of Huggins, saying there was going to be a showdown, with either Huggins or himself to go. In fact, the Yankee management had had a detective following Ruth, and it was reported that Ruth had missed curfew the night before his suspension because he had been with several different women. The Babe started back to New York, granting interviews at train stations along the way and escalating his rhetoric against Huggins. He bragged about how he was going to put Huggins in his place and called Huggins a lousy manager. On his arrival in New York, Ruth was met by a crowd of reporters who followed him up to owner Ruppert for the great confrontation. Ruth was apparently confident that Ruppert would support him. But after the meeting, Ruppert called in the press to take a message from "Root," as the colonel with his German accent called him. Ruth apologized for his conduct and apologized to Miller Huggins. The fine stayed in force, although after Huggins' death Ruppert returned the money to the Babe.

This whole spectacle gave his critics an opportunity to bombard the Bambino. Frank Lane of *Baseball Magazine* had long been disturbed by the fact that Ruth had destroyed "scientific baseball" and brought the home run to such prominence. Lane took this opportunity to try to separate the facts about Babe Ruth from the myth:

> A popular idol fell with a crash to the dust when.Babe Ruth was fined and suspended by Miller Huggins. To the public that surveys its heroes through a golden haze of misplaced admiration this drastic act of the Yankee manager came as a distinct shock. Through this golden haze Ruth loomed big and heroic. He moved as a celebrity, even among prominent people. He was the headliner of lurid sport sheets; the idol of the sandlots. This haze of inaccurate, almost meaningless bunk endowed Ruth with virtues utterly alien to his nature, and softened or obliterated that coarse strain, those crude defects, those fatal weaknesses which made him an object rather of apology and of pity than of admiration to those who knew him best.
>
> Ruth's popularity has become a thing monstrous, formless, senseless. It has been exaggerated beyond all the bounds of sanity. It has made of Ruth a fable; a fiction rather than a man...
>
> Of course his fellow players, the sport writers, those who knew him as he is, were not deceived by all this flamboyant exploitation. They saw in him the poor boy of the charity school, the child of an inferior family, a wilful youngster full of crude, bad impulses who never grew up. When Ban Johnson said Ruth has the mind of a fifteen-year-old boy, he did not exaggerate. Crude, uncultured, ill-educated, unrefined, there is little about Ruth, to those who know him, to suggest Ruth the popular idol. His wild license, his utter disregard of all regulations, his coarse escapades have been a burning theme in baseball to all who knew, since fickle fame first marked him for her favorite. There is little substance for Babe Ruth the myth of popular imagination in Babe Ruth the reality....
>
> When there is so much pure metal unalloyed at hand, why must the public, in the mold of its own distorted imagination, cast a heroic figure with feet of clay?

Lane's closing question may supply its own answer. Ruth was a hero cast in the public's own image. He had all their weaknesses and was still a hero, a success, and rich. He was, in short, a perfect symbol for the common man in America. Read in another light, Lane's lament shows a remarkable similarity to the kind of criticism that was leveled against the participants in the revolt of the intellectuals in the 1920s. The old conventions were under attack. In a curious way Babe Ruth could symbolize both sides, leading both the attack and the defense—Babe Ruth as mythic hero, defending; Babe Ruth the reality, attacking.

Despite its critics, the Ruth legend held together. By mid-September Ruth was back with the Yankees. It appeared to some that he had turned over a new leaf and was redeeming himself. Ruth was "submissive and sensible" and had learned that he wasn't bigger than baseball. The following spring Ruth was off to a good start. *The Sporting News* saw this as yet another lesson in the benefits of good conduct and clean living. Once again, the reform of the sinner made great copy and was added to the Ruthian myth.

Part of the Ruth legend also touches the political scene. The most famous episode in this respect has to do with Ruth's large salary in the early 1930s. There are several accounts of this story, all of which may be apocryphal. Mrs. Ruth, Harold Seymour, and Fred Lieb each has a version. The essence is that while the Babe was negotiating a contract with the Yankees, someone—in some versions, Ruppert—mentioned to Ruth that he would be making more money than President Hoover. Ruth is supposed to have said that he had had a better year than Hoover. Few would have disputed the claim. Another illustration of Ruth's lack of awe of the presidency is illustrated by Roger Kahn's story of an encounter between the Babe and President Coolidge (in some accounts, President Harding). All of the Yankees had lined up to meet the president before a game. As the president approached Ruth, the Babe removed his cap and wiped his brow. The president greeted him with, "Mr. Ruth." The Babe is supposed to have replied, "Hot as hell, ain't it, prez?"

In 1928 Ruth supported his friend Al Smith for the presidency. In Washington, candidate Hoover, seeking to demonstrate his identity with the common man through the National Pastime, attended a game. Someone tried to arrange to have Hoover's picture taken with Babe Ruth. This certainly would have made a nice contribution to campaign literature. Ruth, however, declined the request for the picture. Although his motives aren't clear, Ruth's support of Al Smith seems the most likely explanation. At any rate, the press made much of the incident to the embarrassment of Hoover and perhaps even to Ruth. There is also the tale that during the 1928 campaign Ruth was doing a series of radio spots on Smith's behalf. On one occasion he interviewed Tony Lazzeri, and Ruth is supposed to have said, "Well, Tony, how are the wops going to vote?" This ended Ruth's radio campaigning. Perhaps none of these stories is true, but they have become a part of the Ruth legend. They illustrate the public's belief in the man's simplicity and natural qualities and the sense that Ruth stood above all others in the public mind, even the president of the United States.

The longer Ruth played, the greater the myth became. As his career came to its close there was a kind of uneasiness about the future of baseball and the future of the Bambino, evidenced in an enormous amount of speculation on the inevitable end. As the end approached there was also a considerable amount of myth-enhancing and image-polishing by the sportswriters as they pre-pared for the inevitable canonization of this man who had so domi-nated his times.

Although Ruth didn't finally retire until early in the 1935 season, some saw the end coming much earlier. After the 1930 season W.O. McGeehan, writing in the *New York Herald Tribune*, was beginning to see signs that the Babe was in decline. Ruth had lost his position as leader in home runs to Hack Wilson of the Cubs and had been incapacitated by nagging injuries throughout the season. McGeehan noted that it was a pity for baseball, but Ruth, after all, was a human being and could not last forever. But Ruth still had several great seasons ahead of him. At the beginning of the 1933 season *The Sporting News* noted that Ruth was still on top as a hero. Of those who had entered baseball in 1914 there were only six remaining. While the others still performed well, Ruth's record was even more remarkable because he had maintained a position in the front ranks. Many other heroes had long since fallen from the pedestal. Ruth had displayed the "attributes of a superman." If 1933 were to be his last season, then he could retire "with the satisfaction that he [had] won

such distinction as few men in any walk of life have accomplished"
and amidst the praise, "Well done, thou good and faithful servant."

As the 1934 season developed, it seemed almost certain that it
would be Ruth's last, at least as a player. Ruth himself wanted to
manage, but only in the major leagues. The Yankees, however, were
not interested, as they had demonstrated by hiring Joe McCarthy as
manager in 1931. Mrs. Ruth reports that Ruth felt the job should have
been his, and perhaps this accounts for the resentment the Babe held
for McCarthy. Ruth believed that anyone could have won with the
Yankee players and that McCarthy, who had never played major-
league baseball, was a "busher." Ruth's only major-league managerial opportunity, at the end of the 1933 season at Detroit, is described
by Fred Lieb: Frank Navin, president of the Tigers, got in touch with
Ed Barrow, Yankee general manager, and received Barrow's permission to make an offer to Ruth. Barrow was eager to get Ruth out of the
Yankee organization to avoid future problems. Navin then asked
Ruth to come to Detroit to talk about the job, but Ruth was committed
to go to Hawaii and told Navin he would talk to him when he returned. By then it was too late, as Navin had hired Mickey Cochrane.
Ruth was to spend the rest of his life frustrated by his failure to secure
a major-league managerial position.

In August 1934 *The Sporting News* reflected on the anticipated end
of Ruth's active playing career. It felt the Babe belonged in the game.
There had never been anyone as representative of the game or anyone who had ever so completely caught the imagination of the public
as had Ruth. Undoubtedly, everyone was reluctant to see the Babe
retire; probably no one more reluctant than the great man himself.
But, *The Sporting News* philosophized, "nature takes its toll of high
and low alike and Ruth must bow to the demands of time, as does
everyone else...." But what of his future? The editors thought it
would be a good idea for Ruth to tour the country as a man who could
hit for the pitcher in minor-league games. He would act as a sort of
missionary for baseball, and it would allow his many fans to see him
in the flesh. This, of course, would be a minor inconvenience to
Ruth; but then, not only had Ruth done a lot for baseball, but baseball
had also done a lot for Ruth.

In September 1934 Kenneth D. Fry, writing in *The Chicagoan*, reflected on Ruth and several others who had passed from baseball in recent years, noting that they had played a professional sport, but it was a sport more honest than any of the amateur sports. These men were not to be found in *Who's Who*, "because they never received Ph.D.'s and never wrote books, like any little old two-by-four college professor." No, they took their drinks and chewed their tobacco while receiving the praise and criticism of the people in the stands. Fry said that all of this might seem unimportant, but when Babe Ruth announced his retirement, fans jammed Fenway Park and Yankee Stadium to get their last look at the Bambino. When the Babe failed to hit a homer for them it didn't really matter; what mattered, Fry felt, was that they had come to see him: "It's damn near as important as a stratosphere flight." These men had contributed something. "They might not be the guys you'd want for your church social, but they've

Reprinted from the *New York Post*

kept a lot of kids reading batting averages and forgetting crap games."

Many writers claimed that there would never be another Babe Ruth. Yet, knowing that Ruth would leave a large void in the game, many began to search for his logical successor. Some felt that Jimmy Foxx might be the one. He could hit the home run ball often. He had been raised on a farm, where he had developed large arm and shoulder muscles wrestling with milk cans and doing other farm chores. But Foxx, like so many who came later, lacked the drama of Ruth. As one writer complained in *Literary Digest,* "There are no bright lights and dissipation in the career of Jimmy Foxx.... He could do with a few engaging faults, and a press agent to keep them before us."

Others thought they saw Ruth's successor in Lynwood Thomas ("Schoolboy") Rowe of the Detroit Tigers. Sam Greene, Detroit correspondent for *The Sporting News,* saw the coming of Rowe as a result of "the inevitable law of compensation." Although the two men did not look alike, they did share many characteristics. Both started as pitchers; both hit the long ball; both had a rare gift for showmanship and therefore attracted great crowds on and off the field; both liked to sign autographs; and both were flattered by "the adulation of the mob." Not only that, success had not gone to Rowe's head, and he fully understood his own importance to the baseball public. And, of course, his nickname, "Schoolboy," appealed to the public in the same way that "Babe" carried publicity value for Ruth. It would be great for baseball to have "such a happy transmigration of power—from the Babe to the Schoolboy...." But Rowe did not live up to expectations. So the public had to wait for the next dominant figure to emerge. When he did he wore a Yankee uniform, but he was entirely different in character from Babe Ruth.

As it turned out Ruth did not retire at the end of the 1934 season. Instead, he was lured to the Boston Braves by owner Judge Emil Fuchs, who held out the prospect of a future managerial position as bait so that he might exploit the name of Ruth to shore up the financial problems of the Braves. Naturally, the announcement of Ruth's move to Boston came as a shock and disappointment to many in New York and to Yankee fans around the country. The fact that

Ruth was going to the National League raised even further doubts. It is amazing that other American League owners passed up the opportunity to pick Ruth up on waivers and allowed this great box office attraction to move on to the other league. Many doubted the wisdom of the move and wondered about its effect on the Yankees and the American League. In the end, the impact was negligible.

The opening of the 1935 season in Boston was filled with anticipation. A large crowd turned out to cheer Babe Ruth on in his homecoming. With his special flare for the dramatic, Ruth responded with a home run. *The Sporting News* said this "proved that although a man may be down, he is never out, and that courage and showmanship are ageless." But courage and showmanship could not sustain Ruth through the 1935 season. Finally, in June, following a dispute with Judge Fuchs, Ruth called it quits. It seems appropriate that the immediate issue of the dispute centered on Ruth's desire for a few days off to attend a party on the arrival of the oceanliner *Normandie* in New York. Many mourned his passing from the game, and there were again numerous suggestions offered for his future. For the most part, these centered on some scheme to promote baseball among young boys. *The Sporting News* paid its tribute to the Babe and fairly accurately predicted his future in a June 13, 1935, editorial titled "The Babe Strikes Out":

> Nothing can ever efface, however, the marks he has put into the records. They will stand there until someone else can come along and obliterate them, and it is doubtful whether some of his achievements ever will be surpassed. To those who have been growing old with the Bambino, he ever will remain a glamorous character, who, more than any other individual, put the game back on its feet when it was rocked by a World's Series scandal and who, more than any other player, drew the big gates and attracted the crowds to watch his team perform.
>
> However, the earth went on revolving and the box scores continued to appear just the same after he quit, proving that no matter how great is a man, he is only a tiny figure in the entire picture. It is to be hoped that baseball will find a place for one who once was so close to the hearts of the fans, but that place won't be as a player.

The sands of time have run their course in the Babe's playing career, which will become an even dimmer memory as the years elapse and new idols succeed him. It is with keen regret that the fan bids farewell to the Sultan of Swat, but in the game of ball, as in the game of life, the old must give way to the new. The king is dead, long live the king!

5

Commercialism and the Corporate Player

"There were things about the games I liked.
The crowds, for example. I felt like I was part
of something there, you know, like in church,
except it was more *real* than any church, and I
joined in the score-keeping, hollering, the
eating of hot dogs and drinking of Cokes and
beer, and for a while I even had the idea that
ball stadiums, and not European churches were
the real American holy places."

MAJOR-LEAGUE baseball represented a society seeking to reaffirm
old values and clinging to its fading past. At the same time it was
living in a changing world and was not immune from the effects of
change. The changes were recognized and recorded, and their
relative merits were hotly debated. There were changes in the style
of the game that had been brought on by the home run and changes
in the organizational and business side of the game that reflected the
fact that mass entertainment was becoming a big business in
America. There was a growing concern about competition from
other sports and the position of baseball as the National Pastime.
Above all, there was a change in the nature of the player, as he
became more and more a member of a large corporate venture. The
increased organization and bureaucratization of life in the United
States, as it became more and more an urban-industrial culture, had

an impact on baseball. To borrow the terminology of sociologist David Riesman, the inner-directed was slowly being replaced by the other-directed type of personality. It should be emphasized that this process of change was only beginning, and would not be completed until after World War II.

The coming of Babe Ruth and his home run bat revolutionized major-league baseball. According to the *Baseball Encyclopedia*, the statistics indicate that between 1919 and 1921 there was a significant increase in home runs, runs per game, and batting averages. During the same period there was a sharp decrease in stolen bases. The early Twenties also witnessed an increase in the use of the relief pitcher. Most of these changes were related directly or indirectly to the emergence of the home run. In fact, the home run was considered important enough in 1920 for the Liggett and Myers Tobacco Company to produce a cigarette called "Home Run." It cost fifteen cents a pack and was advertised as having a "cool taste."

Not everyone was as enthusiastic about the homer as Liggett and Myers. What was called the "lively ball controversy" developed and ran hot and cold through the 1930s. Taking note of this controversy early in the 1921 season, *The Sporting News* expressed belief that there had been no change in the ball; the fact that the umpires were quicker to remove balls from play explained the new liveliness. It was also held that most fans liked the change and did not want to see a return to the lower scoring games, as evidenced by record-breaking attendance and "unprecedented enthusiasm." Those who could not keep up with the changing times were chided: "It is a fast age, and we're doing time in jazz, not goose step." The home run was not destroying baseball, only changing it. It brought new excitement and new uncertainty to the game.

The enthusiasm of *The Sporting News* was not totally unqualified. In an editorial instructively titled "The Triumph of the Crass," the home run's popularity was attributed to the love of spectacle by the "ignorant general average of human kind." Since grandstands were built for the "mob," they had to be filled to pay the bills. There were misgivings about the popularity of the long ball. One writer decried "the short right-field-fence hero," who was destroying "real" baseball and promoting "indiscipline." Even more distressed was F. C. Lane of *Baseball Magazine*, who mourned the passing of the stolen base, which he felt was one of the best plays in baseball. He felt that the decline in stolen bases was due to an increasing emphasis on organization and mechanization. The stolen base had allowed the player to be a thinking human being, not just a cog in a machine. Now the stolen base was being "sacrificed on the altar of mechanical perfection."

Despite these complaints the home run continued to enjoy immense popularity. In 1928 John B. Sheridan found the home run as popular as ever, and he described the popularity in terms of the revolt of the Twenties. It was part of the general trend to throw off the restrictions of the past. The possibility of seeing a home run was thrilling to the baseball fan, in the same sense that the "flapper thrills over her cigaret and still shorter skirt."

By 1929 *The Sporting News* was growing weary of the preoccupation with the home run, fearing it was beginning to overshadow the game. The problem was not, of course, Babe Ruth; it was all those players who were emulating him. Criticism mounted. The St. Louis Browns put up a large screen in right field to eliminate what many writers had felt was a cheap home run. (The screen became a subject of some controversy in 1932 when Jimmy Foxx hit 58 home runs and fell two short of Ruth's 1927 record, which had been set before the screen was put up.) One St. Louis sportswriter applauded the action by the Browns' management. He felt that the screen would add to the action of the game by increasing the number of doubles and close plays at second base and that the home run had been cheapened to the point that it was losing its popularity. There was, he said, a trend toward "reversion to rational methods in baseball."

But in 1929 and 1930 there were more hits, runs, and home runs than ever. Team batting averages jumped to over .300. According to Fred Lieb this brought about a "drastic deadening" of the lively ball in 1931 and again in 1933 and resulted in many low-scoring games for the New York Giants, who won the pennant but suffered from low attendance. Some of the drop in attendance was due to the effects of the depression, but Lieb felt that it was also related to the deadening of the ball. On the other hand a 1936 poll by *The Sporting News* indicated an eight-to-five preference for a restoration of the balance between pitching and hitting. In many ways the argument was moot: Baseball had changed, and it would never again be what it was prior to World War I. The same could be said of the nation.

William Allen White chose *A Puritan in Babylon* as the title for his biography of President Calvin Coolidge. That image could be equally apt for some people connected with baseball in the Twenties who expressed alarm over what they termed the "growing commercialism" in baseball. The World Series fix of 1919 had been a sign to some that the commercial element was too strong in baseball, but the criticism was not restricted to this one point. There were claims that commercialism among the owners was affecting the fans, who were coming to regard the home run as the main point of the game. Even more disturbing, some modern fans seemed to regard baseball as a "mere amusement," while another segment was using the game as a vehicle for gambling.

Late in the 1922 season a scandal broke surrounding New York Giant pitcher Phil Douglas. He had written a letter to Les Mann of the St. Louis Cardinals offering to throw games to prevent McGraw and the Giants from winning another pennant—at least this was the charge. Joe Vila immediately called for a reduction of the money in the World Series. He saw it as a source of commercialism that was ruining baseball. He also called for an end to the "greed and avarice of the players." John B. Sheridan did not agree. He reminded his readers that there had been scandal before the World Series even existed. To inhibit or do away with the World Series would have an adverse effect on fan interest in baseball. The big money prizes were the "soul" of baseball and all other successful American enterprises. "Money chasing is the great American game. Professional baseball is based on money chasing." In the same issue of *The Sporting News* the editors voiced their agreement with Sheridan. They suggested that anyone who recommended abolishing the World Series because of commercialism ought to join the Communists or restudy human nature. "The only people we know who don't care whether or not they reap a bit of the yellow harvest are those who look with suspicion on every man who washes his neck and wears a clean collar."

The 1922 World Series was played, of course, but it brought more charges of commercialism. The second game of the series was called on account of darkness—some forty-five minutes before sunset. This caused a great uproar from the fans in the stands. Charges leveled that the game was called so that the owners could milk the public for more money. Commissioner Landis acted quickly and arbitrarily by announcing that all the gate receipts would be turned over to charity. In the face of his action, some of the players complained that Landis had no right to give away money that was rightfully theirs. The only effect of this protest was that the players became another target for those who complained of commercialism. *The Sporting News* was disturbed, not so much by commercialism as by the lack of a "sporting atmosphere" which permeated New York, and it was charged that both the Giants and Yankees had bought their way to a pennant.

By 1926 there was growing criticism about the evils of commercialism in baseball even in *The Sporting News*: The players were becoming overpaid and not keeping their minds on the game. It seemed as though the game had become only an incident in the busy day of the major leaguer. The player still did his job but gave only what was required of him, nothing more. The editors felt the root of the problem was too much money for the winners of the World Series, and the fact that even teams that finished second, third, and fourth received a share of the money. "There was a time when ball players ate, slept, and lived baseball. Goodness how the fans loved them." The excess attention being given to "the show side of sport" was considered bad policy because it neglected the building of sportsmanship among the young men. With the end of the decade the great concern over commercialism faded, as commercialism in the nation at large took a breather during the darker days of the depression.

The 1920s have often been called the Golden Age of Sport. During that decade both participatory and spectator sport enjoyed booming popularity and prosperity. Although baseball reaped the benefits of the trend, it also raised new concerns. Some sportswriters interpreted the rise of the popularity of other sports as a threat to baseball. They voiced the fear that baseball was actually experiencing a decline in the midst of its seeming prosperity or that the American boy was abandoning baseball for other sports. If the owners did not take action to cultivate the youth, the future of baseball was in jeopardy.

But by 1927 The Sporting News no longer feared for the future of the National Pastime. Record-breaking attendance figures for the opening of the 1927 season belittled the claims of those who were still pronouncing the death of baseball. They were dismissed as prophets of doom and "cynical New York writers." By the end of the season it was clear that hero worship was not dead and the American boy was still interested in baseball. It had been the year of Ruth's 60 home runs, highlighted by a season-long home run race between Ruth and Gehrig and capped by Ruth's spectacular record for September. Following the regular season and World Series, Ruth and Gehrig made a cross-country tour, visiting 20 cities and attracting some 220,000 people. The crowds were made up largely of boys. Many schools closed so that these boys could see their heroes. Coupled with the optimistic results of Ban Johnson's survey of playground conditions, this tour led The Sporting News to conclude that in 1927 baseball was still number one with the American boy.

The critics were not silenced, however. In 1929 several articles appeared raising the issue that baseball was a dull game and in decline. Herbert Reed, writing in Outlook, said that baseball had become a circus for the mob, who turned out only to see the heroes and not the game. Reed also said that baseball was a game for the "proletariat" that required little brain power either to play or to watch. Worst of all it was a slow and dull game, and Reed said that he was pleased to see that the younger generation was deserting baseball. This was a serious charge. A slow and dull game could never sustain itself in a society that was increasing its speed and could ultimately find meaning only in intense activity.

Jack Kofoed, writing in the North American Review, saw baseball dying a slow death caused by a number of factors, including the decline in the number of colorful players, the pricing of young boys out of the bleachers, and a loss of intensity and fire by players and fans. Irving Vaughan affirmed this view in *The Sporting News* when he called for more fights in baseball and termed them a "revival of the old spirit of competition." The argument still goes on today. However, lack of speed remained a major criticism. In 1939 *The Sporting News* confronted the issue in an editorial titled "Streamlining the Game." The editors noted that automobiles, trains, planes, houses and even pictures were being streamlined. "It is an age of speed, and baseball, to survive, must keep up with the procession." It was time to streamline baseball.

Streamlining implied more than just physical speed. It also related to organization. In that respect, the late Twenties and the Thirties witnessed a streamlining that touched almost all aspects of baseball except the rules of the game. The process and its impact were reflected in the changes in baseball as a business organization and in player personnel, producing what will be referred to here as the corporate player.

In 1933 *The Sporting News* commented on the death of several of the major-league club owners, saying it seemed that the day of one-man ownership of baseball teams was disappearing. The new times required new structures. Baseball administration must become like that of a business—a board of directors, made up of men of diverse interests and talents, must replace the one-man ownership pattern of the past. Baseball could no longer be a personal venture but must become a cooperative one, run by a "corporation of sportsmen" who were interested not only in the sport itself but also in the benefits that a baseball team could bring to a community. It was necessary for baseball clubs to become community enterprises, surrounded by community pride and sustained by community spirit. Although such an organizational arrangement never fully developed during the years between the wars, there was an awareness that baseball was existing in a changing world.

Probably the most significant organizational development was the chain-store or farm system, pioneered by Branch Rickey, who developed the system for the St. Louis Cardinals in the Twenties. The farm system, like most new ideas in baseball, was slow to catch on among other owners. It was also fought vigorously by Commissioner Landis. But its triumph had an air of inevitability about it. The last of the opponents, the New York Giants, began constructing its farm system in 1937. The development of farms was viewed as a mixed blessing by many and condemned by others. In 1932 Tommy Holmes, writing in the *Brooklyn Eagle*, was not convinced of the benefits of farms. While admitting that the system brought great success to the Cardinals, Holmes questioned whether Rickey might. be "efficiency-experting the Cardinals into smaller and smaller gate receipts." Holmes allowed that Rickey was an expert at handling the St. Louis "machine," but protested that the public was not interested in machines. Rickey didn't understand that baseball's popularity depended on "tradition, sentiment, human warmth, and kindred emotions that it succeeds in arousing in the breasts of its supporters." In 1935 *The Sporting News* expressed the fear that the chain-store system might kill local interest in minor-league baseball because of its centralized nature and resulting lack of community involvement in the teams.

In 1937 Branch Rickey predicted the end of the scout as a means of finding baseball talent. He would be replaced by the summer baseball camps developed by the Cardinals. *The Sporting News* was again alarmed: "Mass production" was threatening to "force the individual to the sidelines." The end of the scout in baseball would be regretted; "but modern progress is no respecter of persons."

There were fears that the farm system might reduce the elements of drama and romance in baseball. Under the chain system, player development had become a highly rational system in which players progressed gradually up the system one or two steps at a time. They no longer appeared out of nowhere to become overnight sensations. This disturbing development diminished baseball's role as "a game of glittering opportunity."

Branch Rickey created the chain system, and George Weiss of the New York Yankees perfected it. During the Twenties the Yankees had relied on the checkbook to create and maintain the great Yankee teams, but by the late Thirties the Yankees had developed a massive farm system which, together with the Yankee bankroll, made the Bronx Bombers the dominant force in major-league baseball for the next several decades. By the end of the 1937 season the dominance had become obvious, and the cry of "break up the Yankees" grew to deafening proportions. Following the 1937 World Series—second in a row for the Yankees—*The Sporting News* expressed fears that the Yankees were becoming a monopoly and killing all competition. If that persisted, it could mean disaster for major-league baseball. But mixed with the fear was admiration. The 1937 Yankees were one of the greatest teams of all times. The Yankees "showed everything and were welded into a seemingly perfect machine, which functioned smoothly, precisely and flawlessly." The metaphor of the "machine" was being used with increasing frequency in the land of the rugged individual.

Yankee owner, Col. Jacob Ruppert, was not impressed by the calls to break up the Yankees or by charges that the Yankees constituted a monopoly. Ruppert said that the Yankees had no intention of break-ing themselves up. Instead they would go on developing talent in order to win pennants by as wide a margin as possible. If baseball really felt the Yankees were a threat, then baseball should lose no time following the Yankee system of organization. And what was the system? The Yankees had developed a farm system that developed replacements "automatically." It had produced Gordon and Keller, and, added the Colonel, "it will go on and on."

And it did. In the midst of the 1939 season Clark Griffith offered the owners two proposals aimed directly at the Yankees. The first called for a ban on trading within the league by the league champion. The second forbade ownership of more than one farm team in each minor-league classification above class D. At their winter meetings, American League owners adopted the first of these proposals but rejected the second, which would have been much more effective in preventing a monopoly on talent. As it turned out, the Yankees failed to win the 1940 pennant, and the rule was repealed. When the ban on trades was adopted, there was a good deal of adverse comment. *The Sporting News*, while agreeing with the motives, did not like the idea of discriminatory legislation. If the Yankees were to be taken care of, it should be done "on the playing field, and not by the club owners in a meeting room." The many writers who agreed with this statement were incapable of releasing themselves from the older competitive values, even though they knew they were functioning in entirely new structural forms. This problem was not uncommon as the American culture of the rural nineteenth century attempted to come to terms with the realities of the urban-industrial twentieth century.

The 1930s also saw an effort to apply the principles of business to baseball, especially in the areas of advertising and promotional techniques. In a 1930 editorial titled "Be Discreet," *The Sporting News* expressed misgivings about promotional techniques in baseball. "Sideshow accessories" had the effect of creating "a counterfeit of genuine interest." Club owners were warned that they must preserve the "sense of dignity" which major-league baseball deserved. This was a warning similar to those against commercialism in the 1920s. But by the end of the Thirties, all such warnings had vanished. The "sideshow accessories" of 1930 had become sound business techniques by 1940.

The first major breakthrough came in 1933 with the institution of the All-Star game. Many owners opposed it, for a variety of reasons. Some managers resented the break in the regular schedule. But those who supported the All-Star game did so on the basis that it would stir interest and serve to promote baseball. Dan Daniel, writing in the *New York World-Telegram*, felt that it was about time baseball did something to focus attention on itself and encourage interest: "What baseball needs is more showmanship, more innovations, in place of mental static and physical inertia which now are found in so many high places in the game." J. G. Taylor Spink, publisher of *The Sporting News*, was equally enthusiastic about the All-Star game. Baseball had been backwards in developing promotional techniques, and Spink hoped that the All-Star game would be "the dawning of a new era of enterprise...."

A few months later *The Sporting News* called for the adoption of an official insignia for organized baseball to use for advertising purposes in the same way that the NRA (National Recovery Administration) insignia was being used. A good promotional manager ought to be able to find numerous uses for such an emblem: as stickers for automobiles, as directional indicators on telephone poles to show the way to the ball park, and on posters. "Any attraction that is worthwhile is worth advertising...," said the publication.

The quintessence of the new approach to baseball was found in two men, Phillip K. Wrigley and Larry MacPhail. During the winter of 1934–35 Charles Drake, Wrigley's assistant, announced an advertising campaign for the Chicago Cubs. The theme of the campaign was to be "sunshine, recreation, and pleasure": "Mr. Wrigley is applying merchandising methods to baseball." Drake went on to say that Wrigley had found in the chewing gum business that the constant repetition in advertising built a desire for the product into the public consciousness. Of course, the product had to come in a nice, clean, attractive package; therefore, Wrigley Field would be beautified. *The Sporting News* believed that the Cubs' president was following sound business methods in thus advertising his team. In 1939 *The Sporting News* reported that Phil Wrigley had introduced marketing research into baseball. "The old days of the 'public be damned' policy have gone, and baseball, like every other enterprise seeking patronage, must find out what the public wants and what it dislikes."

The other great promoter of baseball in the Thirties, Larry Mac-Phail, practiced his art first in Cincinnati and then moved on to Brooklyn. He was an innovator both on and off the field: among his more notable firsts were baseball's use of radio and television, night games for the majors, and air travel. To some traditionalists, these innovations approached madness. In anticipation of MacPhail's arrival in Brooklyn, Dan Daniel's character "Pitcher Snorter Casey" reported in one of his "Dear Hank Letters" that fans in the New York area had heard so much about MacPhail "that they think the Dodgers now is part of the Ringling Circus." Casey also noted that MacPhail had introduced night ball, radio broadcasts, red uniforms, usherettes, cigarette girls in bright-colored satin pants, lunches for the press, field days, and ladies' day in Cincinnati. He sáid Brooklyn fans are "waiting eagerly for them gals in satin pants...." Casey reported that someone in the Yankee office said MacPhail combined the best of the Dodgers and Coney Island, and a sportswriter was predicting "a merry-go-round in center field in Flatbush." *The Sporting News* undoubtedly had MacPhail in mind when they endorsed showmanship in the form of night games, field days, special days, and drum and bugle corps. However, the paper was quick to add that it was not that the game itself had lost any of its appeal, "but experience has proved that a little added showmanship now and then adds to its entertainment value—and gate receipts."

By 1935 the notion that merchandising methods were essential to baseball had gained wide acceptance. At the annual meeting of the National Association, talks and exhibits dealt with promotion. George Trautman, president of the Columbus American Association club, was one of the principal speakers. He pointed out that no one had a better product to sell than baseball, but it was necessary to attract customers. Although baseball people might not like to think so, they were, in fact, in show business. Also, baseball had to compete with other recreational enterprises. To attract people Trautman proposed many promotional devices including bargain days and merchandise giveaways. Answering the objections of those who claimed that baseball itself should be sufficient attraction without any artificial stimulus, Trautman said that he knew no product that could not gain some benefit by promotion and showmanship.

Of course, things could be carried too far. Promotional techniques had been introduced as a result of declining attendance during the depression. With the return of some prosperity in 1937, *The Sporting News* found less need for "the most flamboyant types of promotion." If a team fell in the standings, some means of creating interest might be necessary. But even in those cases, such things as "fan dancers, hog-calling contests, donkey ball," and other activities not even remotely related to baseball should be avoided. Not only might baseball be cheapened, but the fans might come to expect the extra attractions if they were used all the time. The best promotional devices were "those which enhance the comfort of the fans and contribute to their enjoyment of the game," for instance, loudspeaker systems, more complete scoreboards, and neat ushers and vendors.

The Sporting News said that baseball had proven its ability to attract the public over the long haul and that a well-played game was still the best possible attraction.

Devoted fans of baseball who read *The Sporting News* apparently believed that the game itself was sufficient. In a poll of its readers, "Baseball's Bible" found that, of those who replied, 88 percent opposed any added attractions at the ball park. Of the 12 percent who wanted some sort of change, 4 percent asked for a speedup of the game; 2 percent asked for entertainment between games of a doubleheader; 2 percent wanted a little music or comedy injected into the game; 1 percent wanted "novelties." Honoring players and playing the National Anthem were also mentioned. Were these the opinions of the "real Americans" that sportswriters claimed were the backbone of the game and the backbone of America? If so, how was it that the baseball establishment was out of harmony with them? Apparently, the answer is that to the devout fan the game itself will always be enough. But all fans who go to games are not so devoted. It is also possible that the inner-directed men who were production-oriented and who were attracted to this inner-directed game simply saw no reason for the sideshows that were used to keep baseball vital in an increasingly other-directed society of consumers. It seems a matter of more than passing interest that many of the techniques and concerns that were criticized as signs of overcommercialization in the Twenties were being praised as sound business techniques by the late Thirties.

These changes in the front offices of baseball were accompanied by and helped to produce a change in the nature of the playing personnel of the game. Slowly, and perhaps inevitably, the rugged individualism of the Ruthian type gave way to the new-style corporate player. It is the contention here that these changes in baseball reflected changes in American life itself. All this was both noticed and commented on by the sportswriters of the period.

As early as the mid-Twenties there were complaints that the modern ball player was going soft and losing his fighting spirit. In 1924 Dazzy Vance of the Dodgers, chosen MVP in the National League, was hailed by *The Sporting News* as one of those "rough-and-ready chaps" who had helped to make baseball what it was, not one of those "parlor ball players" who seemed to be more prevalent in the game than in the past. The following year Ed Smith of the *Chicago American* accused the players of "simply going through the motions." He complained that there was only rarely a real fight in baseball. No one was interested in "a match between a cream puff and a chocolate eclair…a little more of the old-fashioned 'choke 'em Charley' wouldn't hurt a bit."

Were the players going soft? Surveying an injury list in 1926 that included upset stomach, sunburn, and fear of an ulcerated tooth, *The Sporting News* charged that the players were being "coddled by trainers" and "pampered by managers." The problem was diagnosed as too much psychology—baseball was not a game of psychology and "mental flapdoodle" but an "old-fashioned game to be played with bat and ball." Complaints of this nature were momentarily halted by the tenacious battle between the Tigers and Cardinals in the 1934 World Series. But a few years later *The Sporting News* was once again complaining about "softies." For some reason there seemed to be an inordinate number of sore arms that year. As a cure the editors prescribed "a little horse sense," "hard-boiled tactics" by the men who paid the bills, and "a little intestinal fortitude" by the players.

When in 1927, the Twenties were proclaimed the "era of Ruth," Francis Wallace found it fitting that the "reigning monarch of baseball's Golden Age should be so frankly the type of man who founded the game." Wallace, in an article in *Scribner's Magazine*, described Ruth as a man who played the game out of love for it, a man whose appetites and emotions were comparable to any of the greats of the past, and as the last of the old school. The collegians had arrived, and the public now had to turn to other sports for "the contact stuff. The National Game has lost its vital thrill." By 1927 college men accounted for one-third of all the starting positions in major-league baseball, changing the atmosphere, as the profession was cultivating respectability. This was a great contrast to the "Bowery period." The sophistication of the players and the economic sensitivity of both players and owners were turning the "care-free national sport into an efficient machine which permits commercial sentiment only." Wallace noted that all of these changes had broken the personal bond between player and fan.

Donie Bush, manager of the Cincinnati Reds in 1933, expressed a similar view, saying that the public was tiring of the "business-like baseball" that had developed in the majors. Bush blamed this change on the college player, who had too easy a road to the majors. "They step right into the big money without going through the lean days which make them realize that what they have is worth fighting to hold," said Bush.

The emergence of the collegian and spreading technology were seen as conspiring to make the "busher" an endangered species in baseball. This development was noticed by J. G. Taylor Spink in 1937 as he toured the spring training camps. Spink reported that the "green-horn Rookie" was nowhere in evidence, attributing it to three factors. First, by the time most players arrived in the majors they had spent time in the farm systems, where they had learned all the tricks, as well as how to wear their hats. Second, the automobile and the movies had broken down the isolation of the backwoods farms and country villages, spreading social education far and wide. Third, a big percentage of the rookies were college men, who were themselves capable of teaching the veterans a thing or two. The following spring columnist Dan Daniel's character Snorter Casey commented on the same change:

> Well, come to think of it, Hank, the screwballs is not what they used to be. Kids come in all wised up. Serious business. Hard training. Collegeeans, kids which listen to radio and knows all the answers for Prof. Quizz, and kids which goes to the movies and learns all about wimmen from them.
>
> You can't find a single guy in any camp today to pull the badger. Wow, what do you think about that? The world is getting too wise, and so is goin' nuts.

Another casualty of the new era was "color": many writers complained that the new players lacked that undefined quality. There were no "rollicking roisterers" left on the Yankees to carry on the tradition of "free and fast living" set by Ruth. Instead the Yankees were a group of earnest young businessmen whose idea of a good time was to spend a day golfing at the country club. The only exception was Lefty Gomez. Some blamed the lack of color on the new college players; others blamed the umpires and managers, who had become too quick to eject players from games and to fine them.

Courtesy of World Wide Photos

Managers treated the players like a flock of sheep. Players were severely punished and humiliated for staying out too late, drinking a few beers, or for expressing their own opinions. As a result, the players learned quickly to give the appearance of being nice, tidy, and obedient boys. In short, the umpires and managers were doing everything possible to make and keep the players "subdued and innocuously acquiescent."

In fact as early as 1927 Ralph Davis, Pittsburgh sportswriter, pointed out that because baseball was now a business, the club owner could no longer tolerate "silly temperamentalism on the part of any individual in his employ." Sid Keener of the *St. Louis Times*, commenting on the release of a player for off-field conduct, noted that any ball player who refused to accept the rules and regulations of the organization would not be around very long. As the anonymous "observer" of *The Sporting News* put it: "This is the age where it is not so much what you can do, as it is whether or not you conform to the model of what you should be to do it."

During this decline of individualism, there was a growing notion in sports that the players were not much more than interchangeable parts. Other men were always ready and available to take any given player's place. This tended to undermine self-reliance and could only have a bad effect on sport. The chain system stifled individualism, and baseball was becoming less a sport and more a chain of convenience stores. The chain store was seen to substitute the system for the individual. John B. Sheridan feared what he called the "modern idea of big business," which lived by the doctrine that the company must be greater than the individual. When Branch Rickey instituted such a system in St. Louis, Sheridan believed that the frequent changes of managers was Rickey's way of educating the fans about that doctrine. Pointing out that the Cardinals had almost remade their entire team in only four years, Sam Murphy of the *New York Sun* concluded that the chain-store idea eliminated catering to individual stars. If a player had an off year or did not conform to the rules, he would quickly find himself out of the Cardinal organization. Rickey was interested in team players: "No star, no matter how good he may be, will be retained [merely] to strut his stuff for the fans."

In 1936 *The Sporting News* lamented the loss of the "personal element" in baseball. The "closer spirit of fellowship" between players and fans disappeared with the growth of the stadium and the placing of barriers between the fans and the players. The game had become an "impersonal affair, with 18 automatons, represented by the players, parading before the eyes of the spectators."

Arthur Daley and Frank Graham, writing in the 1950s, both observed this change as they looked back on the history of the New York Yankees. Daley saw the Thirties under manager Joe McCarthy as the time that produced "'the Yankee type,' the cool, precise craftsman." Graham commented on the same development in his *Casey Stengel* and contrasted it with the Yankees of the Twenties:

> McCarthy's Yankees, of whom Lou Gehrig with his stolid power and Joe DiMaggio with his almost lethargic grace were the popular symbols, beat their opponents' brains out with a kind of passionless venom. They were seldom "good copy." McCarthy became famous as "the push-button manager," a term of derision applied to him by a rival because, with his great collection of stars, he allegedly had only to push a button to get the home run or outstanding defensive play needed to win....
>
> The Yankees of the Roaring Twenties were a different breed. It was Babe Ruth who loaned them a part of his own gargantuan personality and made them a nation's favorites. They were as bawdy and combative as any band of roustabouts attached to a wandering carnival. As much as they craved victory, they never let its pursuit blot out their idea of the good life. Ruth was more than their best player. He was their spiritual leader.

In a similar vein Lefty Gomez, quoted by Maury Allen, noted that Joe McCarthy wanted perfection both on and off the field. He required the players to wear tie and jacket on all road trips and became very upset over unbuttoned shirts. McCarthy said that "playing for the

Yankees called for being the same kind of gentlemen who would work in a bank." McCarthy's machine was not only well oiled, it was also well polished.

Lou Gehrig was one of the best of McCarthy's bankers. His career with the Yankees overlapped those of both Ruth and DiMaggio, and to a certain extent he played in the shadow of both of these men. He became a dominant heroic figure only in the tragedy of his death. No one questioned the greatness of Gehrig as a player, yet it is significant that he is most remembered for his endurance: He played in 2,130 consecutive games. This earned him the name "Iron Horse," but he lacked color. Gehrig seemed destined to remain a figure in the

Reprinted from the *New York Post*

shadows. In 1932 he hit four home runs in one game, only to be pushed out of the headlines by the retirement of John McGraw. In the World Series that same year Gehrig led the Yankees with three homers, nine hits, eight RBIs, nine runs scored, and a batting average of .529. But this was also the series in which Ruth hit his designated home run.

In August 1933 the Iron Horse surpassed the old record for consecutive games played. *The Sporting News* described Gehrig's performance as impressive and Lou as a man of Spartan courage, clean-living, a willing worker, and a man who was loyal to his team and to his fellow players. This description of Gehrig summarizes much of what was written about the unobtrusive Iron Horse until his career came to its tragic close. The string of consecutive games ended May 2, 1939, when Gehrig withdrew from the Yankee lineup. He was hitting only .143 at the time and had been under considerable criticism from the press. He did not return. A trip to the Mayo Clinic revealed that he was suffering from what was described variously in the press as polio, infantile paralysis, and amyotrophic lateral sclerosis.

John Kieran of the *New York Times* wrote that he knew it would be no ordinary disease that would stop Lou Gehrig, because Lou had overcome many ailments before "without ever breaking stride." Kieran found in Gehrig's career a reaffirmation of old copybook maxims: "If at first you don't succeed..."; "Early to bed and early to rise..."; "A rolling stone..."; and "A penny saved...." Although some people scoffed at these maxims, Kieran pointed out that Gehrig lived by them and believed in them. Gehrig also believed he was under an obligation to earn every penny his employer gave him in salary. Although some people might call this "apple sauce," Lou Gehrig thrived on it.

July 4, 1939, was Lou Gehrig Day at Yankee Stadium. Gehrig stood before 61,808 people and bared his soul in a tear-blurred speech which has become a legend in the annals of American sport. After several people had paid tribute to him, and a multitude of gifts were presented, Gehrig stepped to the microphone and said:

Fans, for the past two weeks you have been reading about a bad break I got. Yet, today, I consider myself the luckiest man on the face of the earth. I have been in ball parks 16 years, and have never received anything but kindness and encouragement from you fans.

Wouldn't you consider it an honor just to be with such great men even for one day? [he continued, motioning to present-day and past Yankees lined up at the plate].

Sure. I'm lucky! Who wouldn't consider it an honor to have known Jake Ruppert, builder of Baseball's greatest empire; to have spent six years with such a grand little fellow as Miller Huggins; to have spent nine years with that smart student of psychology—the best manager in baseball today—Joe McCarthy?

Who wouldn't feel honored to room with such a grand guy as Bill Dickey?

When the New York Giants, a team you would give your right arm to beat, and vice versa, send a gift—that's something. When the ground keepers and office staff and writers and old-timers and players and concessionaires all remember you with trophies—that's something.

When you have a wonderful mother-in-law, who takes sides with you in squabbles against her own daughter—that's something; when you have a father and mother who work all their lives so that you can have an education and build your body—that's a blessing. When you have a wife who has been a tower of strength, and shown more courage than you dreamed existed—that's the finest thing I know.

So I close in saying that I might have had a tough break; but I have an awful lot to live for."

Reaction to Gehrig's speech was overwhelmingly favorable, although one writer felt that the whole affair grew a bit maudlin. Looking back on that day in Yankee Stadium, James T. Farrell (*My Baseball Diary*) recalled when Gehrig died that Gehrig's words had been simple, and nothing as "meaningful and spoken with such moral bravery, was ever uttered through a microphone from the home base area of a big-league ball park." To Farrell, Gehrig offered an example of "fine manly courage and moral bravery."

In August 1939 Lou Gehrig was named Youth Director of the New York World's Fair and honored as a hero of, and example of, the youth of America. When the season ended Lou was appointed by Mayor LaGuardia to the New York City parole commission, to work as a youth counselor. In an editorial titled "A Hero Becomes a Helper," *The Sporting News* voiced its opinion that Gehrig would be an inspiration to all the boys with whom he came in contact. His life story "is that of an American boy who rose from poverty and adverse circumstances to the top of his chosen profession, through perseverance, clean living and courage."

Lou Gehrig died June 2, 1941. The *New York Times* paid tribute to Gehrig as one of the greatest players of all time, "a shining example of manliness to all young Americans." Behind his success was more than luck and ability: "It was his character, his patient steadiness, his keeping himself in condition for this task...." To *The Sporting News* it was Gehrig's courage that set him apart. It quoted Quentin Reynolds as saying that Gehrig had exhibited courage equal to the people of London during a severe bombing raid. Tributes were offered from such varied sources as Gov. Herbert W. Lehman of New York and Bill "Bojangles" Robinson. Five thousand people viewed Gehrig's body as it lay in state at Christ Protestant Episcopal Church in Riverdale. The *Times* reported that the New York House of Assembly passed a resolution portraying Gehrig as a symbol of "the spirit of courage, clean living, tenacity and fair play." The man who was one of the first of the colorless heroes of baseball in the end served by his tragic death to reaffirm the manly virtues and time-tested values of American society.

When Paul Simon and Art Garfunkel asked, "Where have you gone, Joe DiMaggio?" they were decrying the loss of the grace and order of a simpler universe in the past. Roger Angell wrote in *Ten Years of Holiday* that although DiMaggio was "personally a cold, restrained, almost disdainful man," every move he made on the field seem distinctive and exciting. He raced across the outfield "with huge, easy strides," and at no time did he "look hurried or graceless."

Maury Allen's biography, *Where Have You Gone, Joe DiMaggio*, describes the beauty, grace, style, and certitude that were the trademarks of Joe DiMaggio, the perfect player. But it was not without reason that he was called "Deadpan Joe." He was the colorless superstar par excellence. His attractiveness lay in the flawless perfection of his movement in the field and the mechanical precision with which he swung his bat. Yankee manager Joe McCarthy said that DiMaggio did everything so easily he wasn't fully appreciated. His catches didn't seem spectacular because when the ball was hit Joe knew exactly where it was going and got there. He simply didn't need to make spectacular catches. He was that good.

Joe DiMaggio was a product of the Yankee organization. Purchased from San Francisco of the Pacific Coast League, he was left there for a full season to age, like fine wine. Then in 1936 he came to the American League, where some called him the rookie of the decade. He was touted as the new Babe Ruth, but unlike the Yankee superstar of the Twenties, Joe DiMaggio was the perfect organization man. DiMaggio would never do anything to hurt his name or the Yankees, and Joe felt an obligation to the public, the fans, and his ball club. Although he had his salary disputes with the Yankee front office, Joe was never the discipline problem of his predecessor. Whereas Ruth was a restless playboy, DiMaggio was a quiet, dedicated professional. Lefty Grove said of DiMaggio (in Maury Allen's biography): "He was a guy who knew he was the greatest baseball player in America and he was proud of it. He knew what the press and the fans and the kids expected of him, and he was always trying to live up to that image. That's why he couldn't be silly in public like I could, or ever be caught without his shirt buttoned or his shoes shined. He knew he was Joe DiMaggio and he knew what that meant to the country. He felt that obligation to the Yankees and to the public."

Like all sports heroes, DiMaggio was much in demand for personal appearances, was showered with honors, and was the recipient of massive doses of publicity. What was striking about "Joltin' Joe" was his quiet acceptance of these accolades. There was an almost stoic quality in his public appearances and in his public image. He seemed always to be in the calm eye of the hurricane that swirled about him. One of the strongest hurricanes of his career swirled through fifty-six games during the 1941 season, as DiMaggio set a new consecutive-game hitting streak. It inspired Les Brown's hit recording of "Joltin' Joe DiMaggio." It caused a history class in Cincinnati to name him the greatest American of all time, ahead of Washington and Lincoln. The excitement generated by the streak was so great that it gave some of Joe's teammates the jitters. But, Allen records, Joe remained "outwardly calm. No one could discern excitement or nervousness in his deportment. Years later DiMaggio explained, 'I was able to control myself. That doesn't mean I wasn't dying inside.'" Here was the new American man—always in control, never showing emotion.

What is most interesting in reading about DiMaggio in this prewar period is that the more one reads, the less one seems to know about him, as if the "Yankee Clipper" were all style and no substance—the perfect corporate player for the increasingly other-directed society. The game of the real Americans, the rough and ready men, the rugged individuals of rural America, was rapidly disappearing. In its place came the game of the polished college graduate and the more sophisticated products of the new mass culture. These men were shaped to fit into the organization, sometimes mere cardboard cutouts. By the end of the Thirties baseball had nearly completed its organizational transformation; it presented to the American public the corporate player, complete with gray-flannel traveling uniform. Baseball had now truly become a part of the urban-industrial culture.

6

Novas

And no other activity in the world had so
precise and comprehensive a history, so
specific an ethic, and at the same time, strange
as it seemed, so much ultimate mystery.

ALTHOUGH Babe Ruth was the dominant figure between the wars,
and Gehrig and DiMaggio were symbols of the new order, there were
numerous other heroes offering the public a varying montage of
symbols, examples, and moral lessons. The public image of these
hero figures offers an interesting glimpse of the mores and values of
the times.

One of the dominant figures of the pre–World War I period was
Christy Mathewson, great pitcher of the New York Giants. Christy's
playing days ended in 1916, but he remained active in baseball until
near his death in 1925. Because of his continuing association with
baseball, Matty was often held up as an ideal for the youngsters of
America. Late in 1920 Matty's stay in the hospital fighting the
tuberculosis that would ultimately take his life prompted a massive
Christmas card mailing by his many fans. Reacting to this, Hugh
Fullerton, writing in the *New York Evening Mail*, paid tribute to "Big
Six" as the man who embodied the ideal player and stood for all the
best things in baseball. Matty was not only a great pitcher but also a

"clean, right-living man." Matty willingly helped the younger players with the skills of the game and in their dealings with the dictatorial manager, John McGraw. But Fullerton did not want to leave the impression that Matty was a "mollycoddle." On the contrary, he was "100 percent male he-man. He smoked a bit, drank a bit, at times gambled and swore."

Mathewson recovered from this preliminary bout with TB and took up duties as president of the Boston Braves in 1923. But in 1925 he was confined to his home in Saranac Lake, New York, where he died on October 7. That was opening day of the 1925 World Series—a fact that held symbolic meaning for many fans. At the annual meeting of the Boston Braves a few weeks later, Boston Mayor James M. Curley, longtime friend of Matty and one of the club directors, offered a memorial resolution: Matty's life presented an ideal and inspiration for youth and "a stainless record of loving service for God and country." He typified the qualities of resourcefulness, science, and ingenuity, and raised the game to new and higher standards. "His game of life was called by the darkness of death, but the Great Manager of all, releasing from mortal pain and travail, has taken him home, and signed him to an eternity of light and happiness." This great tribute, not only to Matty, but also to baseball and the nation, unblushingly proclaimed the virtues of Americans, practiced under the watchful and approving eye of the "Great Manager."

Death among the personnel was frequently an occasion for moralizing. Pat Moran, manager of the Cincinnati Reds, died unexpectedly during spring training in 1923. He had been a player for the Chicago Cubs in the legendary days of Tinker to Evers to Chance. Both Tinker and Evers were at the hospital at the time of Moran's death. Cincinnati sportswriter William A. Phelon provided the readers of *The Sporting News* with a tribute to the Reds' manager by describing Moran as "one of Nature's noblemen," a plain and rugged man with a keen wit and a soft heart. He had been like a father to his players and was loved by all who knew him. In his private life Pat Moran was a model citizen, loyal husband, and kind father. On the field he played cleanly. Baseball had benefited from Moran's presence in it. When

Moran was called out by the "Great Umpire," whose decisions are never reversed, Mrs. Moran was there holding her husband in a "last embrace." At the end Pat's eyes opened for just an instant, "and as the Death Angel spread his sable wings Pat Moran, blameless man and honored leader, knew that the woman he loved was with him at the end."

In September 1923 Moran's colleague Frank Chance, "the Peerless Leader," died. *The Sporting News'* tribute to him was as a "clean, hard, conscientious, manly fighter." Chance loved and gloried in combat on the field of play. He grinned when he won and gritted his teeth when he lost. He, too, played the game cleanly and squarely.

Even more shocking than the death of a former player or a manager was the death of an active player, especially if it happened on the field. The death of Ray Chapman, Cleveland Indian shortstop, was just such a shock. Chapman died on August 17, 1920, from being hit on the head by a pitched ball. Carl Mays of the Yankees was the pitcher. Chapman was also described as one of Nature's noblemen, who had "a character of sterling worth." His background was Algeresque: Chapman had come out of the coal mines to success on the baseball diamond and had become a "civilized gentleman." In an editorial the *Cleveland Plain Dealer* called Chapman the greatest shortstop of his day, whose personality as much as his skill made him a great player. He always gave his best, never gave in to temperament, and never sulked or shirked. Of course, he did make an occasional error. But anyone who did his best and tried to do what could not be done would inevitably err.

As for Carl Mays, most players showed charity toward him at first. But Mays was not well liked. He threw the ball submarine fashion— side-arm and underhanded—so that it looked like it was coming from third base. Mays had a reputation for throwing at the heads of batters, and one of his former catchers was reported to have said that Mays had a signal for his bean ball.* When the Yankees defied public opinion by putting Mays in to pitch just one week after the beaning

*Halsey Hall 1972; personal communication.

of Chapman, the Cleveland players tried to organize a boycott and demanded that Mays be ejected from baseball. *The Sporting News* was shocked by Mays' apparent insensitivity as well as that of the Yankee management. It was a "heartless act," they said, and made a mockery of the mourning for Ray Chapman. Worse yet, Mays was cheered by Yankee fans and responded with a smile. He had the bad taste to explain that he had not suffered a nervous breakdown over the death of Chapman, "merely a headache." The furor passed, but it seemed fitting that Cleveland went on to win the American League pennant. In a front-page cartoon in the October 5 *Plain Dealer*, a Cleveland player was depicted holding the pennant. On a cloud behind him was Ray Chapman, saying, "Carry on." The caption read simply, "It pays to play clean."

The death of Yankee manager Miller Huggins in 1929 prompted a chorus of praise in the *Times* for his honesty and integrity. Mayor Jimmy Walker described Huggins as a clean sportsman. Congressman Fiorello LaGuardia said that the nation needed good clean sport, which Huggins personified. He was, said LaGuardia, "the first inspiration for fair play, idealism, and honesty to the youth of America." Lou Gehrig called Huggins the squarest shooter he had ever known in baseball. Mayor Walker, at the dedication of the Huggins memorial in Yankee Stadium in 1932, said that Huggins would be remembered for his sportsmanship, that Huggins had "demanded nothing but fair play and a square deal."

The other great New York manager of the 1920s, John J. McGraw, presented a different set of characteristics for public admiration. McGraw's nickname, "The Little Napoleon," indicated one aspect of his character. On McGraw's twenty-fifth anniversary with the Giants, *The Sporting News* called him the "little fighter of baseball." He might fight in a losing cause but was still a "dynamo of relentless action, a foe of the quitter and loser." Following McGraw's resignation from baseball in 1932, Hugh Bradley, writing in the *American Mercury*, recalled that McGraw did not believe in the "good loser" philosophy. Instead, he felt that the only way to popularity was to win; therefore, the philosophy to follow was fight to win.

When McGraw died in 1934, *The Sporting News* paid tribute to him by praising his raw aggressiveness. He was a "firebrand, a stickler for discipline, a fighter...." He would let nothing stand in the way of victory. McGraw hated failure, laziness, and any "lack of intestinal fortitude...." Complete dictators, however, are not good democratic heroes, so McGraw's image had to be modified. Therefore, McGraw was also described as a man of "gracious personality," loyal to his friends and players, generous, and with a paternal affection for his players.

In an article in the *New York Times*, Judge Landis commented on McGraw's place in baseball and put him into the context of the times. Landis felt that the man who first talked of rugged individualism must have had McGraw in mind. McGraw was one of the players who helped lay the foundation of baseball as the National Game. McGraw played a "ripping, tearing, charging" kind of baseball; he asked no quarter and gave none. Landis concluded: "I can think of no man whose name was more universally associated with the virile, competitive spirit of baseball than John McGraw."

The most enduring character of baseball through all these years was Connie Mack, owner and manager of the Philadelphia Athletics. Mack could be seen daily with scorecard in hand, wearing street clothes in the dugout, directing the up-and-down fortunes of his ball club. In 1920 the A's finished last in the American League. In 1930 they were world champions for the second straight year. In 1940 they were once again last in the league.

Philadelphia honored Connie Mack in February 1930 with the Edward Bok Award for his service to the city. Previously the award had gone to scientists, educators and leaders in the arts. According to William Dutton, writing in *American Magazine*, the Bok Award was given to Mack not just because the A's had won the pennant, but because Mack was clean living and a square shooter and had given "distinguished service to American sport and youth." Mack was in his forty-eighth year in baseball and his thirty-seventh year as manager. He neither smoked nor drank; he was a family man and was devoutly religious. There was a rumor that Mack had a fund to provide for old ball players, widows of players, and kids from the street whom he sent back to school. In addition, under his regime the right-field grandstand in Shibe Park was always filled with kids from schools, hospitals, orphanages, the Boy Scouts, and other youth groups. On the field, Mack believed in good sportsmanship, clean, aggressive play, and fighting the other team, not the umpire. He felt that breaks and close decisions tended to even out over the long run. Mack said that to be a winner, a player must first think like a winner.

The combination of success and failure made Mack an attractive

Courtesy of World Wide Photos

advertisement for the competitive spirit: He was the archetype of the man who didn't quit. Jim Nasium of *The Sporting News* felt that Mack's career offered great inspiration in this respect. Mack had reached the top, fallen to the bottom, and then, refusing to give up, had climbed back to the top. This spirit was more impressive than that of a man who had only known success because it requires force of character to triumph over adversity.

Ban Johnson, the president of the American League, also served as a moral force. As a founder of the league, he had done his best to elevate the stature of the umpire. He also spent much of his career in well-publicized campaigns to rid baseball of gamblers. By the Twenties his leadership was coming under fire—as demonstrated in the Mays case mentioned in chapter 1.

The appointment of Judge Landis as commissioner was a defeat for Johnson, and the two men never got along well. Baseball was not big enough for two moral leaders, especially when their views of morality differed so widely. Johnson was often in open conflict with Landis and criticized him publicly. At the 1924 winter meetings both leagues gave Landis a public endorsement for his work. This was followed by Johnson's removal from the Advisory Council of the American League—another vote of confidence for Landis. Johnson was allowed to remain as American League president only on the condition that he refrain from any further criticism of the commissioner. In 1926 Johnson returned to the Advisory Council but was soon again in conflict with Landis. In January 1927 the American League owners sent Johnson on a vacation, citing his poor health as the reason. He returned as league president for the 1927 season, only to be forced to resign in July, effective November 1.

The involuntary vacation was generally interpreted as the end of Johnson's career as a baseball executive. *The Sporting News*, a longtime supporter of Johnson, published his picture on page one with the caption, "His Honors Will Endure." In an accompanying editorial, Johnson's departure was compared with the death of Julius Caesar, with clear implications as to who were Brutus and the senators. It was pointed out that Johnson had been so effective at cleaning up baseball that "even the whisper of scandal" rocked the entire sporting world. The editors called him a lion whose roar "struck terror" into the hearts of wrongdoers. When Johnson announced his retirement in July 1927, Baseball's Bible once again paid tribute to him as a symbol of "decency, honesty, and earnest effort." It noted Johnson's only regret was that "sporting sense" had not been able to prevail over commercialism. *The Sporting News* concluded that the owners had removed Johnson because he fought "to keep the game and his league clean." Time had passed this great man by. "Ban Johnson belonged to a day when ideals stood on righteous ground—he faced a day when ideals do not mean so much...."

Another Johnson, Walter, offered a multitude of lessons to the American public. Known for his blazing fastball and gentle manner, Walter Johnson was a favorite of both fans and sportswriters. One story that has become part of his legend was that he threw the ball so hard that he constantly feared he might hit and severely injure a batter. Ty Cobb, aware of Johnson's fear, allegedly crowded the plate and forced the "Big Train" to walk him.

From the time Walter Johnson began his major-league career in 1907 until 1924, he was never in a World Series. Ten of those years Washington had finished in the second division of the American League—seven times in seventh or eighth place. Despite his team's poor showing Johnson amassed impressive statistics, soon winning recognition as one of the best men ever to throw a ball from a major-league pitching mound. Therefore when the Senators finally won an American League pennant in 1924 there was great anticipation and excitement over Johnson's first World Series opportunity. Johnson started the first game against the Giants, who pitched Art Nehf. For twelve innings the two men battled. Johnson struck out twelve, but in the twelfth inning he gave up a bases-loaded single and lost his first World Series start 4 to 3. In game five he was again the starting pitcher; he went the distance, but with an unimpressive losing performance of 6 to 2. Johnson's supporters were dismayed. He would probably not get another start even if the series went the full seven games. But game seven, back in Washington, saw the Senators and Giants go another twelve innings; Walter Johnson pitched the last four. Several times he pitched his way out of trouble. Then in the twelfth inning the Senators scored on a bad-hop single over the head of Giant third baseman Freddie Lindstrom. Walter Johnson was the winning pitcher, and the typewriter ribbons of sportswriters across the country turned to syrup.

In 1925 the pattern was reversed. Johnson was the winning pitcher in the first game of the series, defeating the Pittsburgh Pirates in a ten-strikeout performance, 4 to 1. In the fourth game, he shut out the Bucs, 4 to 0. In the seventh game, on a cold, dark, rainy day in Pittsburgh, Walter Johnson was back on the mound, but he struggled to a 9 to 7 loss, giving up a two-run double to KiKi Cuyler in the eighth inning that produced the deciding runs against an obviously tired pitcher.

In 1925 Chester Crowell, writing in *American Magazine*, tried to answer "Why is Johnson the best loser and best winner in baseball?" Johnson was respected by everyone; he was a man who never lost his temper, even when his teammates lost games for him that they should have won. Johnson always gave his best. He was a man of "steady nerve," a "sterling character" with a "simple philosophy of life." He had defied bad luck, defeat, and the ravages of time. Crowell quoted Johnson as saying that no man can give his best when he is worried, angry, or resentful. These emotions eat into a man's strength. "Baseball," said Johnson, "is simply a dramatization of the life struggle of a man."

Grantland Rice found Johnson the perfect hero. Here was a man never touched by scandal, whose record of conduct both on and off the field was unmatched. He was, according to Rice's article in *Collier's*, more than just a great pitcher. Humble in victory, he made no excuses in defeat. He served as "a 20-year inspiration for right living, clean conduct, unspotted sportsmanship, and loyalty to the job."

But then not all heroes were necessarily men of great virtue and good examples for the youth of the nation. Rogers Hornsby started his career with the Cardinals, first as a player and then as player-manager. He traveled far and wide from there, wearing several different hats over the years. Hornsby was a heavy gambler; his career as manager was marked by controversy; there were stories of dissension among those who played for him. Yet he had some of the stuff of which a hero could be made. He was another of the rugged individuals who played the game in the 1920s.

J. Roy Stockton of the *St. Louis Post-Dispatch* called Hornsby "one of the most pleasing characters that the great game of baseball has ever produced." A loner, who swore "like a trooper, a Texas trooper," Hornsby's outstanding characteristics were courage, honesty, confidence, determination, and bluntness. He neither smoked nor drank, but he was no paragon of virtue. He was stubborn and bullheaded. Rogers also had a strong anti-intellectual streak: "If a man comes from a university, he's dumb, and the higher the university the greater the degree of dumbness in Hornsby's estimation," claimed Stockton. Yet for all Rogers' weaknesses, you couldn't help but like him. "He's just an honest-to-goodness person, without guile or subterfuge. People trust Hornsby."

It was Hornsby's gambling that got him into much of the trouble he had with club owners and the commissioner, but he considered betting on horses his recreation and would not stop. On one occasion, Judge Landis called Rogers to task, pointing out that betting on horses was a form of gambling. Hornsby retaliated by pointing out that playing the stock market was also a form of gambling. "Landis, who happened to have been playing the stock market, gave Hornsby an indignant glare from beneath his white locks, and Hornsby went on betting on horses and knocking the pitchers loose from their moorings" (Douglas Wallop, *Baseball, An Informal History*). This incident shows that rugged individualism was not yet dead and the age of the corporate player had not yet arrived. No player today could exhibit that kind of defiance to Bowie Kuhn or Pete Rozelle and survive in professional sports.

In Pittsburgh during the Twenties there were many great players, but one in particular embodied many of the most important characteristics and ideals of the National Pastime. Pie Traynor played his first full season in Pittsburgh in 1922 and remained the regular Pirate third baseman until 1934. By 1923 Pie had emerged as one of the idols of the Pittsburgh fans. He was portrayed as a man who had a great love for the game of baseball. If Pie had been in another profession, he would have been out on the sandlots every evening, "for he simply can't keep away from the diamond." Equally important, success was not spoiling Pie Traynor. As the adulation increased, his reaction was to work even harder to merit the honors. He did not develop a big head. Not content to bask in the limelight in the off-season, he attended Boston University to earn a degree. His hope was to become a manager some day and he felt that education would help him prepare for it. Pie Traynor was "an upstanding young ball player of clean habits," the kind of man you could bet would achieve his goals in life. Here was a man who was a worthy inspiration for the boys of America. "He is clean, ambitious, and is forever striving to improve himself physically and mentally." In 1926, when Traynor was chosen to succeed Max Carey as captain of the Bucs, it was a popular choice among Pittsburgh fans. Under Pie's picture, The Sporting News commented that he was a throwback to another day, when the players played the game for glory and lived and loved baseball. On the field Traynor displayed nerve, spirit, and energy. Off the field he was a gentleman and was always ready to talk baseball.

In 1933, on the death of former White Sox manager Kid Gleason, one writer lamented the changes he saw engulfing baseball and, by implication, American society. Kid Gleason had been worthy of the days when the players shared the "honest urge to battle that flamed in the breasts of our pioneer ancestors in an age when men lived by conflict...." It had been a time when moral and physical courage were the highest virtues; fear of an opponent was dishonorable. "His was an age when you had to meet bluster with bluster in order to survive, when the surest way to avoid rough tactics was to take the initiative and spread the gospel of fear in the ranks of your opponents—and be ready to go through with it if your bluff was called." But times were changing, and physical prowess was no longer a vital factor in survival.

Sportswriters had a field day whenever they were writing about St. Louis' Gas House Gang, especially the 1934 version of the Cardinals, who won the World Series. Their reputation as rough-and-tumble players and light-hearted adolescent pranksters has become legendary. They too were celebrated as throwbacks to the earlier days. But their role as revivers of days past may have been more symbolic than real. From a survey of the literature on the Gas House Gang, especially that concerning their spiritual leader, Dizzy Dean, there emerges the uneasy impression that there was too much calculation and prepackaging for them to be authentic. The Gas House Gang was, at least in part, only a calculated imitation of the days of Kid Gleason and Ty Cobb.

The Gas House Gang was led by player-manager Frankie Frisch, the Fordham Flash. According to Frisch (in the *Saturday Evening Post*), the Cardinals were not really tough, and, in fact, they had less trouble with umpires than most teams. They were a colorful group of players who put on a great show while fighting for a pennant. There had been numerous stories of personal conflicts on the Cardinal team, particularly involving Frisch and Dizzy Dean. But Frisch said that in baseball there was just no room for likes and dislikes. "You don't like your players or dislike them. You can't go far with a friendship team. There's no room for sentiment in baseball if you want to win." If fights in the Cardinal dugout and locker room were any indication, the Gas House Gang was certainly not a "friendship team."

John Pepper Martin emerged as a Cardinal hero in the 1931 World Series. Known as "The Wild Horse of the Osage," Martin, with his daring base-running, led the 1931 Cardinals to the world championship over the favored Philadelphia A's. Martin eventually teamed with Dizzy Dean as the leading prankster of the gang. After the 1931 World Series, St. Louis sportswriter J. Roy Stockton predicted that Martin would become a favorite of the fans because he had "the showman instinct" that would serve him well when he joined the dean of showmen. Martin was confident and yet modest, a man who did all he could to satisfy his admiring public. He always had time to sign autographs and exchange pleasantries with the fans. Martin did not care much for dance halls, cabarets, or the drawing room. He was instead a natural man who felt most at home when tramping through the woods hunting deer. "Pepper is not without his share of quick wit, and he is naively sincere, outspoken, and unafraid to voice his thoughts...." To J. G. Taylor Spink, the Pepper Martin of 1931 was a perfect example of Algerism in baseball. He had served his apprenticeship in the Cardinal farm system. With ambition and determination he emerged as one of the outstanding figures in baseball in 1931, with a comfortable fortune in the making. In many ways he was just an average young American.

In 1939 Arthur Mann (in *The Saturday Evening Post*) wrote that Leo Durocher was the most hated man in baseball. Undoubtedly there were many who had felt that way about "The Lip." Durocher broke into the big leagues with the Yankees. Miller Huggins called Leo the greatest infielder ever to play the game. Plagued by poor hitting and a preoccupation with the bright lights of Manhattan, Durocher's stock fell with the Yankees, and after Huggins' death Leo was moved to the Cincinnati Reds. He took some $20,000 in debts with him to his new home. Over the next few years he worked hard to pay them off. He also worked hard on the field, something he had always done, and he lost some of the cocky, loud-mouthed quality that he had displayed in New York. In 1933 he went on to the Cardinals, where he met Grace Dozier, a local dress designer. They were married just a few days prior to the 1934 World Series. (This was considered most unorthodox behavior by baseball purists, who apparently feared that sexual intercourse adversely affected playing ability.) By 1934 Leo had emerged as an important leader of the Gas House Gang. The man who had once been called "the hitless wonder" became a terror at the plate with men on base. He remained with the Cardinals until 1938, when he became too powerful a force on the club, and Frisch let it be known that either Leo or himself would have to go. Leo's career up to that point offered some moral guidance to the boys of America. In 1936 J. Roy Stockton wrote that there was a new Leo Durocher, "who has learned what he knows in the school of hard knocks." That year Branch Rickey had chosen Durocher to go to the United States Naval Academy as a coach, prior to reporting to the Cardinals' spring training camp. Leo had come a long way from the mistakes and blunders of his early career: Horatio Alger would have been delighted to write a story about Durocher.

If it was Pepper Martin who provided the fire and Leo Durocher who provided the lip, it was Dizzy Dean who was both master of ceremonies and the leading act of the Gas House Gang. Tristram Coffin, in *The Old Ball Game*, noted that Dean was lucky because all he had to do was remain true to his roots to be what people wanted him to be. The only danger to continued success was that it and money might change Dizzy Dean. This danger of course might be minimized by marketing, packaging, and institutionalizing the image of Dizzy Dean. "Ole Diz" himself took the lead in this process. Before the 1934 season he predicted that he and his brother Paul, whom he named "Daffy," would win forty-five games—instead they made it forty-nine. As an encore, the Deans were the winning pitchers in the four Cardinal World Series victories. Dizzy performed countless tricks both on and off the field, and the press quickly fell into line. When he was struck in the head during the 1934 World Series against Detroit, the headlines proclaimed "X-rays of Dean's Head Show Nothing." Dean explained that he saw stars, moons, and all kinds of animals when he was hit, but no Tigers. "I still can't see the Tigers," he added.

The year 1934 was a good one for Dizzy off the field as well. Under the highly skilled direction of his wife, Pat, Dizzy became a master at exploiting the media and cashing in on endorsements. There were "Me and Paul" sweatshirts and toothbrushes, a "Me and Paul" vaudeville tour, Dizzy Dean caps, shirts, and booklets—all promoted by radio and personal appearances. On one occasion it was arranged to have a professional golf tournament finish early so that everyone could rush to the ball park and watch Dizzy pitch. Through it all, J. Roy Stockton reports, Dizzy was capable of insulting "friend and enemy without slightest provocation.... Wisecracking, breaches of discipline, popping off, had paid him large dividends. Occasional outbursts of temper had helped establish him as an athlete of color." He was playing the calculated role of "American frontier literature—the lovable, careless, amoral bumpkin who somehow found himself in a twentieth-century world" (Coffin, *The Old Ball Game*). Few have ever played that role so well. But then, it came so naturally to Dizzy.

At first the reaction of the baseball press was highly favorable to Dizzy and his antics. After all, he was good copy. During the 1934 World Series, Bill Corum reported that Dean's "boastfulness is not the annoying sort at all. He is rather inclined to be modest and shy and polite." Corum reported that in the presence of Babe Ruth, Dean had been humble, even calling him "Mr. Ruth," while throwing in a

They May Sing Pennant Duet

DIZZY. —CAPABLE— AND COLORFUL !!

PAUL· —THE YOUNGER OF THE DEAN BOYS, THREATENS TO OVERSHADOW BROTHER DIZZY ON THE MOUND.

THESE BOYS HAVE PROMISED THE CARDINALS FORTY·FIVE GAMES THIS SEASON

All Rights Reserved by The Associated Press

Courtesy of World Wide Photos

few "gee-whizzes." Corum felt that people had Dean all wrong: he was just a simple fellow who said what was on his mind and who did not mean to brag. *The Sporting News* expressed its pleasure that success had not gone to the heads of the Deans, and saw Dizzy as the logical successor to Babe Ruth as the dominant figure in the public mind.

By the middle of 1935 things had begun to sour. Some writers were tiring of the Dean braggadacio, especially when Dizzy started to criticize some of his teammates. Two incidents in particular provided targets for criticism. The first took place in Pittsburgh in June. Dizzy began to serve up fat pitches to the Pirate hitters because he had become disgusted with either the umpiring or the play of his teammates. In his first appearance in St. Louis following this incident he was greeted by lemons thrown on the field. The second incident was in July, when he refused to come out of the dugout during an exhibition game in St. Paul, Minnesota. A number of writers around the country expressed anger over Dean's behavior. One was Ed Shave of the *St. Paul Daily News*, who lectured Dizzy on his duty to the fans, especially the little boys, and his duty to the game which had taken him "from obscurity and poverty into notoriety and affluence." Shave compared Dizzy's performance with that of Babe Ruth, who had played an entire game in the rain with a sprained ankle, not wanting to disappoint the St. Paul fans. Following the St. Paul incident Dean issued a public apology to the fans of that city and gave assurances to the St. Louis fans that he hoped to remain with the Cardinals. *The Sporting News* thought the apology sufficient, feeling that he had had too much pressure on him because of his fame. After all, he was only "a callow youth just a few years from the sticks." It was certain that Dizzy would never "go high hat" because he was "too close to the grass roots of his origin for that."

By early 1936 it was more difficult to excuse Dean's transgressions as a product of his rural naiveté. *The Sporting News* now called him the "once-poor cotton picker" who had surrounded himself with "pomp and circumstance" and indulged in "yellow cars and winters in Florida." Dizzy was warned that money should not become the focus of the game. He must learn to give, as well as to take, from the sport that "opened to him such wide vistas of wealth and fame." The contract troubles that prompted these comments passed, and by the end of the 1936 season Dizzy was earning his way back into the good graces of the public.

A brawl in a hotel lobby between Dean and his teammates and a New York writer who had been unkind to him started Dean on what had promised to be another great season in 1937. In fact, it was his best season. Then he was starting pitcher in the All-Star game in Washington. Hit on the toe by a line drive, he returned to the lineup too soon and suffered a sore arm trying to protect the toe while pitching. It was the virtual end of his career, and that shrewd trader Branch Rickey dumped him off on the Cubs before the start of the 1938 season.

In an editorial titled "Dizzy Dean at the Crossroads," *The Sporting News* tried to assess Dean's career. He was a pitcher of great contrasts. On the one hand he had the necessary competitive spirit and desire to win. On the other hand he "found himself unable to acquire that esprit de corps which submerges self for the benefit of all, and he...continued to be a rugged individualist regardless of the consequences to himself and his teammates." Times had changed. No one had criticized Babe Ruth for failing to submerge the self. However, by the late Thirties, when the corporate player was displacing the rugged individual as the baseball ideal, Dean was a transitional figure. He played the role of rugged individual but did so by exploiting the techniques of the emerging corporate society. He continued to attract the attention of the Chicago fans and performed his swan song in the 1938 World Series. But his baseball career had actually ended in Washington at the 1937 All-Star game. He went on to a new career as a prepackaged bumpkin on radio—and later television.

Then there were the stars who lacked color or, if they had it, always kept it within the bounds of the organization. These were the new mechanical men of baseball, the corporate players of the Gehrig and DiMaggio type. If there were ever a stereotype of this player, it was Charlie Gehringer, the perfect second baseman of the Detroit Tigers.

Called the "Silent Knight" by Harold A. Fitzgerald, Gehringer looked like a "Hollywood Star" and was dubbed the quiet man of baseball. Charlie did everything the right way: Naturally, he eschewed alcohol and tobacco. He played conservative baseball and was not given to eccentric behavior. In 1937 Gehringer was named MVP in the American League, and Detroit fans held a dinner in his honor. On that occasion, The Sporting News pointed out that Charlie was not a "seeker of the limelight." He went to the other extreme, starring for the Tigers "quietly, unassumingly, and efficiently." It could be said of Gehringer that he always gave his best, "without ostentation."

In 1932 Jimmy Foxx hit 58 home runs and was seen by many as the logical successor to Babe Ruth. Foxx remained among the leaders in home runs through the decade. "Double X" was a farm boy from Maryland's Eastern Shore who came to Connie Mack's A's with arm and shoulder muscles developed by farm work, which gave him his hitting strength. But Foxx lacked color. He had no dissipating habits and was not corrupted by the bright lights of the city. One writer complained in Literary Digest that Mack had never lost a night's sleep over Foxx. In 1938 Foxx was named MVP in the American League, and, according to The Sporting News, he had earned it several ways. Not only did he take the field while suffering from severe sinus trouble, but his activity on behalf of baseball did not end on the field of play. He responded with enthusiasm to requests to appear at the banquet table or on the speakers' platform. In addition he spent a good deal of time both winter and summer promoting baseball. In short, Foxx was a good organization man who understood the need for public relations in the new world of baseball.

The achievements of Carl Hubbell as a pitcher for the New York Giants were most impressive. During the 1936 and 1937 seasons King Carl won twenty-four consecutive games in regular-season play, which may explain why he was often called "The Meal Ticket." Then there were his heroics in the 1934 All-Star game, when he struck out, in order, Ruth, Gehrig, Foxx, Simmons, and Cronin. But for all of that, sportswriters complained that he lacked color. C.M. Black, in

Scribner's: "On the pitching mound he was a robot. He never changed expression. He just reared back and threw that ball. He had no mannerisms, nor did he indulge in any dramatics when things went against him." Off the field King Carl was described as an ultraconservative dresser who talked little. He looked "more like an office worker than one of baseball's number-one performers." When asked what he did at night, Carl replied that he read a book, went to a movie, or when in New York he might go to a show. When writers tried to make him into an off-season farmer who milked cows at

dawn, Carl was quick to point out that actually most of that sort of work was done by the hired hands. And yet Hubbell was one of the biggest drawing cards in the National League. It could be argued that his great crowd appeal was based solely on his tremendous skills as a pitcher, but Black thought there was more to it. The baseball public had changed, and Hubbell's "absolute lack of color" appealed to this new public. "His modesty, his quietness, and his refusal to indulge in histrionics of the Dean or Ruth brand have all made him a lovable figure, not only in New York, but all around the circuit."

Another of the great pitchers to come along in the Thirties was the high school sensation from Van Meter, Iowa—Bob Feller. His blazing fast ball earned him instant success as well as the nickname "Rapid Robert." On August 23, 1936, at seventeen, Bob Feller made his first major-league start and struck out fifteen St. Louis Browns. This was only one strikeout short of the American League record set by Rube Waddell in 1908. Three weeks later Feller struck out seventeen Philadelphia Athletics, surpassing Waddell and tying the major-league record held by Dizzy Dean. It was a perfect setting: Feller's father, mother, and little sister were sitting in the first-base box seats. The Cleveland fans roared on every pitch. "What a head-whirling experience that must have been for these unpretentious farm folks. What memories!" wrote Ed McAuley of the *Cleveland News.* And who was this Bob Feller? He was "just the average 17-year-old boy." Feller was just a bit under six feet tall, weighed 160 pounds, had dark brown hair, "apple cheeks, and dimple in his chin." Despite the apple cheeks, he had "a girl back in Iowa." McAuley found Feller difficult to interview, for he had "an abiding horror of appearing cocky." No country Rube this boy! He knew from the start the importance of appearances.

When the season ended, Bob Feller returned to Van Meter, where he resumed his education as a high school senior in Adel, Iowa. But now he was "the storybook ball player of the generation," said J. Roy Stockton in *The Saturday Evening Post.* How did this come to pass? According to Stockton, Bob's father, Bill, had "manufactured" a major-league pitcher. When Bob was a young boy, Bill Feller did not plant corn and oats. Instead he turned to wheat so that he would have more time to play catch with young Robert. Bob himself revealed part of the secret when he told young boys "to get plenty of rest, and eat, sleep, and think baseball." Bob also told Stockton that the biggest thrill of his young career was his 3-to-1 victory over Detroit in the last game of the season. After that game he felt that he had made good for himself, his dad, and his mother. Stockton rhapsodized: "Just an Iowa farm boy, talking from the heart and sincerely giving credit where credit is due."

Courtesy of World Wide Photos

In 1937 Feller developed arm trouble and many feared that his career might end as rapidly as it had begun. But when by the end of the season his troubles had passed, *The Sporting News* thought Feller's comeback remarkable. A young boy who "had never been called on to face life's difficulties" was able to survive the ordeal, when many other young men of his age would have proven unequal to the test. Feller had demonstrated his maturity and shown that he had "that extra something which makes geniuses, prodigies, and stars...." In 1940 Feller added to his records by pitching a no-hitter on opening day against the White Sox. *The Sporting News* called Feller's career a reaffirmation of the value of hard work and the power of the will. It all proved that baseball was like life, "a test for the survival of the fittest, and, again like life, one gets out of it only what he puts into it."

Mickey Cochrane was considered by many the greatest catcher of all time. In 1934 Cochrane, as player-manager, led the Detroit Tigers to the American League pennant. J. G. Taylor Spink described the Detroit star: Cochrane had overcome the severe obstacles of physical ailments and tremendous financial losses on Wall Street. He was an aggressive leader who had established a reputation as a manger of both men and events: "Loyal, truthful, aggressive, a fine sportsman, and a great athlete." A few years earlier, as catcher for Philadelphia, he was the first member of the A's to receive the league's MVP award. Bill Dooley, Philadelphia correspondent for *The Sporting News*, saw in Cochrane a man who had "literally lifted himself by his bootstraps from obscurity to the peak of his profession...." He had never wanted to be a catcher, but by determination and self-discipline he made good. Cochrane was "the personification of the ideal diamond athlete....the picture of sublime courage, of energy, pep. Eyes flashing, his fist quivering as a flaunting pennon of battle, Cochrane in the thick of things personifies faith, fight, confidence, courage, and give-'em-hell and victory!"

In the Thirties the parade of Horatio Alger heroes continued. *The Sporting News* profiled, for example, Aloysius Harry Szymanski, one of six children of the "Widow Szymanski" of Milwaukee. Mrs.

Szymanski provided for her family by working Saturdays in a bakery and scrubbing, cleaning, and what other housework she was able to get during the week. One cold winter day, she was facing the "cruel and hopeless task" of working out the family budget, she felt a tug at her sleeve. It was her eldest son, Aloysius, the nine year old.

> "Don't you cry, mamma," he said, "When I get big I am going to be rich and buy you a house. You just see if I don't."
>
> In South Milwaukee today there is a beautiful house on a pretty street. There are servants and, too, a big automobile in the garage. Friends, relatives and little children seem to be forever arriving or departing and there is always gay laughter and merry making. There lives the Widow Szymanski, the mother of Al Simmons, mighty slugger of the Philadelphia Athletics.
>
> "The fundamental factor of my success in baseball," said Simmons, "was my determination to care for my mother.
>
> "As a boy, my natural love for baseball prompted me to seek a career in the field of professional sport. Always ahead of me as a goal was that house which, when a little boy, I promised my mother."

At the end of the decade was the story of Red Ruffing. In 1939 he pitched a four-hitter as the Yankees beat the Reds in the opening game of the World Series. Red had not pitched for two weeks because of a sore arm, but that day he pitched well even though in pain. But what was a little pain to a man who had come out of the coal mines near Nokomis, Illinois? Red Ruffing had lost four toes in the mines, nearly lost his left foot, and had narrowly missed decapitation. He had seen his father emerge from the mines with a broken back, his brother's kneecap and fingers smashed, and the death of his twenty-year-old cousin. Now he was pitching for the New York Yankees in a World Series—another story of "Pluck and Luck."

There was also the man called "Teddy Ballgame": Ted Williams was one of the bright new stars of the late Thirties. Remembered now as a great player who had a running war with the press, Ted Williams was a dedicated professional. If there was ever anyone who ate, drank, and lived baseball, it was he. In 1939 Jack Mulaney of the *Boston Post* revealed that Williams swung an imaginary bat morning, noon, and night. He would come out of a shower swinging a towel, or maybe swing his knife before sitting down to dinner. He was a serious student of hitting. Williams incessantly asked questions about hitting of anyone he could find who might know something about it. He was also a serious young man who out of uniform was a "quiet, unobtrusive citizen." He was one of the most sought-after speakers in the Boston area. Williams viewed himself as a student of the game, constantly learning something new about baseball. He viewed baseball as something more than a game. "It's one of the arts," he said, and many believed that he proved just that. Halsey Hall, who knew Williams as a minor leaguer in Minneapolis, felt that Ted fell victim to the fact that five newspapers were competing in Boston. The writers were too busy trying to scoop one another.* Therefore he was miscast as a screwball. But whatever the case, Ted Williams was one of the new breed of dedicated professionals, even though he still had some of the rough edges of the rugged individual.

These men paraded through the sports pages of the daily newspapers and the mind's eye of radio. Relatively few people saw them in the flesh. As a result they were largely the product of imagination—the fan's and the sports reporter's. If the realities did not measure up, who would know? It was not reality but a world of myth and ideal being portrayed, a world where the values of American interwar culture found expression. There was the clean living and honesty of Mathewson and Moran; the aggressiveness of McGraw or Cochrane; the hard work and endurance of Mack; the rugged individualism of Hornsby; the Alger qualities of Simmons or Traynor. And there were the changes implicit in the merchandising of the frontier-bumpkin hero like Dizzy Dean; the new colorless heroes like Hubbell; the image-conscious young players like Feller; the dedicated professionalism of Williams. It was a new ball game in many respects, but the attachments to the old values were still very much alive, much like in the real life of the American nation.

*Halsey Hall 1972: personal communication.

7

Problems and Tensions

He wants to quit—but what does he mean,
"quit"? The game? Life? Could you separate
them?

THE end of World War I let forces loose that altered American society
in many ways. The Eighteenth Amendment sought to create a nation
free from the curse of demon rum. There was a gradual liberalization
of attitudes toward the observance of the Sabbath. The Nineteenth
Amendment was one indication of the changing role of women in
American life. The Red Scare let loose strong antilabor and
antiforeign feelings that echoed through the 1920s. These antiforeign feelings challenged the myth of the melting pot and pointed
to racial discrimination in American life. All of these forces, to
greater or lesser degree, affected baseball and were reflected in the
baseball literature.

The coming of Prohibition was seen by members of the Anti-Saloon
League as the arrival of the millennium. Great predictions were
made concerning the general moral improvement of the United
States. In the world of baseball the death of demon rum was viewed
with less enthusiasm although not total alarm. Former manager
Frank Bancroft, although not a Prohibitionist, felt that the coming of

Prohibition might take people out of the beer gardens and saloons and return them to the ball parks. Ban Johnson expected an increase in attendance of 10 to 15 percent. But others, like Joe Tinker, saw bad side effects for baseball. Tinker mourned the loss of the bar owned by the former ball player, where fans could stop for a drink after a game and chat with the man who had once been their hero. On the other hand Oscar Reichow of the *Chicago Daily News* saw a number of benefits accruing to the National Game. First, the drunks, with their habit of shouting obscenities and getting into fights, would no longer populate the stands. Second, the players would keep in better shape, thus easing the burden of the managers.

During the 1919 season Washington was already dry. In June an incident occurred which *The Sporting News* viewed with some alarm. Reacting to an unpopular decision by the umpire, the fans in the stands showered the field with whiskey bottles, with the malicious intent of hurting the umpire. *The Sporting News* expressed the fear that the incident might be a preview of things to come elsewhere:

> A return to the days when every other man carried potent trouble in his hip pocket—not only a six-shooter these times, but a half-pint of bootlegger's rotgut.
> A half-pint of the stuff in the man's insides, the consequent inflammation of temper, the emptied bottle as a weapon. A fancied bad decision by an umpire as the spark.
> It is a condition for which baseball is not responsible, yet one it may have to meet.

H. C. Walker, writing in the *Detroit Times*, viewed Prohibition and other social reform measures with tongue in cheek. Walker wondered if all these reforms might produce the super athlete: Liquor destroyed the life and sapped the strength of athletes; cigarettes destroyed the nervous system; cigars produced headaches and indigestion; snuff made the athlete sneeze so much that his joints were loosened; tea was bad for the liver; coffee caused insomnia; soda water made the athlete effeminate; and chewing ruined the eyesight and made the athlete an old man before his time. Most

American athletes indulged in at least some of these things. Yet the American was the best athlete in the world. If these things could be eliminated, Walker asked, "Can it be imagined what new heights he can reach?"

In the United States athletics and the consumption of alcohol have been associated with manliness and with one another. Not surprisingly then, the ball players, like most other Americans, were not inclined to take Prohibition seriously. The drinking prowess of Babe Ruth revealed the tip of the iceberg as well as the general attitude toward liquor. Even Judge Landis, who had a judicial reputation as an opponent of bootleggers and an enforcer of Prohibition, shared the attitude. At a dinner party following a World Series, where there was considerable liquor in evidence when Landis arrived, some of the guests felt that the judge might put a damper on the occasion. Instead he rose with cocktail in hand and proposed a toast to the Eighteenth Amendment (Spink, *Judge Landis*). While Ruth defied the Prohibitionists by public conduct, the judge flaunted the law only in semiprivacy, thus living up to the hypocrisy of officialdom on this aspect of American life in the Twenties.

While the fundamentalists were trying to take liquor away from the people of America, there was an increasing tendency to take Sunday out of the hands of the ministers. This trend was supported by the sporting press and the baseball establishment. They organized their power to stop the passage of blue laws where Sunday baseball was already played, and they were active in the fight to liberalize the law where Sunday ball was prohibited. It was one of the hot issues from the end of the First World War until the early Thirties and revealed one way in which the baseball establishment attempted to exploit its identification with the forces of democracy.

In 1919 the local blue-law proponents in Washington began a campaign to pressure Congress to make the Lord's Day holy in the District of Columbia. This group had statistics to support their case: only 7,000 people attended church on one Sunday, while the same day there were 50,000 at the movies. One writer in *The Sporting News* informed the Sabbatarians that the figures were the result of their own fanaticism, which was driving the people out of the churches. He called Sabbatarianism an invention of the devil and claimed that the Bible did not forbid Sunday amusements. He also said that it was another case of the minority trying to impose its will on the majority. These groups were antidemocratic and therefore anti-American.

About the same time, the New York legislature was considering a bill for local option on the question of Sunday baseball. *The Sporting News* saw it clearly as a case of the minority stifling the majority and drew an analogy to the Prohibition issue. If the New York law were passed, *The Sporting News* felt that it would be "a great victory for democracy, right here in America." Major-league baseball organized a lobbying effort to push the New York legislature. Johnny Evers, Christy Mathewson, and others were scheduled to appear before the lawmakers. Also, the men still in uniform overseas were flooding the legislature with mail on behalf of local option, fighting against those who had "cooked up laws that would nullify everything the boys were fighting for...." The editors of *The Sporting News* were pleased by this turn of events and called for all-out victory. It was time to go "over the top for Sunday baseball."

Sunday baseball was also interpreted as a class issue. The opponents of Sunday ball had argued against it on the basis that it would be dangerous to allow a large group of workers to come together in one place. When the local-option law was passed in New York it was hailed as a victory for the working class. They had gained "the same privileges that even idlers are permitted." Sunday ball would increase baseball attendance as new fans could now be drawn from the working classes. Revealing its own nonproletarian roots, *The Sporting News* warned the workers that it was "up to them to prove they can behave as well as a crowd of brokers or daintier gentry."

In 1920 the state of Massachusetts passed a local-option law that allowed Sunday ball as long as no admission was charged. Although pleased with the law, *The Sporting News* took the opportunity to attack the Bay State Puritans in a tone imitative of H. L. Mencken. It began by reviewing the history of the state, which was termed "one of the original seats of intolerance." The first settlers were Puritan fanatics that "even a seventeenth-century England could not stand."

When they landed they were opposed only by "a few unsophisticated Indians, who promptly were killed off for the glory of God or driven to the tall timber." The sons and daughters of the original fanatics continued in the ways of their parents. Massachusetts was saved by the influx of Irish, French-Canadians, and Italians, whom the fanatics regarded as aliens. But these aliens "flourished and multiplied." Now the majority in Massachusetts was no longer descended from the Puritans. "This majority, with saner ideas of life, has made a long fight against an arrogant and intolerant minority, a fight against Seventeenth Century prejudices and practices, and the passage of a law permitting Sunday sports is a marker in its step toward Twentieth Century democracy."

Massachusetts wasn't the only state to come under such vituperous attack: Pennsylvania was described as "Cossack-ridden and graft-burdened." Georgia was pictured as a place where slavery still existed and where the "murder of a black man who seeks his freedom is considered less of a crime by a good many people than is the taking of a drink or the playing of a Sunday game." It was only the West, "where Americans are as free as anywhere," that *The Sporting News* saw as a bastion and guardian of democracy, at least on this issue.

The Sunday issue was important enough to touch the White House. Baseball fan Calvin Coolidge attended most of the World Series games played in Washington. On October 15, 1925, Harry S. Foight of Pittsburgh sent a letter to President Coolidge expressing concern over a report that the president had attended a World Series game on a Sunday. Foight said that he did not believe the report, knowing the president was a "conscientious observer of the Fourth Commandment," and that as the leader of a Christian nation Coolidge would not help desecrate Sunday. Foight was reassured by the president's secretary, who wrote that the report was "without foundation," and the president did not, and would not, attend a Sunday game.

Jimmy Walker, New York's flamboyant mayor, spoke of Sunday baseball at a baseball dinner in St. Petersburg, Florida, in 1926. Walker claimed that nothing in his political career gave him a greater sense of accomplishment than his role in the passage of New York's local-option law. There were great benefits, he said, in Sunday baseball. People could "forget their cares in the zest of a red-blooded baseball game, our national sport...." Certainly there were worse ways to spend a Sunday. Besides, "I defy any one to say that the morals of New York have been lowered since Sunday baseball was given to the people." Doubtless the cynics would reply that it was impossible to lower New York's morals.

In November 1928 Massachusetts finally capitulated and passed a local-option law for Sunday sports, and in December the Boston city council approved Sunday sports for its city. It was a hot political issue. Before it was settled, Judge Emil Fuchs, president of the Braves, was caught in the middle of charges of corruption: first, that Boston city council members had solicited bribes from the Braves; then, that the Braves had violated the Massachusetts corrupt-practices act by supplying money to a fund used to promote passage of the local-option law during statewide elections in November. It was also charged that the picture of one of the men running for the state senate appeared on the back of Braves tickets in an attempt to defeat an opponent of local option. City council members were cleared of the charges against them. As for Fuchs, he admitted spending some $200,000 of his own money to secure passage of the law. He pleaded *nolo contendere* to a charge of spending money to influence the vote on Sunday baseball. The Braves were fined $1,000 in municipal court on similar charges (*The Sporting News* and Kaese, *Boston Braves*).

So Boston got Sunday baseball. The Red Sox played the first Sunday game in the city on April 28, 1929. However, according to Kaese, the game had to be played at Braves Field because Fenway Park was too close to a church. The final holdout at the major-league level was Pennsylvania, which finally collapsed in the face of a statewide referendum in November 1933. There was more support for repeal of the Sunday blue law in some areas of the state than there had been for the repeal of Prohibition.

In the aftermath of World War I and the Red Scare, the labor move-ment in the United States declined. Unions had become associated in some quarters with dangerous radicalism and even Bolshevism. It was to be expected then that unionism would not find much favor in baseball. In 1922 the National Baseball Players' Association of the United States was formed. Ray Cannon, the Milwaukee attorney and former player who headed the group, was also the lawyer for several of the Black Sox players who had been banned from baseball and were seeking reinstatement and redress. Cannon's association with the Black Sox cases did not enhance the image of the Players' Association. Initial reaction from *The Sporting News* suggested that the union was simply exploiting the players to enrich its own treasury. It also regarded Cannon's connection with the union as an indication that the union might be a front for the reinstatement of the Chicago players. The guardians of the establishment painted the union as a conspiratorial group. What possible grievances could a baseball player have? they asked. And if, in fact, there were any, they ought to be taken to Commissioner Landis, not some union. It was also reported that John McGraw, surprised that any of his "liberally paid Giants" were involved with the union, condemned the union "in no uncertain terms."

By the spring of 1923 the Players' Association claimed a membership of 225. It issued a demand for a vote in the governmental structure of organized baseball. Such a demand was rejected as "preposterous." Here was a group of men drawing a collective salary of over $2 million who took no financial risks of their own. On the other hand, the owners had to be considered. They were the guardians of the public trust, safeguards of the National Game. It was these owners who had restored public confidence in baseball after the 1919 World Series fix. It had been the "high-salaried stars" themselves who had caused the scandal. At the heart of the union movement was greed; at its head was Ray Cannon, infamous defender of the Black Sox. It was all too much for the sportswriters to take. As Harold Seymour has pointed out, the reaction stemmed from unnecessary anxiety: The union soon collapsed. The players were not interested.

During the Thirties, the labor movement came into more public favor and was legitimized by the New Deal. Thus, when the question of a union for players was again broached, the reaction was less hostile, but it was again rejected, simply because it was inapplicable to baseball. *The Sporting News* acknowledged the right and desirability for unions in industry, but noted that "there were certain individualistic endeavors in which the plan is not practicable...." In a later editorial it outlined the reasons why unions could not succeed in baseball. First, unions implied the leveling of wages. This could not be done because of the differences in wages between a Dean or a Gehrig and a rookie or a fading veteran. Players of great skill would never accept salaries equal to those of lesser players. Second, economic reformers wanted a thirty-hour work week. Players who worked only two or three hours each day would consider that oppressive. Third, the "sit-down" tactic employed by unions carried little appeal to players who were already tired of sitting on the bench. Fourth, and the biggest obstacle, was a lack of sympathy from the public. The average citizen found it difficult to become indignant over the oppression of someone making $10,000 annually for a few hours work a day for only part of the year. Finally, players were unlikely to surrender proven "benefits of individual bargaining" for the collective bargaining that would lead to uniform pay scales. Although for the most part this line of reasoning avoided and distorted issues, it still fairly accurately reflected attitudes that would survive well into the post–World War II era.

Of more concern than unions to at least some of the players in the Twenties was real estate. Because a majority of major-league teams trained in Florida, it was perhaps inevitable that baseball people would get involved in the Florida land boom. When they did it was at two levels, that of investor and that of salesman. In 1925 it was reported that eight members of the Brooklyn team were involved in Florida real estate. Both Jacques Fournier and Milton Stock had interests in a large land company in Sarasota, with Fournier serving as assistant sales manager. Spittin' Bill Doak, a Brooklyn pitcher, was quite successful in real estate in the Bradenton area. He quit baseball in 1925 to devote his full time to land sales. Uncle Wilbert Robinson, the Brooklyn manager, was said to get a cold chill every time anyone even mentioned Florida: there were rumors that several more of his players were quitting baseball to join in the land boom.

In the spring of 1926 Francis Powers reported from Cleveland that no class of people was so infected by the Florida land boom as major-league ball players. These players were not just investing on their own but were very effective salesman, using their baseball fame to lure the customers. Powers predicted that major-league owners would have to offer higher salaries to retain their players "in the more plebeian life of a baseball player." That spring several full-page advertisements appeared in *The Sporting News* announcing the virtues of Florida land being sold by John J. McGraw. Managers were not above trading on their name. In fairness to McGraw, it should be added that when the boom collapsed he paid back every penny to those who had invested in his project.

The reaction to this player involvement in real estate was not entirely favorable. It was frequently pointed out in the press that the real estate deals were taking players' minds off the game and adversely affecting their play. And if the players were distracted in boom times, when the market began to shake in 1926 it was predicted that batting averages would suffer in direct correlation with land values. Another problem involved personal relationships: "One can imagine the strained relations between Pitcher Jones and Outfielder Smith, Jones having induced Smith to put his savings in some diluted Florida sand, the price of which declined many points per gallon."

The Sporting News addressed itself to the problem in an editorial titled "Base Hits or Sand?" It pointed out that baseball required more concentration than "dealing in sand." A head full of real estate terminology was likely to be devoid of base hits. Those who were preoccupied with land simply could not compete with those "young men who are the cream of the United States as ball players, and who enter their summer vacation with no purpose in mind other than to give the best they have."

After the 1926 hurricane ended the boom, *The Sporting News* looked back to survey the wreckage. It hoped that Florida would welcome back with "a glad hand and a warm climate" those players who had lost so heavily. There was, of course, a lesson to be learned. "Ball players have yet to learn to be Spartans and slam out a home run with three men on bases when the fox of slipping values is eating at their speculative hearts, as they wonder why they did not stick to the simple life and not venture into the realm of Get-Rich-Quick-Wallingford." But the collapse of the land market was good for Brooklyn, for Bill Doak returned to the pitching mound. He had discovered "that a baseball salary check in hand is worth ten lots in the backwater." He and other players were lucky. They could return to baseball, where, along with much of the rest of the nation, they remained untouched by the economic crisis until the Great Depression.

If land speculation could distract players, then certainly so could women. The Nineteenth Amendment to the Constitution, giving women the right to vote, was a symbol of the changing role of women in American society after World War I. Baseball had always been a man's game, serving the red-blooded American boy. There was no doubt that from the standpoint of participation it would remain so. But the increased incidence of men and women in public and social affairs resulted in increased attendance by women at major-league baseball games. Owners sought to exploit the new pool of potential fans through such devices as ladies' day and the introduction of radio broadcasting, through which, it was felt, the housewife could be reached. In the terminology of today's feminism, the reaction could only be characterized as clear evidence of male chauvinism.

In July 1919 *The Sporting News* published a short poem called "Quite So." It sets the general tone on this subject:

> When women enter baseball
> They'll shake a batter's nerves;
> I never knew a player
> Who could catch on their curves.
>
> When women enter baseball
> The time to take your heed
> Is when by chance you tackle those
> Who have both curves and speed.

Slightly more serious was an editorial in the same publication reacting to the announcement that two women would serve on the Ohio grand jury investigating the 1919 World Series. The editors welcomed the women to the investigation, seeing it as a chance for the "deadlier sex" to demonstrate that it was worthy of the new sexual equality. Although noting that women had a tendency to lie about their age, the editors were confident that the high ideals of the woman fan would be of great assistance in cleaning up the game.

In 1929 Al Demaree, a former player, wrote an article titled "Grandstand Girls" in which he examined the role of women in baseball. Starting from the premise that baseball is a man's game, Demaree expressed the opinion that when the ladies intruded into the game there was usually trouble, which could take the form of cliques of wives, jealousy over salaries, or simply a comment by one wife about seeing one of the other husbands with a good-looking girl. In addition, family affairs could be a distraction for a player and hinder his performance. Getting married during the season was considered bad luck.

But women could be useful by sitting behind the dugout of the opposition and acting as spies. Demaree also described what he termed the "baseball daisy." These women served as the "fifth pitcher" for a team by dating the opposing pitchers. The "daisy" would take them out "for a round of the cabarets" the night prior to their pitching assignment and thus impair their effectiveness. According to Demaree certain pitchers simply could not win in certain towns because of this subterfuge.

The "Grandstand Girls" could also be a distraction on the playing field. When in his best-selling exposé, *Ball Four*, Jim Bouton revealed to fans the practice of "beaver shooting," some baseball people were shocked Bouton should make such revelations. However, Demaree had suggested a similar practice in the late Twenties. According to him the players were constantly on the lookout for "sex pots" in the stands. Occasionally players cut peepholes in the back of dugouts in order "to spot the 'knockouts.'" Others carried field glasses to survey the prospects from the bench. When one player was asked by his wife why he carried the field glasses, he is supposed to have replied that he needed them to catch the signs. Demaree also revealed an ingenious device used by Phil Douglas to attract the good-lookers. Before each game Douglas would throw three or four baseballs to the best-looking girls in the stands. On each ball he had written his name and telephone number. He claimed a fairly high response from this approach. Apparently, Al Demaree—and several of the players—had great difficulty thinking of women in baseball as anything other than sex objects.

By the late Twenties women were regarded as an important part of fandom. Ladies' day was an established institution. Probably the greatest success with this promotion was in Chicago, where the Cubs made extensive use of ladies' day and the radio. The response was so great that there were mob scenes at the gates of Wrigley Field every Friday. In June 1930 over 30,000 women appeared at the gates, nearly causing a riot. The Cubs were finally forced to distribute ladies' day tickets in advance at outlets around the city. Later they changed to a mail-order system (Brown, *The Chicago Cubs*).

In addition to increased numbers of women at the games, one woman joined the organizational structure of baseball, advancing to the vice-presidency of the Philadelphia Phillies. This was exceptional and probably due to the fact that she was the wife of Phillies' president, Gerry Nugent. A feature article on Mae Nugent that appeared in *The Sporting News* concentrated on such things as her views on ladies' days and how to make the game more attractive to women. Mae Nugent's area of expertise was narrowly defined.

If there were any doubts about the proper role for women in the National Pastime in those years, an incident in the spring of 1931 should have cleared the air. In Chattanooga, Tennessee, a young woman pitched in an exhibition game against the New York Yankees. *The Sporting News* doubted the value of such "bawdy publicity" and reminded everyone that the National Game must be "treated with respect." Forrest Cain of the *New York Evening Post* did not take the event so seriously, saying that she didn't throw the ball very hard and was unable to throw a curve. Then he added, "It takes curves to pitch baseball, and Miss Mitchell's aren't that kind." But one letter-writing fan from Missouri did take the whole affair very seriously. He felt that the "stunt at Chattanooga" would have a bad effect on baseball. He said that the game was already "too feminine" and ventured the opinion that men like Rogers Hornsby would never have been responsible for bringing females into the game. "It's a he-man's game, and it seems like we even have to have real red-blooded he-men to even promote it, as well as play it." The irate fan went on to predict that women all over the country would now be signing baseball contracts. Women would "do anything from shaving their heads to shooting their husbands, just for the thrill of getting their names in the paper." The role of women in baseball was clear to the fans of the day. It would not be confused by changes in other social customs. As in the larger society, baseball was not yet ready to take equality for women seriously.

Another of the results of World War I was a preoccupation with 100 percent Americanism and a general intensification of antiforeign feelings. Nurtured by both George Creel's committee and A. Mitchell Palmer's drive to the White House, these undemocratic aspects of the crusade to make the world safe for democracy lived on in the Twenties. They took such grotesque forms as the Ku Klux Klan revival and the Sacco and Vanzetti case, received legal sanction in the Immigration Act of 1924, and gained middle-class respectability from the Chamber of Commerce mentality. Baseball considered itself the game of democracy and Americanism, and at different stages in its development baseball provided various ethnic groups with a means of upward mobility. It was natural that baseball at times concerned itself with questions involving various ethnic groups.

In 1921 one club owner complained that the increase of unruly behavior at baseball games was due to the increased number of foreigners attending the games. The owner felt that these "squareheads" did not understand the true values of American sportsmanship. In reply to this charge, The Sporting News pointed out that unruly behavior could be found even in "bastions of 100 percent Americanism" like the South or such cities as Philadelphia. The editors did, however, recognize that there was an increasing resentment against immigrants and some ethnic groups. The Sporting News cited, as an example of the trend, charges that the bribers of the White Sox had been "conspicuously of one certain nationality." But, said the journal, "They're all 'Americans' here."

In The Sporting News in 1924, one writer decried the increased rowdyism at games, charging that the worst transgressors were foreigners and that seldom did one "have the appearance of a well-bred American-born man." The attacks on umpires were blamed on young people who were "born of foreign parents and high-pitched emotionally."

For the most part, however, sportswriters chose to emphasize the more positive side of this issue. Baseball was portrayed as a force for democracy, opportunity, and Americanization; it was a microcosm of the great American melting pot. Foreigners should not be rejected but assimilated, and baseball had a role to play. In 1923 it was revealed that the Philadelphia A's were torn by dissension between those who were members of the Ku Klux Klan and those who did not qualify for or desire membership. *The Sporting News* produced a long editorial on the subjects of the Klan and baseball as melting pot. The journal was disturbed that in a "democratic, catholic, real American game like baseball," the "hideous monster of racial or religious prejudice" could raise its ugly head. It was claimed with pride that any player could be admitted to the game regardless of race—with the notable exception of the "Ethiopian." The editors did not want to comment on this exception except to say that it did deny opportunity to some of the "greatest players the game ever has known." It was also pointed out that religion was not an issue when a player signed his contract. The fans would accept any player, judging him only on his ability. "The Mick, the Sheeney, the Wop, the Dutch and the Chink, the Cuban, the Indian, the Jap or the so-called Anglo-Saxon—his 'nationality' is never a matter of moment if he can pitch, or hit, or field."

However, at times the players could not restrain themselves. The editors were disturbed by this and by the influence of the Klan. But they were also optimistic that things would return to "normalcy." There might be some fanatics among the players, but the editors did not think they would do much harm. They would be suppressed by the "normalcy of fandom" and the Americanism of baseball that would lead to tolerance and democracy. It is not known how widespread Klan influence was in major-league baseball, although several prominent figures have been mentioned as Klan members.

In 1931 sportswriter Tommy Holmes developed the melting-pot

theme by pointing to Brooklyn as an "all-nations team." There was
Ernie Lombardi (Italian), Al Lopez (Spanish-American), Val Picinich
(Czech), Adolfo Luque (Cuban), Del Bissionette (French-Canadian),
Babe Herman ("Teuton"), Frank O'Doul (Irish), Al Cohen and Max
Rosenfeld (Jewish), and an assortment of "Anglo-Saxons." Holmes
felt that the addition of Lombardi was particularly significant be-
cause of the large number of Italians who frequented Ebbets Field.
Italians, Holmes noted, made great baseball fans because of "their

Reprinted, courtesy of the *Chicago Tribune*

natural capacity for great enthusiasm." Holmes also found it strange that there were so few outstanding Italian players. But by mid-1931 *The Sporting News* saw the "Sons of Caesar" moving to the forefront of major-league baseball. The publication warned the Irish that the Italians and Poles were about to challenge them to prove their racial superiority. There would always be the Smiths and Browns, of course: "They represent Uncle Sam."

But if American baseball was a melting pot, the Jew had difficulty melting, and the black American never got into the pot. As Harold Seymour has pointed out, in the early part of the century Jews were accepted into baseball, but they were not joyously welcomed. Many found it prudent to change their names to avoid harassment.

Then there was the connection some had made between Jews and gamblers in baseball at the time of the Black Sox scandal. Even before that, an item appeared in *The Sporting News* reporting the arrest at the Polo Grounds of six gamblers, named Herman Kellman, Joe Koskie, Sidney Stroelley, Moses Bresher, Joe Meeter, and Lester Litt. "Do you get those names?" the reader was asked. "If you do you get the idea of what sort of people it is that are generally most active in trying to besmirch baseball with their gambling operations." However, even if Baseball's Bible was willing to lend itself to this barely subtle innuendo, it was not willing to accept the more overt attacks by Henry Ford. In an editorial in 1921, *The Sporting News* responded to charges made by Ford in the *Dearborn Independent*. Ford claimed that the 1919 World Series scandals were evidence of Jewish corruption and that other publications did not attack the Jews because they were muzzled by the Zionist conspiracy. *The Sporting News* took the position that all Jews were not responsible for the actions of a few corrupt Jews. It noted, with an interesting twist, that to condemn all Jews for this action would be the same as condemning all Italians because of the actions of "Dago hootch-makers." To combat Ford's charges, the journal gratuitously advised each Jew to live his life by such high principles that he could point to a "crooked member of his 'race' as a remarkable exception."

In 1923 John E. Wray, in the *St. Louis Post-Dispatch*, sought to explain why there were so few Jews in professional baseball. Wray talked with John McGraw, who had constantly searched for a Jewish star to attract New York's Jewish population to the Polo Grounds. McGraw said that Jews stayed out of baseball because the monetary inducements were not sufficient. Wray, however, found intolerance a more important reason, as well as the "natural tendency of the race to play a lone hand." Jews were simply not inclined to team sports. Francis Richter claimed that he could find no reason for the lack of Jews in the "virile, mind-developing, and muscle-building sports" which attracted so many of the young people of America. But he found Jews prominent in only one sport, "pugilism, the most commercialized" of sports.

In 1928 it appeared, at least for a short time, that John McGraw had found a Jewish star for the New York Giants. A young boy named Andy Cohen came from the University of Alabama to replace Rogers Hornsby, who had been traded at the end of the previous season. When the Giants opened at the Polo Grounds, Cohen at second base was the hero of the day. Fans came on the field at the end of the game and carried Cohen around on their shoulders. Giant players had to rescue Andy from his followers. In commenting on Cohen's success, W. O. McGeehan of the *New York Herald Tribune* saw the young man as the answer to McGraw's dream of a Jewish hero for the Giants. Will Wedge, in the *New York Sun*, profiled Andy Cohen as yet another Alger hero, Wedge dealt heavily in stereotypes as he pictured Cohen as "keen" and a "sharp" businessman. Burris Jenkins, Jr., writing in the *New York Evening World*, said Cohen was a man working under several handicaps: he was harassed by the fans because he was Jewish; he had a hooked nose; he was replacing the popular Rogers Hornsby. But according to Jenkins, these obstacles did not bother Cohen, "the earnest young Jew." To Jenkins, Andy Cohen was the perfect Jew. The implication was that Andy was not like other Jews: "He has exactly the correct mixture of modesty and self-assurance. There is nothing crawling about his nature. Nor is he the least bit boastful." And these were supposed to be favorable comments!

Cohen's stardom did not last. He joined the long list of players who enjoyed only transient glory in major-league baseball. Although there were other Jewish players in the majors, none achieved superstar status until the emergence of Hank Greenberg in the early 1930s. Ironically, Greenberg was from the Bronx but escaped the Yankees and Giants and was signed by the Detroit Tigers. In 1934 Greenberg captured the headlines as he led the Tigers to an American League pennant. Dick Farrington wrote a feature story on Greenberg for *The Sporting News* just prior to the start of the World Series. Farrington told of Greenberg's ambitions to go to Princeton, the same institution that turned out Woodrow Wilson. Hank had earned scholastic and athletic scholarships which he hoped would get him into Princeton. But the Ivy League school did not accept Greenberg. Hank said he wasn't sure if it was because he was Jewish.

Farrington used Greenberg as an example of the tremendous opportunities offered by the National Pastime. Here was the son of Rumanian immigrants who had found great success in baseball. But

Reprinted from the *New York Post*

Farrington could not escape the straitjacket of the stereotypes, either. He began his article on Greenberg: "This is the story about a Manhattan Jewish boy, transplanted into the Bronx, who made good without going into the ready-to-wear line." Farrington reported that Greenberg didn't look or even sound Jewish: "There is little suggestion of the Jewish characteristics in his appearance, the nose being straight, and he speaks with more of a Harvard than a so-called East Side accent." Presumably these were redeeming traits.

Unlike Greenberg who did not look Jewish, the black American always looked black. His exclusion from the most American of sports mocked the myths of equality and democracy which the sportswriters loved to extol. But that went unnoticed until the Thirties. As in so many areas of American society, the unwritten law of exclusion was taken for granted by baseball men everywhere.

During the Twenties the issue was only rarely mentioned. In 1921 *Baseball Magazine* commented on the formation of the new Continental League, to be open to the Negro player. Although the publication favored this idea in principle, it felt it would never work in practice: "Through all the ages the effort to mix oil and water has failed. In this country at least all efforts to mix black and white on an [equal basis] have also failed." At the end of the 1921 season, some of the St. Louis Cardinal players took part in an exhibition game with "colored players." *The Sporting News* commented that it might be all right for the players to pick up a few extra dollars. On the other hand, in the eyes of the Cardinal fans it was "bad stuff" to see their heroes participating in "the grand African show...." A similar comment by *The Sporting News* followed a 1923 exhibition game between the St. Louis Browns and "a bunch of Negroes." The journal was particularly disturbed by the "spectacle of white major-league players taking the abuse of mobs of our colored brethren and liking it or seeming to because of the few dollars netted." This comment preceded by only two months the previously cited editorial in which *The Sporting News* stated that they did not wish to comment on the wisdom of the exclusion of Negroes from organized baseball.

But for the most part the entire issue was ignored in the Twenties. During the Thirties the subject was once again brought to the fore. In

1931 Westbrook Pegler, writing in the *Chicago Tribune*, made one of the first attacks in the white press against the color line in baseball. Pegler asserted that the exclusion of black athletes from baseball was difficult to reconcile with baseball's claim to be the National Pastime. He noted that there were great black players in football, basketball, and track, yet the black athlete was excluded from baseball without explanation. To those who argued that the Negro was more likely to engage in conduct detrimental to the game, Pegler countered that there were no Negroes working for Al Capone or Legs Diamond. Pegler was amazed that the great sportsmen of America had not raised their pens against the color line. While white collegians could compete and associate freely with the great black athletes, "professional ball players must be protected by a regulation which the magnates haven't the gall to put on paper." Pegler wanted to know why.

At the Baseball Writers' Dinner in New York in early 1933 the issue was taken directly to the writers by Heywood Broun. To the claim that no color line existed in baseball, Heywood Broun pointed to the attempt by John McGraw to use a Negro named Monroe when McGraw was managing the Baltimore Orioles. McGraw protested that Monroe was not a Negro, but the rest of the league members knew otherwise, and they forced McGraw to remove Monroe from his team. At the same dinner New York sportswriter Jimmy Powers took a poll. The only important baseball figure to object to the admittance of Negroes into the major leagues was, ironically, John McGraw. That same year John Heydler, president of the National League, had the temerity to say that baseball never excluded anyone on the basis of race, creed, color, or religion. He claimed that major-league baseball only required good character and good habits of its players (Robert W. Peterson, *Only the Ball Was White*). It is interesting that the *New York Times'* report on the dinner made no mention of Broun's remarks or the poll taken by Powers. Nor did *The Sporting News*. Joe Vila, in his weekly contribution to *The Sporting News*, criticized Broun without mentioning him by name. Vila also praised John McGraw as the only man "who had the guts to say that Negroes should not be permitted to play on teams with white men."

Occasionally a letter from a fan appeared on this subject in *The*

Sporting News. Shortly after the publication of Westbrook Pegler's column, a fan from Columbia, Missouri, wrote to voice his objections. He demanded an immediate apology from Pegler to baseball, for the insults that Pegler had directed at the game. In 1934 a fan from West Somerville, Massachusetts, wrote urging the admittance of "the colored man" into professional baseball, arguing that Negro players would increase Negro attendance and the availability of talent. A year later another fan called for the admittance of "colored boys" on the grounds that they would add to baseball as an entertainment form. There was almost everything else in the game, "so let's be fair."

In the midst of growing sentiment for the admittance of Negroes, the major-leagues were embarrassed in 1938 by an incident involving Yankee left-fielder Jake Powell. It was near midseason, and the Yankees were in Chicago for a game with the White Sox. Bob Elson in a pregame radio interview with Powell asked him how he liked his off-season job as a policeman in Dayton, Ohio. According to the *New York Times*, Powell replied that he derived considerable pleasure from his job of "cracking niggers over the head." The program was immediately cut off the air, and the station was flooded with protests. The next day a group of Negroes at the ball park demanded that Powell be barred from baseball. Commissioner Landis suspended Powell for ten days. League officials considered banning pregame radio interviews, and Joe McCarthy, the Yankee manager, did issue such a ban covering his players. McCarthy also criticized radio stations for bothering players before a game. As for Powell, he claimed that he could not recall the remark and said that he hoped he had not offended the Negroes of Dayton, Chicago, or anywhere else. Powell concluded with this inevitable comment: "I have some very good friends among the Negroes in Dayton."

The only other indication of fan reaction to the incident was reported in the *Times* after Powell's first appearance on the field after his suspension ended, in the second game of a doubleheader in Washington on August 16. Powell did not receive a particularly warm welcome from the crowd: In his first appearance at the plate he was booed. In the sixth inning, when the Yankees took a 3-to-1 lead, pop bottles descended on Jake as he returned to left field. (It was a nice irony that Negro grounds keepers had to be called to remove the bottles.) Then in the seventh inning, when Powell reached first base on a single, a bottle just missed him there. After Jake advanced to third, a large pail was thrown at him. In his next appearance in the Yankee lineup, Powell played both games of a doubleheader without incident.

The late Thirties saw an increase in the criticism of baseball on this issue. In 1938, according to the *Times*, the American Youth Congress passed a resolution condemning professional and amateur baseball leagues for their exclusion of Negroes. The following year Sen. Charles Perry of New York City introduced a resolution in the New York state legislature voicing disapproval of discrimination against Negroes in the major leagues. The *Times* reported that copies of the resolution were sent to the two league presidents and to Commissioner Landis. Meanwhile, sportswriter Jimmy Powers continued his campaign to open baseball to blacks. In a 1939 article in the *New York Sunday News*, he recommended that instead of worrying about minorities in distant lands, some attention ought to be paid to the Negro minority at home. He suggested that those interested in baseball could begin by going to Yankee Stadium to watch the All-Star game between the Negro National and American Leagues. After reviewing the talents of various players, Powers expressed the hope that some day, some owner would have the courage to sign a young player like Josh Gibson, all-star catcher. "Then baseball will be a truly National Sport."

In 1940 the *New York Times* wrote that a group of sports editors from New York college newspapers added their voices of dissent by passing a resolution condemning discrimination against Negro athletes by major-league baseball and by American colleges. Also in 1940 the magazine *Friday* published comments from major-league managers and players who approved of the elimination of the color line from major-league baseball (Peterson, *Only the Ball Was White*). Public pressure was beginning to mount.

But to Dan Parker, sports editor of the *New York Mirror*, all the talk was cheap. It was the Yankee management that was really helping the Negro players by providing reasonable rental of Yankee Stadium to the Negro National League. In addition Parker reported that the Yankees were offering the Col. Jacob Ruppert Trophy to the team with the best record in the Negro league. Parker felt that such actions as these would help "colored baseball much more than cheap words."

Despite the growing volume of criticism, *The Sporting News* ignored the obvious contradiction and welcomed the arrival of the 1941 season with an editorial titled "A Wide Door of Opportunity." Baseball was celebrated as the "great leveler, bringing together lads in tweeds and denim, from mansion and farmhouse, out of college or backwoods, some seeking sport, others a livelihood." Baseball was a means of escape from economic hardship, and each year the lineups contained new names representing groups that were making their way up the economic scale. No matter how humble the origin, said *The Sporting News* all a young man needed in baseball was the necessary energy and talent. "That is the American way, and baseball, as America's National Pastime, offers an easy entry into the field of opportunity."

That such comments could be made in the face of the trend of nearly a decade of protest is tribute to the resilience of the myth of opportunity and the matter-of-fact approach with which most Americans accepted racial discrimination and separation. It also offered ample evidence that the time was not yet ripe. But the next war would change a lot of things.

8

Crisis, Change, and Continuity

> Beyond each game, he sees another, and yet
> another, in endless and hopeless succession.

> ...like Cuss says. Centennial of everything
> these days. Enough to give a guy the creeps.

THE Great Depression has become a major reference point in the lives of those who lived through it. Anyone of the present generation, hearing his parents, grandparents, or great-grandparents speak of those days of economic hardship, knows that the depression left a permanent mark. The depression also had an impact on baseball: It affected attendance, dislocated a baseball dynasty, and sped change in the game. Naturally, salaries were affected. These surface changes were accompanied by deeper effects, which can be seen in the role that the sporting establishment saw for itself in these difficult times. The resilience of the American character in the face of a crisis is also revealed by the literature of baseball in the Thirties.

The Wall Street Crash of late October 1929 hurt many people, but the gravity of the situation was not generally realized at once. The severe economic dislocations were more slow to develop. The year 1929 had been a good one in baseball. The National League had experienced the second best attendance in its history and the American League its third best. Baseball salaries were higher than they had ever been. So, despite the Great Crash, *The Sporting News* called for more talk about baseball and less about "irrelevant misery." Business conditions in baseball were very good, and they would get better. It was that simple. Indeed, by the middle of the 1930 season it was apparent that the major leagues were headed for record attendance. It was equally clear that the country was heading into a depression. Some writers found these two facts were related, holding that often business depression was a harbinger of a good baseball season. The 1930 season was confirming that belief. It was also proving that baseball was "a good tonic game," as it attracted the "more or less depressed mind to watch its fascinations." As the depression deepened, the role of baseball as tonic proportionately increased.

Following the 1930 World Series the players' share was reported at over $300,000. *The Sporting News* called this "a sermon [in] itself." And what were its lessons? First, it proved that it was a generous public that paid a third of a million dollars to see these very lucky young men play. "What country, or nation in the world, treats its athletes as handsomely?" Second, it raised the question of whether or not hard times did in fact exist. On this point the journal was skeptical. The National League had set a new attendance record; the American League had also had a very good year. The skepticism of *The Sporting News* increased, and it began to be smug. It reported that the managers of other amusements were amazed by baseball's success, but then, as all good baseball men instinctively know, there is nothing in the world that brings out the crowds like baseball. "When other enterprises fail, baseball goes on." However, the major-league teams were going to reduce the number of coaches, the explanation being that overhead had expanded beyond reason.

Barney Dreyfuss, owner of the Pittsburgh Pirates, was equally enthusiastic as he surveyed the 1930 attendance figures. However, his Pirates did not share in the general National League prosperity. Dreyfuss had been around a long time and recalled that baseball had always come through depressions in fine style. Barney explained that a relatively cheap form of amusement like baseball appealed to the common people. When these people were employed daily they could not come out to the ball park. When they were "loafing" and in need of entertainment, there was nowhere else they could get so much for their money. Barney Dreyfuss did not speculate on what would happen when the loafers ran out of money.

Some awareness of the seriousness of the economic crisis surfaced during the winter of 1930–31. There were indications that the owners were not above using the depression to their advantage in contract negotiations. Reports circulated at the winter meetings that players seemed anxious to sign their contracts. Cincinnati sportswriter Tom Swope wrote that the players realized that the depression could affect salaries and that baseball attendance might drop in 1931. Meanwhile Ed Barrow, Yankee general manager, predicted that there would be no difficulty signing players in 1931. He noted that contracts were generous considering the hard times and the presence of apple vendors on the street corners. Ralph Davis, who had only a few weeks earlier reported the optimism of Barney Dreyfuss, developed a rationale for lower salaries. He said that if poor economic conditions continued, baseball would be adversely affected in the 1931 season. Therefore it was perfectly understandable that the owners should not offer salary increases for 1931, despite the record attendance in 1930.

All of these pessimistic predictions vanished with the opening of the 1931 season. Attendance records were set for opening day in the majors. Yankee Stadium attracted the largest crowd ever to see a Yankee home opener. Fred Lieb, writing in the *New York Evening Post*, found interest in baseball stronger than usual, and he attributed this increase in interest to the public's tiring of depression talk. Marshall Hunt of the *New York Daily News* found the turnout at Yankee Stadium, the traffic jams around the stadium, and the well-dressed fans reason to doubt the portrayal of New York as a city suffering from the depression. The *Chicago Herald and Examiner* rejoiced that there was such a thing as the National Game. No one in the record opening-day crowd in Chicago even seemed aware that there was a depression anywhere near the ball park. Ed Wray, in the *St. Louis Post-Dispatch*, found an old saying true, that baseball prospered during periods of high unemployment. It looked as though 1931 was going to be another banner year for baseball.

By midseason, optimism was confirmed. *Baseball Magazine* boasted that baseball was the most prosperous industry in the country, and explained it in several ways. First, in boom times there was a preoccupation with "pipe dreams," but a man worried about his job or his stock-market losses needed the ball park for relaxation. Second, baseball offered entertainment at an attractive price to people watching their budgets. "Great is baseball, the national tonic, the reviver of hope, the restorer of confidence."

In late July the Cubs turned away 35,000 fans for a Sunday doubleheader. The Cardinals set a new attendance records for St. Louis. In Philadelphia some 60,000 fans had to be turned away from Shibe Park. In the face of these events, Edgar Brands asked, "If baseball is dying, as the croakers would have it, then, death, where art thou sting?" Within a month there was evidence that the sting was about to be felt. In late August Dick Williams in the *Philadelphia Record* was predicting that Connie Mack would break up the world champion A's as he had done in 1914. In mid-September Joe Williams reported in the *New York World Telegram* that club owners facing red ink and rising payrolls were preparing salary cutbacks for the 1932 season. If salaries were to be cut, one Chicago fan felt it was time to cut admission prices. The nickel ham sandwich had returned and was enjoying increased popularity. The fan from Chicago saw a lesson in that for baseball.

When the World Series ended, the *St. Louis Post-Dispatch* commented on the value of the series as a liberator of the national mind from the "cares and anxieties" of the depression. From Broadway to Main Street, the country was talking about the exploits of Pepper Martin. The Cardinals upset the Athletics in the "series of the century." Baseball added other services as the depression mounted. Not only did it continue to be a tonic for the people, but it was contributing directly to voluntary relief efforts. A number of interleague games were played to raise money for unemployment funds. An estimated quarter of a million dollars was raised by baseball in this way. In addition, contributions to community chests and welfare organizations were made by individual owners.

The more immediate concern was for the welfare of the game

itself. At the winter meetings the major leagues passed a resolution
calling for a reduction of players' salaries and other expenses. In a
more direct economy move, the player limit for each team was cut
from twenty-five to twenty-three.

When the question of players' salaries was raised, it naturally led

Reprinted, courtesy of the *Chicago Tribune*

to consideration of the most famous salary of all. In 1931 Babe Ruth was making an estimated $80,000. When the economy moves came in late 1931, Colonel Ruppert let it be known that Ruth would have to take a cut in pay. Joe Vila predicted that the Bambino's salary would come down to $50,000. Vila justified the cut by claiming it would still be the largest salary in baseball and pointing out that Yankee management needed to safeguard itself against the future. As the story of Ruth's salary developed, it was reported that Ruppert was offering $70,000. Some members of the press and some fans expressed the view that Ruppert was a cheapskate and using the depression to try to save himself money. They claimed that Ruth was worth more than $80,000 in gate receipts to the Yankees. Others said that Ruth was a boor who was insensitive to what was happening in the country. Everyone else was suffering, so the Bambino should be willing to try to get along on $70,000. In the end Ruth signed for $75,000.

Ruth was not the only player asked to take a cut in pay. In some cases the owners moved ruthlessly to cut salaries, despite the fact that financially 1931 had not been a bad year for most clubs. The owners generally had public sympathy with them. As George Trevor put it, "Somehow, in these days of breadlines and jobless heads of families, one cannot sympathize too deeply with the well-fed, bankroll-padded baseball holdout."

For all the gathering clouds, *Baseball Magazine* remained optimistic as the 1932 season approached. It felt that baseball was emerging from the depression stronger than ever. Its view of the depression seemed to be that people had to make a more realistic assessment of their lives than they had in the previous decade. There were some problems, but these were "relatively unimpressive." The journal concluded that baseball continued to carry universal appeal. Never before had it more deserved its title as "Our National Game." At *The Sporting News* there was a great awareness of the gravity of the problem. Publisher J. G. Taylor Spink suggested that in addition to cutting expenses the owners needed to find ways to increase income. He rejected the notion of lowering all prices, pointing out that prices had not risen drastically during the prosperous Twenties. But Spink did suggest that the owners pay special attention to the bleacher fans, who undoubtedly were being hardest hit by the depression. He recommended that bleacher prices be dropped to twenty-five cents at least once a week or some other special arrangements be made for these fans.

In what was for them a radical departure *The Sporting News*, in an editorial titled "Taxes," commented directly on politics, alluding to proposals coming out of Washington that would increase revenues by taxing a number of items—bat, ball, uniform, and the game admission price. The editors said that this was being done "because it seems to be the easiest way out for the capitoleers." This was not a political statement, they declared, only the simple truth, which was more than was coming from Washington. The editorial concluded with the hope that the players would "vote not to tax themselves into the poorhouse in 1933 if they can avoid it, and remember the capitoleers." At least one segment of the baseball press was beginning to grasp the gravity of the situation facing the country.

By the middle of the 1932 season it was clear that baseball was no longer immune from the depression. Fred Lieb, writing in the *New York Evening Post*, reported that several minor leagues were folding up and that attendance at major-league games was down for the second consecutive season. Lieb felt that in previous economic depressions baseball had benefited because people thought they would be out of work only a short time. They were able to raise four bits for the admission price. During the 1930 and 1931 seasons this same psychology had worked well for baseball. However, by 1932 the same people were still unemployed and unable to raise four bits even for food. In these circumstances they obviously could not afford to go to the ball park. The realities of the depression had arrived on the diamond.

During the winter months of 1932–33 the talk of salary cuts was more prevalent than in the previous year. If there had been interest in Babe Ruth's salary in 1932, it became a near obsession in 1933. The spotlight on salaries also caught Commissioner Landis. In early 1933 *The Sporting News* raised the issue of the commissioner's salary and the high cost of running the commissioner's office. The players were asking why they should take a cut while the commissioner did not. At the same time fans were asking why they should continue to pay high admission prices to support "an unnecessary costly appendage." Within a week Landis voluntarily cut his salary 40 percent to an estimated $40,000. *The Sporting News* now turned its attention to the Bambino's salary. It noted that some had objected that Ruth's salary should never fall below that of Landis because of Ruth's central role in the game. With Landis' action, the Bambino would be "compelled to fall in line and take his cut, too."

But Ruth felt no such compulsion and returned his contract unsigned. He rejected an estimated $50,000. *The Sporting News* was incensed. It felt that by refusing to sign, and calling $50,000 small change and beneath his dignity, Ruth was "jabbing the sore financial sensibilities of John W. Fan." On the other hand, if this was just part of the usual ballyhoo that accompanied the signing of Ruth in the past, then it was in "doubtful taste." Millions of people in the country considered $50,000 "the mint itself." Joe Vila echoed this view. In the midst of "breadlines and human misery," the extravagant talk about Ruth's salary was out of line. Newspapers were receiving hundreds of letters from fans, who felt that Ruth and other players were overpaid and should "conform to new and imperative conditions." Ruth was still holding out in March. Publisher J. G. Taylor Spink addressed an open letter to the Bambino urging him to accept the cut to $50,000. Spink told Ruth that baseball was the game of the common people. Millions of them were unemployed and could not get fifty cents together. "Too much publicity for your holdout would be bad for yourself, bad for baseball."

Spink might have added that it would have been bad for the owners. They were anxious to see baseball's biggest paycheck take a cut to justify cuts all down the line. In the end Ruth signed for $62,000. As for fan resentment over the holdout, there was little evidence of it when Ruth, in his first day at spring training, was mobbed by 2,000 fans, who gave Ruth his biggest welcome to spring training in fourteen years as a Yankee.

Other players of course did not fare as well as Ruth. Pay cuts in some cases were severe, as there was little the players could do but accept their contracts. As Ed Bang reported from Cleveland, most of the players were happy to have any employer at all. The old threat to retire from the game and go into business rather than accept an unsatisfactory contract could only draw a laugh. Despite these unfavorable conditions the decline in baseball salaries did not match the decline in the cost of living. According to Ralph Andreano's "Money and the Folk Hero," real wages at the lowest point in the depression were higher than the 1929 level and continued to rise throughout the depression.

Despite the realization that the time had arrived for baseball to confront the reality of economic crisis, baseball men were not dismayed by the prospect. The Sporting News cautioned against the cries of the "Calamity Janes" whose pessimism could only tear things down and not build them up. The depression was viewed as a "cleansing process," because it eliminated those dreamers who thought that everything they touched would turn to gold. The dreamers would be replaced by the "optimistic realist" who had the courage to invest in the future. Baseball must, said The Sporting News, look forward to the future if it expected to move ahead. Joe Vila shared this opinion and called for less "knocking" and more "boosting." If all would put their "shoulders to the wheel" and boost baseball, Vila felt that everything would be fine. Franklin D. Roosevelt said virtually the same thing to the nation a little later when he told people they had nothing to fear but fear itself.

When the new season opened with a new president, The Sporting News smelled new confidence in the air. It predicted more earning power for the masses—which would mean more people at the ball parks. The president, vice-president, several cabinet members, and many congressmen attended the season's opener in Washington. The Sporting News bragged that this was greater recognition for a sport than the country had ever seen. Such confidence in baseball placed a heavy burden on baseball's leaders to provide "the most interesting divertissement they are capable of producing." This meant offering a colorful team and the employment of "modern methods of showmanship."

As the New Deal agencies geared up, baseball men sought their role in the recovery process. A suggestion from Joseph Addleman of San Francisco attracted the attention of *The Sporting News*. Addleman proposed that the federal government provide a loan of $25 million to sixty-one cities to build 3,850 baseball diamonds. Baseball's Bible felt that the plan fitted well with the general approach of the New Deal. If the New Deal was seeking increased employment and shorter working hours, then there must be provision for "healthful and interesting" use of leisure time. If the New Deal was offering funding for the building of material things, then "character building should go hand in hand with prosperity building." If reforestation was important, and if the back-to-the-land program was important in relieving slum conditions, then surely the "promotion of character and physical rebuilding of the youth of the land" were also important. *The Sporting News* felt that Mr. Addleman's proposal would serve all of these functions and urged the baseball hierarchy to promote such a proposal in Washington.

Things were improving; but the off-season months of 1933–34 provided further evidence that baseball was still suffering financially. Sidney Weil, president of the Cincinnati Reds, was forced to resign after suffering through several difficult seasons with the Reds and his creditors. Connie Mack, facing financial difficulties in Philadelphia, found it necessary to begin the breakup of the A's. He sold catcher Mickey Cochrane and pitcher Lefty Grove. By March it was evident that lower salaries were once again in order. The situation was severe enough in some clubs that Dan Daniel urged caution lest salaries get too low. He feared a repeat of the Black Sox scandal, which in his opinion had been caused by low salaries.

As spring training approached, *The Sporting News* commented on a new phenomenon which had appeared the year before. In 1933 large numbers of young men had made their way to Florida hoping to find employment with a baseball team. Many had arrived half-starved and in rags, without money, gloves, or shoes. They were "fortified only by their confidence in themselves." Some of them collapsed on the field from exhaustion and lack of nourishment and thus had no chance to show their abilities. *The Sporting News* tried to discourage these young men from coming again in 1934. It urged people to help out any young men of ability who they felt might have a chance to make it in baseball.

The year 1934 brought the first real signs of improvement. The opening of the season was greeted with optimism by sportswriter Rud Rennie, who said that the "National Road to Ruin now is a thriving thoroughfare." Rennie reported that the trip north from spring training in 1933 had been grim. People did not come out even to see Ruth, Gehrig, and the Yankees. But in 1934 it was a different story. The Yankees were greeted in city after city by brass bands and were paraded through the streets. In addition, for the first nine home games New York Giant attendance was up 73,000 over the previous year. At the close of the 1934 season the Detroit News praised Tigers owners Frank Navin and Walter O. Briggs, honored with a banquet given by the Detroit business community. They had invested heavily in the Tigers while most of Detroit had been worrying about bank failures. But the trouble was not over. There was a call for the establishment of a revolving fund for the use of teams in financial difficulty, to prevent these teams from having to sell their star players in order to survive.

Although there were more signs of improvement in 1934 and 1935, they were certainly not conclusive. After the 1935 season Connie Mack was forced to continue the dismantling process of his A's. He sold $400,000 of baseball talent to the Boston Red Sox, including his star first baseman, Jimmy Foxx. But apparently the worst had passed for most clubs. It was 1936 that brought the first clear indication that baseball's prosperity had returned. The American League reported an increase of nearly one million in attendance, with the Yankees going over a million at home and over 800,000 on the road. The National League showed similar gains. In the face of the improvement Colonel Ruppert of the Yankees predicted a better year in 1937, maybe even a record-breaker.

At the end of the 1938 season The Sporting News was able to call the depression a thing of the past. It paused to assess the role that baseball had played in those troubled times: "Baseball may well be proud of the part it has played in bringing the nation back to normalcy, not only economically, but spiritually, as well, if one may be permitted to use that term. While other businesses of the nation were in the doldrums, their leaders singing songs of lamentation and looking gloomily toward the future, the proverbial optimism of those in the national pastime refused to be dimmed, enabling the sport to take a leading place in the march forward. Furthermore, the ball parks furnished a place where surcease and relaxation could be found, thus creating a new spirit of morale."

Baseball had survived the crisis. With some exceptions, it probably suffered less than most businesses. But baseball did not emerge from the depression unchanged. There were at least three significant changes related, at least in part, to the depression experience. There was the aforementioned emergence of the corporate player and the introduction of modern business techniques into the game. The other two changes were the introduction of radio on a large scale and the inauguration of night baseball.

The relationship between radio and baseball goes back into the Twenties. However, it was not until the Thirties that radio broadcasting of baseball became an established commercial enterprise. The first radio broadcast of a baseball game was August 5, 1921. Harold Arlin did the play-by-play on station KDKA from Forbes Field in Pittsburgh where the Pirates were playing the Phillies. Regular broadcasting of major-league games did not come until 1924, when William Wrigley opened the Chicago Cubs to the men of the airwaves. As early as 1922 John B. Sheridan foresaw the impact and potential of the radio for baseball. He noted that radio had increased baseball interest in the rural areas of the country. He believed that radio, coupled with the automobile and good roads, would prove a boon to major-league attendance, particularly on weekends and holidays. Sheridan's predictions were confirmed by the statistics in Chicago, where as many as seven radio stations were broadcasting Cubs games at once. Wrigley, feeling that all of this would increase interest and create new fans, charged no fees for the broadcasting rights. Cub attendance did increase 119 percent in the years 1925–31. During that time the Cubs had not substantially improved their position in league standings. Over the same period other clubs reported an attendance increase of only 27 percent (Red Barber, *The Broadcasters*, and Warren Brown, *The Chicago Cubs*).

Others did not share Wrigley's enthusiasm for radio. In 1925 Ban Johnson decided not to allow radio broadcasting in the American League, and *The Sporting News* agreed with his decision. It claimed baseball was more "inspirational" through the eye than the ear. There was a danger that people would stay at home to listen to the games, making them lazy and sluggish and denying them the oxygen they could get in the open air at the ball park. More serious was the charge that "A Nation that begins to take its sport by ear will shortly adopt the white flag as its national emblem, and the dove as its national bird." The journal was willing to concede that at times, such as during the World Series, radio was needed, but "we say the less of it the better."

In 1927 the American League reversed its position and decided to allow broadcasts. The reversal was prompted in part by the belief that the excitement generated by the broadcasting of the 1926 World Series had created many new fans, especially among women. It was established that there were some six million radios in the country capable of reaching twenty million people. By 1927 many believed that these twenty million were a source of attendance that could be tapped through the radio, but not everyone was convinced. Each year as the winter meetings approached there was talk of banning broadcasting. Some minor leagues did so. The biggest criticism of radio was just the opposite of what the radio boosters were saying. The critics claimed that attendance was actually being hurt by the radio. But to the purists more than just body count was at stake—it was a question of aesthetics. To illustrate this criticism, *The Sporting News* printed a fictional radio broadcast of a painting. Following the printed broadcast were the lessons to be learned from such a cumbersome effort:

God made some things to be seen and not to be heard and some things to be heard and not to be seen.

A painting is to be seen and not to be heard. So is a ball game. There is no divine chorus, no immortal sonata, in a ball game unless it be, "Kill the umpire." It hardly seems necessary to us for that to be broadcast.

As game broadcasting increased the opposition to it stiffened, and in 1932 broadcasting was nearly legislated out of the majors. But as often happened both leagues sought to sidestep a controversial issue. In effect the owners accepted local option as a compromise solution. The strongest opposition to radio came from the New York area teams. In 1934 the Yankees, Giants, and Dodgers signed a formal five-year pact banning broadcasting and Western Union re-creations of their games (Barber, *The Broadcasters*). In 1932 *The Sporting News* conducted a poll of its readers seeking opinions on radio. The results of the poll seemed to indicate three things. First, radio was responsible for making women into new baseball fans, and it served to educate them about the game. Second, the radio had reawakened and held the interest of youngsters, who it was said had been increasingly turning to other sports. Third, these new fans were not content to sit by their radios but would prefer to see the games in person. They would be flooding the ball parks when prosperity returned. *The Sporting News*, although still not ready to endorse broadcasting, urged the owners to consider the poll before making any final decisions on this question.

Despite these and other positive indications, the opposition remained strong. After trying radio, St. Louis backed away from it in 1934. This left only Chicago, Boston, and Cincinnati with regular broadcasting at the major-league level. The evidence on the effects of radio on attendance was inconclusive. The only thing certain, according to *The Sporting News*, was that "a winning team, or one with colorful personalities among its players, profits by radio reporting of its game." On the other hand, broadcasting tended to crucify a losing or colorless club.

Although the controversy continued unabated throughout the Thirties, three separate developments indicated that the marriage of baseball and radio was permanent. First was the emergence of the practice of selling commercial rights to broadcasting of games. It was not until 1934 that the World Series was broadcast commercially. In that year the Ford Motor Company paid $100,000 for the commercial broadcast rights. It also paid $50,000 to both NBC and CBS to carry the games over their networks. In addition, in 1936 the American League announced that it would sell all rights to the broadcasting of its games. With money coming in from radio contracts, there would naturally be less objection to any adverse effect on attendance. The second significant development was the breakdown of the anti-broadcasting pact in New York. Red Barber describes what happened. Larry MacPhail, baseball's great innovator, arrived in Brooklyn from Cincinnati in 1938. In 1939 he refused to renew the pact with the Yankees and Giants and sold the Dodger broadcast rights for $70,000. The Yankees and Giants reluctantly followed suit. The final barrier was down. The third development was an important indication that the radio-baseball relationship was acquiring permanency. In November 1936 the American League announced that not only would it sell the broadcast rights but it would also exercise control over what the announcers said. This decision undoubtedly stemmed from the conclusion by the league that radio was here to stay and that instead of fighting the development it would be much more profitable to control it. Baseball had come to terms with the new medium and had begun a conscious effort to exploit it to its own advantage. It also indicated a new sensitivity to image and the maturing of the corporate-organizational consciousness of those in baseball.

No sooner had baseball come to terms with radio than it was confronted with yet another technological innovation in communications which would have profound effects on the game. Baseball had its first contact with television on February 11, 1937, when the Philco Radio and Television Corporation staged a demonstration in which Connie Mack was interviewed by news commentator Boake Carter in the Philco factory in Philadelphia. The picture was transmitted several miles to the Germantown Cricket Club, where some two hundred editors of newspapers and magazines "saw and heard the pair almost as clearly as though they were in the same room."

The first major-league baseball game was televised two years later on August 26, 1939, when Larry MacPhail allowed NBC to air a doubleheader between the Dodgers and the Reds from Brooklyn.

The broadcast was announced by Red Barber. The picture was transmitted into the Dodger club offices and press room, into a theater on Broadway, and out to the Television Building at the New York World's Fair. Public response was described as "instantaneous and amazing." The theater was crowded with spectators, and the Television Building had to close its doors to restrain the crowd. Some regarded this as just another in the series of stunts by Larry Mac-Phail. Others, including MacPhail, saw its great potential. But further developments between baseball and television were forced to await the conclusion of World War II. There were few who foresaw the profound effects the new electronic medium would have on the National Pastime.

Another major change in baseball in the Thirties was the use of arc lights to replace sunlight, as the major leagues moved cautiously into night baseball. The first night game ever was played in Nantasket Beach, Massachusetts, in September 1880. It did not start a trend; there were only a few other night games on record over the next fifty years, but night ball did not become significant until the Thirties.

During the winter of 1929 Des Moines of the Western Association announced that it would become the first team in professional baseball to play a regular-season game at night. But Des Moines opened its season on the road, and Independence (Kansas) beat Des Moines to the honor by playing a night game against Lincoln on April 28, 1930. The Des Moines game, however, attracted greater national press attention when it was held four nights later (Turkin and Thompson, *The Official Encyclopedia of Baseball*). Five years passed before major-league baseball took the final step into the night, and during those five years the issue was debated heavily in the baseball press.

The Sporting News set the tone of the debate shortly after Des Moines announced their intentions. First, it was pointed out that baseball needed no added attractions. It was spectacular enough in its own right, able to create its own showmanship. Second, everyone knew that "real" sport was played in the outdoors, where there was plenty of fresh air and a broad range of vision for the spectators.

Third, what would be the effect on the fans? "The night air is not like the day air; the man who goes to baseball after he has eaten a hearty meal is apt to have indigestion if he is nervous and excited; the disturbed and misanthropic fan will not sleep well after a night game. Who wants to go home in the dark when it is twice as pleasant to drive leisurely in the approaching twilight, to sniff a good meal cooking on the range when the front door is opened and the aroma of a sputtering steak spreads all through the house?" All of these arguments might have been sound, but the following spring an item appeared in The Sporting News which was more telling in the long run than all the other arguments. It was reported that sixteen minor leagues would have teams playing night ball, and there were predictions that 90 percent of all minor-league teams would be playing night ball by midseason. The reason was simple: "Night ball proved a lifesaver financially in the 1930 season." However, by midseason 1932, The Sporting News claimed that the novelty of night baseball was wearing thin. Everyone ought to realize that baseball was essentially a daylight game. It was also a fundamentally sound game with no need for "hippodroming."

As the financial problems of baseball mounted and the effects of the depression were felt in the big leagues, the argument for night ball became more compelling. The advent of the shorter work week meant that there would be increased leisure on the weekend. It also meant that there would be less chance for diversions during the daytime the rest of the week. Yet, the working man would still be looking for relaxation during the night hours. He might be attracted to the movies, but that was indoor entertainment. In the summer months people preferred the outdoors. In addition, it was now possible with advancing technology to make the field almost as light as if sunlit. But the clincher was in the attendance figures. Weekday attendance was off, and the problem needed serious examination.

Sid Keener in the St. Louis Star Times called on club owners to stop sitting around awaiting for the boom days to return. He told them to have the courage to go ahead with night ball and reap the handsome profits. If high school football was a success at night, certainly baseball could be too. The most important voices were heard at the winter meetings of 1934: the National League voted to allow seven night games for each team in the 1935 season. This opened the way for Larry MacPhail to install lights in Cincinnati just as he had done in Columbus in 1932.

The decision by the National League was generally welcomed by *The Sporting News*, which called on MacPhail to secure the best possible lighting system for the Cincinnati ball park and called on the fans and baseball people to give night ball a fair chance. But in the same issue Snorter Casey in a letter to his friend Hank remained skeptical. He explained that Cincinnati was eager to have night ball because when Reds fans got a look at the team in the daylight they were refusing to come back. At night the fans would mistake the Reds for the visiting team, and in the confusion there would be an increase in gate receipts. Snorter also saw the coming of night ball as the first admission by the owners that times had changed since "the Spanish-American mess." Snorter's main objection was that night ball was bad for the players. It would produce confusion in their daily regimen. "It ain't natural. But Hank—the Dough!" Meanwhile, over in the American League, which did not make the change, Yankee owner Col. Jacob Ruppert promised to keep an open mind and watch the National League experiment closely. Ruppert said that he was always open to any new idea that would help the game of baseball, but that he was in the business of selling baseball, not vaudeville.

The first night game was set for Cincinnati on May 23, 1935, but rain and cold weather postponed the event for one more night. It was a festive occasion complete with bands and fireworks, the climax coming when the lights came on. By prearrangement President Roosevelt pushed a telegraph key in the White House at 8:30 EST. This activated the lights in Cincinnati, and night baseball arrived in the big leagues. Most reports indicated the evening was an overwhelming success. The field was lighted just as well as in daylight and without glare. The doubters went away convinced, and the uncommitted went away enthusiastic.

Not everyone agreed. One report noted that many players complained about conditions. Some fans were unhappy because it was a

cold and hazy night. A poll by the Cincinnati Post found a majority of
fans against night baseball. A report in Literary Digest claimed that
lights changed the perception of the game. "The game became a
strangely colorless, synthetic affair. Like the lights it was artificial,
mechanical. Personal characteristics and facial expressions of the
players became vague in the haze which hung over the field." If this
was true, then it might be argued that the coming of night ball was
well timed, for the decline of individualism and the coming of the
corporate player also tended towards the synthetic, mechanical,
expressionless, and artificial.

The success of night ball could only ultimately be measured in the
same terms that had led to the experiment in the first place. Did it
improve the gate receipts in Cincinnati? Total attendance at the
seven night games was 130,337—figures that exceeded the total
home attendance for some teams that year. The Sporting News observed that the opponents of night ball would have a difficult time
laughing off such figures for a second-division ball club. As for the
fans, another Cincinnati paper found that 99 percent of the fans
approved night baseball. Other arguments against night ball faded.
The lighting was adequate, the insects did not take over, the evening
air did not produce sore arms, pitchers did not enjoy an advantage
over batters, and finally, no one was injured in the action. Nonetheless, The Sporting News qualified its endorsement of night ball and
warned against overuse of this novelty. The seven-game limit was a
wise one because it limited night ball to one game per week during
the hottest part of the season.

The success of night baseball in Cincinnati did not produce a rush
to install lights in other major-league parks. In 1937 Fortune reported
that many of the players continued to oppose night ball and that
opposition, in fact, went much deeper than that. It involved funda-
mental philosophy: "Those who favor it, with its 'shopping' type of
fan, its brass bands and fireworks, feel they can cash in on baseball as
a form of general amusement. But the majority who oppose it see
baseball as a tense competition involving violent partisanship, and
prefer to put all their eggs in the basket of the staunch partisan. He
doesn't want brass bands; he doesn't think of baseball as just an

alternative to the movies; he regards it as something permanent in his life." The future, of course, was with the amusement industry. Only Mr. Wrigley held out against lights. Corporate America dealt in what it could measure—things like dollars and bodies. It found it difficult to deal with matters of the spirit. Increasingly, baseball was part of that corporate world and less the heart-throbbing National Pastime.

But night baseball came on, although slowly. The second city to turn to it was Brooklyn. Again it was MacPhail's innovation. The inauguration in Brooklyn was more spectacular than in Cincinnati, even without FDR turning on the lights. Babe Ruth was there. And pitching for the visiting Cincinnati Reds that night of June 15, 1938, was young Johnny Vander Meer, who in his previous start in Boston had pitched a no-hitter. This game had two distinctions: Vander Meer's second consecutive no-hitter and Brooklyn's first game under the lights, a spectacular beginning for night baseball in Brooklyn.

In the winter of 1938 the American League turned to night ball. It was expected that both Philadelphia and Cleveland would turn on the lights in the 1939 season. But a few days later the Giants and Yankees signed an agreement against night ball in Gotham and agreed to refuse to participate in night games on the road—a practice already in use by the Giants. By 1940 there were only five holdouts: the Tigers, Yankees, Washington, and the two Boston teams. The Giants had ended their agreement with the Yankees and adopted night ball even though Giant manager Bill Terry was not convinced. His article in *Collier's* was called "Fly by Night." Terry felt that night ball added nothing to the game itself. It was a backward step taken merely to draw the crowds, and he felt it would have serious effects. "To sacrifice the game itself for temporary economics means that future concessions may bring bingo, sets of dishes, and finally door prizes for the women." Terry was right, he merely had his commodities wrong.

Bill Terry, of course, realized that night ball had arrived to stay. He had no illusions about that. The game was changing, the country was changing, and the fans were changing. Frank Graham, writing in the

New York Sun in 1940, saw a new type of fan in the ball parks, one who no longer displayed intense loyalties to the home team. He came to see a good game, good entertainment. "He wouldn't have been tolerated in the old wooden bleachers at the Polo Grounds when the Giants under John McGraw ruled the National League." But those bleachers and McGraw were gone. The lights had arrived with the new type of fan who applauds a good play by the opposition. The new fan wanted entertainment and if he could have it at night, "so much the better."

But for all the new consumership, and all the changes in the game and the fans, there still remained baseball's connections with the past. These connections were reaffirmed and celebrated with the Centennial of Baseball in 1939. The historical record and the legend do not agree on the origins of the National Pastime. In this case the legend dominated. The children's magazine *St. Nicholas* provided this version of the legend in 1930: "Abner Doubleday, who later became a general in the Civil War, was attending a military school in Cooperstown, New York. He was fond of games of all kinds, but one day he had an inspiration. Gathering a group of boys together, he led them to an open field in the village and proceeded to make the rules of a new game. First of all he told them there would be nine players on a side. Then he took a stick and drew in the dirt the outline of the playing-field, marking it out in the form of the present diamond-shaped field. Later Abner made an outline of the game on paper, together with the rules—rules which are not vastly different from those of today."

The Doubleday myth is attractive for several reasons. First, it provides the National Pastime with purely national origins, whereas historical researchers attempt to show that baseball was an evolutionary development out of the English game of rounders. Second, the legend shows baseball as the inspiration of a boy, demonstrating that the important link between baseball and the boys of America existed from the beginning of the game. Third, it connects the National Pastime with a military figure who became a general in the war to preserve the Union, thus establishing the patriotic link.

Finally, this myth provides the game with rural origins, whereas the historical record suggests an urban genesis with Alexander Cartwright of New York City drawing the first outlines of the diamond in the mid-1840s. The power of the myth is attested to by its durability in the face of fact. The historical record also shows that Doubleday was at West Point in 1839. There is no evidence that he wrote the rules or ever drew a diamond. It is possible he never had anything to do with the game. But this myth became the basis for the national celebration of the Centennial of Baseball in 1939. Pushing this version of baseball's origins were the people of Cooperstown, New York. In 1934 they used New Deal funding to aid in the restoration of the "original" field and dedicate it as the "birthplace of baseball." Then they began a campaign to have a major-league game played there as part of the 1939 celebration.

As the anniversary approached, plans were made for a fitting celebration. At their winter meetings in 1937, the major leagues appropriated $100,000 for the celebration and set up a committee representing the major and minor leagues to develop a program. Also, the first five members of Baseball's Hall of Fame were named. The celebration reached its climax at Cooperstown, June 12, 1939. Two games were played at Doubleday Field, one under old-time rules and one under modern rules. Also, the National Baseball Museum and Hall of Fame, built by the Otsego Historical Society, was dedicated.

Over 10,000 people gathered for the celebration. Among the dignitaries were Commissioner Landis and the baseball immortals who were the first to be inducted into the Hall of Fame. Commissioner Landis dedicated the museum to "all America, to lovers of good sportsmanship, healthy bodies and clean minds. For those are the principles of baseball."

Although unable to attend because he was addressing the graduates of West Point, President Roosevelt officially recognized the event with a letter to the museum to honor its opening, and another message appeared in the program for the day's ceremonies. In this message, the president acknowledged the debt of the nation to Abner Doubleday for his part in developing the great American sport of baseball. Roosevelt pointed out that Doubleday had been a soldier in both the Mexican War and the Civil War and noted that "peace has her victories no less renowned than war." In his letter to the museum, the president noted that not only was baseball the "great national sport, but also the symbol of America as the melting pot."

So baseball appropriately celebrated its one-hundredth anniversary and prepared to launch itself into its second hundred years. As it did so, war was on the horizon, and America's national game found it necessary to gird itself for yet another test of democracy.

9

Baseball Diplomacy

> Oh yes, boys, it was on! He was sure of it! More
> than just another ball game now: *history*!

IT may seem farfetched to suggest a link between baseball and the
foreign policy of the United States, yet as the National Pastime
baseball was linked to all aspects of American life. It took its role in
the First World War quite seriously, seeing itself as the game of
democracy. Also, if it was America's mission in the world to spread
democracy, and certainly many Americans held such a view, it is not
surprising that the game of democracy should see itself playing a
role in that American mission. The baseball community was certainly as active as the business community in expanding American
influence around the world in the decades between the wars. Baseball also saw itself as a game of peace, played by a peaceful people,
and capable of promoting peace wherever it went. However, if
provoked to war, baseball was ready.

In the immediate aftermath of World War I, there was some discus-
sion of the spread of baseball to the areas south of the United States.
In early 1919 *The Sporting News*, commenting on the increase of
baseball in Mexico, concluded that if an American army invaded
Mexico it would have an easy time spreading the National Game.
This report was also critical of American "imperialists" who were

trying to "grab off" the wealth of Mexico and then were upset when the Mexicans complained. Tom Rice, Brooklyn correspondent of *The Sporting News*, saw a relationship between United States policy and the success of baseball in Latin America. Rice reported that baseball was becoming a very popular sport in Panama, pushing out bullfighting and cockfighting. He concluded that the popularity of baseball in Panama was due to the fact that Panama owed its independence to the United States, and the construction of the Panama Canal was bringing great prosperity. On the other hand, in Santo Domingo and Haiti, where the United States Marines were an occupying force, baseball was not popular. "The military occupation by Marines is regarded by the natives as a bum decision. It interferes with their national sport of revoluting so to speak." Rice felt that the dislike of the Marines spilled over into baseball.

In early 1922 American League President Ban Johnson made a goodwill trip to Mexico. He was very well received. *The Sporting News* was delighted and modestly concluded that the trip had done more to promote peace and good feelings "through love of sport, than all the intercourses of officials and exchanges of government memoranda in a half century...." There was a feeling that baseball had a special power to spread peace on earth and goodwill among men. But baseball could spread more than that. On May 12, 1921, the New York Giants turned over all of their gate receipts to the Irish relief fund, which was used for those suffering during the rebellion against British rule. The Irish-Americans of New York City may have seen this as an opportunity more to help spread rebellion than to spread peace and goodwill.

However, this concern with Latin America and Europe in the early Twenties was marginal. The main focus of baseball attention was in the Far East, where Americans had long felt they had a special civilizing mission. In May 1919 Adachi Kinnosuke reported in *Everybody's* magazine that Japanese wrestlers were developing a passion for baseball. This led Kinnosuke to conclude that the Japanese had traveled "pretty far in the right direction, on the highway of civilization!" Two years later a baseball team from Japan toured the United States playing against American college teams.

One Japanese baseball enthusiast felt that baseball would be more important to peace between the United States and Japan than all the efforts of diplomats combined. The *Literary Digest* pointed out that even anti-American university students in Japan welcomed professional baseball players from the United States. The following spring *The Sporting News* quoted a Japanese source on the power of baseball to promote friendship and understanding between the two nations. A high-water mark was reached following the 1922 season when a group of players toured Japan, China, and the Philippines. At the conclusion of the tour, Baseball's Bible felt that the baseball missionaries had helped to bring about friendly feelings and better understanding between the United States and these nations: "It has been proven that most of human nature is akin, that we all are brothers under the skin and sons of the one Adam and that if left to our natural impulses without greed of exploiters and machinations of politicans to manufacture hatred we could and would live in peace and happiness."

Following the same reasoning, H. G. Salsinger noted in the *Detroit News* that baseball was a cosmopolitan sport appealing to all nations and all races. He felt that the popularity of the game among the "children of yellow races" opened the possibility of a truly World Series. Such a development would increase the prospects for world peace, since nations that have much in common were not prone to go to war with one another. Those with nothing in common "generally manage to start one."

Of special concern for the United States in the Far East were the Philippines. During the summer of 1923 *The Sporting News* reported that baseball was dying in the islands, adding that there was probably a connection between Philippine high commissioner Leonard Wood's problems of administration and the decline of baseball. Either baseball suffered from a general anti-Americanism, or perhaps its decline was an indication that Filipinos would never accept the American way of life. If the latter explanation were true, then the United States ought not to attempt to hold the islands. Any people who did not take to baseball "never will be suited to live under the Stars and Stripes." If the explanation were the former, then the United States ought to admit that it had failed and baseball had failed as a civilizing force, because of "the blundering and tactlessness of a lot of politicians." The lessons were obvious. Those who were sent to govern and to teach did not give baseball enough encouragement. They lost the great opportunity before them because they hadn't realized that "the quickest and best way to make 'Americans' of any set of people is to get them out on the baseball diamond."

Baseball diplomacy in the Far East was put into further jeopardy when Congress passed the Immigration Act of 1924. Francis Richter, writing in *The Sporting News*, concluded that all of the advances made by baseball in China and Japan could be written off as of little consequence. The declaration by the United States government that these people were nonassimilable had destroyed all the good work in Asia. Richter now favored concentrating the efforts of baseball in Latin America, and he called for off-season tours to the area by major leaguers.

Baseball Magazine ran an article by Irving Sanborn, who looked at it from another perspective. He felt that baseball tours to Japan should continue because they would help lessen Japanese resentment toward the immigration laws and would show the Japanese that not all Americans were racially prejudiced. Sanborn also offered the proposition that baseball, by spreading the sporting spirit among the nations of Europe, could do a lot to help solve the complex problems facing the European nations. Sanborn defined the sporting spirit as the style of being a good loser and being able to wait till next time, as well as being a good winner. The United States government ought to aid the spread of baseball. Sanborn also recommended cultural adaptations; for instance, in England the seventh-inning stretch might be replaced by a tea break. But baseball never really did take hold in Europe. Bucky Harris, the Washington manager, confirmed that fact after he returned from a European trip late in 1926. Ireland, reported Harris, was the one exception.

Nevertheless, the signs of the internationalization of baseball continued. In early 1931 the announcement that the Italian government was sending forty-three instructors to the United States to learn the game was interpreted by *The Sporting News* as proof that European attitudes toward sports had undergone a profound change as a result of the example provided by the American soldiers during World War I. The journal asserted that, although the English were a sports-loving people, they did not play their sports with a democratic attitude. As a consequence, English sports influence had not been strong on the continent. On the other hand, Americans had demonstrated that officers and enlisted men could join together for fun on the baseball diamond without loss of discipline in the ranks. "This was a mental condition that was new to central Europe, which had thought discipline could be enforced only by force...."

In 1931 the Far East saw another tour by major leaguers, this one led by Lou Gehrig. Although the tour was well received, the greatest impact came in 1934 when Babe Ruth, after years of Japanese requests, made his first Far East tour. Ruth was a legend in Japan, and Fred Lieb correctly predicted that the Babe would receive one of the most impressive welcomes ever accorded a foreign visitor to Japan. "To these ... fans," wrote Lieb, "he is some kind of a demigod who dwells in a distant land, a man so strong that he can drive the ball over fences, houses and tree-tops whenever he comes to bat." The tour by Ruth and other American League all-stars was a grand success. To some sportswriters it was more than just a baseball success. To Bill Dooley of the *Philadelphia Record* it promoted respect for America more effectively than any politicians could. *The Sporting News* shared Dooley's optimism. It claimed that the tour was another important step in the attempt to establish universal peace. It served to demonstrate to both the American and the Oriental that under the skin they were both the same. Some writers looked forward to the day when a team from the Orient could come to the United States and compete on equal terms with the best players in the United States. This would "prove to the Americans that the so-called 'yellow peril' wears the same clothes, plays the same game and entertains the same thoughts. In other words that we are all brothers." And once that was accomplished the Japanese and the Americans could "sing together 'Take me out to the ball game.'"

Despite these feelings, the winter meetings of 1934 saw the banning of tours of this type. *The Sporting News* was appalled by the decision, as were others. The journal expressed the opinion that baseball should be in the forefront of all movements designed to promote sportsmanship and brotherly love. It noted that there were some "jingoists" who were talking about strained relations between Japan and the United States. If such talk were true, the Ruth tour would have the effect of either delaying or preventing conflict. "We like to believe that countries having a common interest in a great sport would rather fight it out on the diamond than on the battle field." This sort of idealism was certainly not unique to baseball and reflects the same atmosphere that produced the Kellogg-Briand Pact, the Nye Committee Report, the revisionist historians, and the peace movement of the Thirties. It was also an idealism that would be subjected to a good deal of reexamination under the press of events in the years 1935–41.

By 1935 there was mounting evidence that the dream of universal peace and brotherhood was not to be achieved. Bill Cunningham of the *Boston Post* found that, while wars and rumors of wars were circulating abroad, things were not well on the home front either. He wondered if getting all excited about baseball might be a case of fiddling while Rome burned, but he concluded that it was not. There was a need for escape and relaxation during times of tension. He also felt that long after the "Hitlers of this crazy age are only academic names," people would still remember the highlights of the 1935 baseball season. In addition, baseball was a link to the past, to America's forefathers. Cunningham felt that, by reestablishing that link, Americans might also reestablish the horse sense of the past.

The 1935 World Series offered an opportunity for similar reflection. H. J. Boyle in the *Pittsburgh Post-Gazette* undoubtedly had the Italian-Ethiopian War in mind when he contrasted the enthusiasm of the Detroit fans celebrating the World Series victory with the enthusiasm of a people cheering a dictator "who wants them to go out and have their eyes shot out, who want[s] mothers to cry over bloody and lifeless messes that were once their sons and whose aim is to stay in power, regardless of what misery [he brings]." *The Sporting News* also was pleased that the World Series could stir people and offer them escape rather than wars, five-year plans, and nationalism.

There was a growing feeling that the United States was fortunate to be separated from Europe geographically and a reaffirmation of the long-held American belief that the spiritual separation of the United States from Europe was even more important and more profound that the physical. There were embellishments on this theme. In the winter of 1936 Branch Rickey, addressing the minor-league meetings in Montreal, contrasted Europe with America. The United States had seen a steady growth of liberty and freedom of speech. In the United States sports were substituted for preparations for war. Rickey called for the building of young manhood on the field of play rather than the field of battle. The need for conquest must be redirected toward winning games rather than killing men. Rickey also praised the British sporting spirit and "pounded home the necessity of better understanding between the two English-speaking nations...." Rickey was apparently ready to choose up sides.

In 1937 *The Sporting News* again found occasion to compare the European and American scenes. Baseball was one of the crucial differences. The record opening-day crowds proved that Americans had not lost their "mental equilibrium and sense of values." As long as the United States had baseball to act as a "safety valve," the future of the country was safe. While Europe faced a civil war in Spain and other conflicts between fascists and communists, dictators and revolutionaries, the United States was concerned with Bob Feller strikeouts and pennant winners. A few weeks later *The Sporting News* reprinted a cartoon by C. D. Batchelor of *New York Daily News*, which juxtaposed the national sport of Spain, bullfighting, with the national sport of the United States. The *Daily News* concluded that the Spanish familiarity with blood contributed to the ferocity of the Spanish Civil War. Although disclaiming any intention of adopting a "holier-than-thou" attitude, *The Sporting News* pointed out that in the American Civil War there had been no warfare on women and children, less cruelty, and many instances of "sportsmanship," or gentlemanly honor. When that war ended, baseball had been one of the factors that had helped to reunite the nation. The writer also felt that Batchelor's cartoon showed that "any nation that finds its thrills on the sports field, rather than in the bloody exhibitions of the bull-fighting arena, will show little inclination to follow the sword-waver." Despite the disclaimer, the sporting press did have a holier-than-thou attitude—and a good deal of smugness. These attitudes grew in 1938 and 1939.

As the 1939 season opened, the celebration of baseball as an alternative to war continued. A cartoon by McCutcheon in the *Chicago Tribune* pictured a man in the upper deck of a baseball stadium saying, "Ah! At last I've found a safe sanctuary from war hysteria." The *Chicago Herald and Examiner* commented that America each spring mobilized its young men for baseball, not for war. Americans preferred the call of "Batter Up" and screaming against the umpire to the call of "Shoulder Arms" and the screaming of men dying on the battlefields. Similar attitudes were expressed by *The Sporting News*. But an editorial in the *Feather River Bulletin* of Plumas County, Quincy, California, while praising the pacifistic aspects of baseball, also included a warning:

> Baseball is more than a National Game. It is America's anchor. It keeps the ship of state fast to its moorings in a balanced life. American boys are not conscripted into army service, they play baseball. "Play ball" is their battle cry, not "Heil Hitler." While little Fascists are learning how to toss hand grenades, little Americans are learning to groove one over the plate. But woe betide the enemy when an American boy finds it needful to throw hand grenades!
>
> This point is that the American boy learns how to use his eyes and his good right arm, and can use it in battle if he has to do so, but first of all he will use it for the constructive purposes of life.

The beginning of World War II in September 1939 was largely neglected by baseball writers. James C. Isaminger, traveling with the Philadelphia A's, did file a story on the reaction of the A's and pitcher Chubby Dean to Hitler's invasion of Poland. According to Isaminger the A's were shocked. Dean's reaction was typical of major-league players. Dean told Isaminger that he was sorry to see war had started, because he did not believe in war. But Dean said that if the United

States became involved in the war, he would be the first to enlist and trade his baseball uniform for khaki. So in 1939 the general attitude seemed to be that the United States was fortunate to be separated from Europe. But there were already some small indications that some people connected with baseball were beginning to prepare themselves mentally for possible involvement.

Reprinted, courtesy of the *Chicago Tribune*

During the 1940 season this mental preparation for war increased its pace. *The Sporting News* in May called on baseball to respond to the appeal of the American Flag Day Association for a fitting observance of Flag Day on June 14. It noted that the flag raising had always been a part of opening day ceremonies and other special occasions in baseball. Observance of Flag Day was "a natural," because the flag was a symbol of the freedom enjoyed by the American people, and baseball was a symbol of the unity of the nation.

There was also growing sentiment for the playing of "The Star-Spangled Banner" before each game. International League President Frank Shaughnessy suggested this practice in June, already in use in the Canadian cities of that league. *The Sporting News* received a letter from Cpl. Ernest LaPointe, stationed at Schofield Barracks, Hawaii, seconding Shaughnessy's suggestion and claiming that he had made the same suggestion back in 1934 when the Brooklyn Dodgers installed a public address system. LaPointe noted that "The Star-Spangled Banner" was being played at Madison Square Garden before hockey games; baseball could surely do the same. He also pointed out that the anthem brought everyone to attention and gave them time to cool off. By 1941 the practice seems to have been fairly well entrenched, as the National Game and National Anthem were combining to make baseball fans of the United States more nation-conscious in preparation for a possible entry into the war.

Late in the summer of 1940 *The Sporting News* took cognizance of the fact that the United States government was seeking to increase unity and goodwill in the Western Hemisphere. The journal suggested that baseball do its part by organizing two teams of stars to tour the Americas in the off-season. This would serve to promote the game and contribute to building good fellowship, mutual understanding, and brotherhood.

A few months later a more ominous report appeared, although its full implications were not entirely clear until December 7, 1941. Baseball in Japan had undergone significant changes. Radio broadcasting of professional games had stopped. In an attempt to remove American influences from the game, such terms as "play ball," "strike," and "out" were being replaced by Japanese words. In addition the uniforms were to become more drab and carry Japanese lettering. The nicknames of the teams were being changed; Senators, Tigers, and Giants were abandoned for Japanese names.

During the 1940 season, concern continued to grow. When questioned on the probable effect of the war on baseball if the United States should enter the war, Commissioner Landis would not speculate. He would say only that if such a situation should arise, baseball would meet it at that time. But J. G. Taylor Spink reminded his readers that one only had to look back to baseball's record in World War I for an answer to the question: baseball "would loyally meet any test that might arise, and like the rest of the nation, would never hesitate to do its part in any emergency."

Before the season ended, baseball was called upon to do its part in somewhat less than an emergency—Congress moved to conscription. Baseball's relationship to the new draft law stirred up a number of suggestions. While various bills were still before Congress, *The Sporting News* disclaimed any need for draft exemptions for baseball players or participants in any other sport. However, the journal did not believe that the nation would be served by wholesale disruption of baseball while the United States was still at peace. Sports, after all, were an acknowledged outlet for the stress and tension of the populace. In this spirit, Baseball's Bible called for serious consideration of a plan presented by Joe Williams of the *New York World-Telegram*, who said that baseball players should be given a leave of absence from their one-year training period during the regular baseball season. If acted on before the end of the 1940 season, such a law would allow six months of training to be completed before the beginning of the 1941 season. *The Sporting News* found this a reasonable peacetime request and urged baseball officials to present it or a similar plan to Washington. In a later editorial, it was pointed out that baseball had been founded by a patriotic citizen who was a West Point graduate with a distinguished record of military service to his country. Certainly Abner Doubleday had not created baseball "as a pastime or subterfuge for slackers." It would not be allowed to become so in the face of the present crisis.

Meanwhile, *Baseball Magazine*, anticipating an increase in the size of American military forces, noted that high morale could be maintained by healthful recreation to supplement the rigors of military life and that baseball could best fill this role. The publication noted another important facet of baseball's contribution:

> The Royal Air Force in defending England from the Nazi raiders has proven itself one of the greatest fighting units in all the history of war. Time and again, although outnumbered, they hurled back the invaders and immediately braced themselves for future attacks. Calm, confident, game to the core.
>
> It was once said that Britain won its battles on the football fields of Eton. But that was in the long ago. In 1936 the playing of *baseball,* the number one American sport, was made compulsory for the students of the Royal Air Force Cadet Training College at Halton, England.

On October 16, 1940, when the baseball players joined fellow citizens and registered for military service, it was page one news. But the feeling was that baseball would not be seriously affected by the draft in 1941 due to exemptions for those with wives and dependents. There was some sentiment for granting the same exemptions to ball players as those given to other entertainers and those involved in essential occupations. In the midst of these preparations for war and increases in war production, *The Sporting News* called for calm among the owners and for business as usual. A boom at the gates was anticipated as employment rose. Baseball was reminded that it had an important role to play in preparedness. It must provide the country with continued diversion in the time of stress. *Baseball Magazine* also found little to fear from the draft, noting that preparedness to fight to preserve the democratic way of life was consistent with the philosophy of baseball. Baseball was still the National Pastime, the bulwark of democracy, and "a common leveler," and it would do "its full share to preserve the democratic way of living. War or no war."

Joe Williams of the *New York World-Telegram* was not quite as enthusiastic. He pointed out that hockey players from Canada were able to fulfill their military obligations by a two-week militia service.

Williams wondered why this arrangement was possible in Canada, which was at war, while in the United States, which was not at war, such an arrangement was not being made for baseball. So baseball moved into the winter of 1940–41 facing the increased likelihood of war. Uncertain of its future, baseball was generally optimistic that, at least for the near future, the preparations for war would not adversely affect it. On the other hand, no one doubted the seriousness of the situation.

As if to highlight that seriousness, Commissioner Landis, for the first time in eight years, addressed the joint meetings of the major and minor leagues held in Atlanta in December. He warned of war's unsettling effect on society, especially on moral standards, and called on everyone associated with baseball to develop a high sense of responsibility in order to maintain the integrity of the game, if and when war came to the United States. In Chicago a short time later, the major-league owners extended the commissioner's contract to January 12, 1946. *The Sporting News* praised this action as an attempt to preserve strong and able leadership for baseball. It was "a fitting and timely demonstration of Organized Baseball's national unity," and it served notice that baseball was ready to do whatever might be required of it. "It is comforting to know that Landis, as its Commissioner, provides a strong bulwark for the sport against the difficulties which may lie ahead."

Shortly after the New Year, news came that the War Department was ordering $1 million of athletic equipment, including baseball gear. In addition, professional teams would be asked to play exhibition games at the army camps. The Dodgers had already offered to play at Camp Dix and Camp Upton. Speculation also began as to who would be the first major-league player inducted into the service. Many believed it would be Hank Greenberg of the Tigers because of his lottery number. *The Sporting News* was elated over the prospect that Greenberg might be first, because "the Detroit outfielder not only typifies the game but also its spirit of self-sacrifice and team work for the good of all." Greenberg's career was extolled, including his 1940 switch to the outfield, after which he finished the season as MVP. Hank had already proven he was a "good soldier." It was reported that he would seek no favors from his draft board and was ready to go whenever the army called.

Also in January, President Roosevelt sent a letter to be read at the annual dinner of the New York chapter of the Baseball Writers' Association. It was fortunate, the president wrote, that interest in baseball had not declined. The country should be more grateful than ever to Abner Doubleday for having invented the game. He said that recreation must continue to play its important role in the maintenance of national morale and that this was the proper role for baseball.

The continuing issue for baseball was the draft and its effects on the game. In late February it was reported that there had been no requests for deferments of players on any grounds but that some baseball people and some draft officials were developing differences of opinion on how to handle the baseball-draft relationship. Most baseball men were inclined to leave the entire issue alone. However, the flamboyant Larry MacPhail went on record as saying that the draft was unfair to ball players. While he believed that no player should escape the draft, it ought to be handled so that a player would miss no more than one season. MacPhail himself was no slacker, the report continued, but was a veteran of World War I and had been part of an effort to capture the Kaiser. Other owners were quoted as saying that no deferments would or should be granted to baseball players. The owners cloaked their comments with such words as duty to country, taking their medicine, and not interfering with the government or national defense. All of these developments were reported by The Sporting News in a new feature column: "From Army Front."

It was probably inevitable that ball players would be charged with draft evasion. One of the first of those charged was Morrie Arnovich of the New York Giants. Arnovich was upset by the charge and called a press conference to produce documents showing that he had been rejected by the army because of his bad teeth. He even removed two bridges from his mouth for the reporters. Arnovich had not sought a deferment but had actually tried to enlist. It was reported: "As a Giant, he doesn't like being called a dodger, particularly a draft dodger."

Asking for a deferment, of course, made news. In late February the *Detroit Free Press* broke a story that Hank Greenberg had asked for a deferment. This was confirmed by two members of his draft board and denied by one. Hank also denied the story but did not rule out the possibility of such a request in the future. Tiger management would not comment on the story, except to make it clear they would not seek deferments for their players. The baseball press was very sensitive on this subject.

In April, in an editorial titled "Those Who Live in Glass Houses," *The Sporting News* addressed another troublesome issue—athletes who received physical exemptions from the army. The journal deplored the razzing and criticism these men received, pointing out that physical defects disqualifying a man for the army might not necessarily disqualify him for baseball. There followed a vigorous defense of the patriotism of baseball players. Baseball's Bible concluded that the unthinking critics ought to hold their tongues. This was not an attempt to stifle free speech, a freedom fully exercised in American ball parks; however, "there were limits beyond which no moron should be permitted to go."

On deferment the official line was consistent: *The Sporting News*, Commissioner Landis, and baseball officialdom all agreed that baseball and baseball players should make no effort to receive special treatment. With the exception of Larry MacPhail this public posture was maintained. However, in the April 24 issue of *The Sporting News*, under the headline "U.S. Likely To Keep Draft from Heavy Inroads on Majors," Dan Daniel quoted Senators owner Clark Griffith as saying that the War Department was aware of baseball's problems and was willing to help. Griffith wanted to make it clear that baseball had not gone to the War Department for relief; he went on to say that the authorities understood the importance of baseball as entertainment in troubled times and recognized that baseball was a big business, representing large investments and important tax revenues for the government. "Yes," said Griffith, "we deserve some consideration, but we are not going to the War Department to seek it." But, although he said these things in public on April 24, Clark Griffith had already sent a letter to Gen. Edwin Watson, secretary to the president, on April 12, making two specific proposals for special treatment for baseball. First, Griffith proposed that an army sergeant be assigned to each team to drill the players, the salary of the sergeant to be paid by the ball clubs. Griffith argued that the physical training of the players along with the drills would keep the players three months ahead of the average citizen in conditioning, making it possible to defer those players to be drafted during the summer until the baseball season ended. He pointed out that this would be similar to deferments offered to college students. Also, the drilling of the players before each game in World War I had been an inspiration to the youth of America and had precipitated many enlistments. These drills would have the added benefit of creating interest in the national defense program. If this plan was not feasible, Griffith had a second proposal: he asked the army to devise some system that would restrict the draft to one player from each team in any one season, as long as the United States was not at war. In reply to these proposals, the government pointed out that the question of deferment and draft policy was a matter for the local Selective Service agencies. In regard to the drill proposal it said, "The science of modern warfare is hardly that which can be attained on the baseball lot" (Franklin Delano Roosevelt Library, Hyde Park). A notation on the letter of reply indicates that General Watson had talked personally with Griffith on these matters.

Although these official channels were reluctant to give baseball any special treatment, and despite the reluctance of baseball officialdom to seek such favored treatment publicly, a Gallup Poll indicated in May that the general public was in fact sympathetic to deferments of players for the duration of the baseball season, as shown by figures of 84 percent favorable to 16 percent unfavorable. Among those who followed major-league baseball on a regular basis, the figures were 79 percent favorable and 21 percent unfavorable.

Baseball headed into its last prewar season uncomfortable with the possible effects of the draft. It maintained a public image of contentment and emphasized baseball's firm commitment to America. The opening of the season brought with it a barrage of print contrasting the scenes in the ball parks of America with the battlefields of Europe. Dan Daniel described how "Baseball Follows the Flag" in *Baseball Magazine.* At the ball parks the American flag was raised and "The Star-Spangled Banner" was played, and in Brooklyn the fans rose to pledge allegiance to the flag. In Washington, President Roosevelt threw out the first ball, prompting Daniel to ask in *The Sporting News,* "Where else could it have happened except in free, democratic United States?...The head of the greatest nation, amid wars and strikes, griefs and troubles, coming to a ball park to toss a ball and sit around relaxed for a couple of hours watching the drama of the great national pastime!" Daniel was so impressed that he suggested the midseason All-Star game in Detroit be made a patriotic affair. The president could be invited to come to the game and address the entire nation by radio before the game started. It would be a "great festival for Americanism."

This concern for Americanism invaded the ball parks as the American public prepared to go to war. It was also invading the sporting press. The playing of the National Anthem before each game was now a regular feature. Dan Daniel found special meaning in this pregame ritual:

> Five minutes in the Stadium...2:55 o'clock. Someone shouts through the public address system, "Ladies and gentlemen, the national anthem!" Out of the loud speaker pour the stirring, yet caressing, thrilling strains of the hymn of American independence which Francis Scott Key composed on a British frigate outside of Baltimore. "Oh say can you see, by the dawn's early light." The spectators are on their feet, at attention. The players, umpires, stand transfixed, all eyes on the Star-Spangled Banner as, slowly, it rises on the flagpole in center field.
>
> The Maytime breezes catch those red and white folds and they spank out. "What so proudly we hailed." The flag seems to throw out a message. Out of the Psalms it shouts, "Hide not thy face from me when I am in trouble; incline thine ear unto me; in the day when I call, answer me speedily."
>
> The blue skies arch over the arena in peaceful glory. Suddenly, a noise. The drone of a motor high in the air. The spectators gaze Heavenward, and for the moment Yankee Stadium is a cathedral, the fans worshippers in silent thanksgiving. To a

man, to a woman—yes, to a child—they have one thought. "This plane might be the spearhead of a blitz. But it can't be." Just folks flying to peaceful Boston, where Harvard crews would be gathering at Weld Boat House, and the Charles would be matchless today.

"The rockets' red glare, bombs bursting in air." They aren't playing games any more in the Olympic Stadium in Berlin, where more than 100,000 persons saw a demonstration of baseball only a few years back. They are using Berlin Stadium for malodorous rallies and hate-begetting speeches.

"Gave proof through the night that our flag was still there." The cricket fields at Eaton, at Harrow, Rugby, are drill grounds. No boys over there any more. Only men. They should be at their wickets. "He shall send from Heaven and save me from the reproach of him that would swallow me up." They will play cricket again.

They used to make such pretty toys in beautiful Nuremburg. Now they build motors for planes. In Oberammergau they gave the Passion Play and Christus once again went out of Galilee to utter the message of Peace on Earth and good will to men. Maytime in Vienna...Men the world over dreamed of spring on the Danube. They were heiling on the Prater.

"Whose broad stripes and bright stars." You think back to that line. The stars are blacked out over there, and the broad stripes are lash-marks on the backs of men in Poland. Starvation stalks and children die where the waltzes of Straus[s] used to be the theme songs of a gemuettlichkeit which has fled that world. They don't play rugby or cricket on the Lords Club grounds in London, and Wimbledon's tennis ghosts look down on a pock-marked terrain.

Paris in the spring...The Bois in the hour after dawn...They aren't playing games there, either. The conqueror throws a sinister shadow across both banks of the Seine. "Oh say, does that Star-Spangled Banner yet wave?" They are playing baseball this afternoon in America from coast to coast. In every city, in every town, at schools and Army camps. "O'er the land of the free and the home of the brave."

The music dies out. The crowd sits back and in its heart it sings, "I love thy rocks and rills, thy wood and templed hills." The Yankees take the field and the first batter of the opposition comes to the plate. They are dropping bombs again over London. "Protect us by thy might, great God, our King." Play ball! Free, beautiful America.

In addition to the regular playing of the national anthem, there were other special features. On May 18, "I Am an American Day" was observed at Yankee Stadium. Over 30,000 fans turned out and were treated to "martial tunes" by the Seventh Regiment Band and a speech on the advantages of the American way of life by James J. Lyons, borough president of the Bronx. Miss Lucy Monroe sang "Keep the Home Fires Burning" and "I Am an American"; and Edward Lamont of the Seventh Regiment Band sang "The Star-Spangled Banner," while the crowd stood at attention as the flag was raised in center field. This stirring event was reported in the *New York Times.* In June, Will Harridge, president of the American League, announced in the *Times* that all American servicemen would be admitted free to the remaining American League games. On August 28 baseball participated in "Defense Bond Day" and, according to *The Sporting News,* "showed Uncle Sam it [was] with him 100 percent and that national defense and the national pastime are synonymous."

In August, more bad news arrived from Japan. By decree of the "war lords" baseball was abolished. *The Sporting News* was dismayed. Baseball had been seen as developing into the national sport of Japan. The journal also noted that baseball had served to create goodwill between the United States and Japan. But Baseball's Bible recalled philosophically that in the past the "spirit of Mars" had been so powerful that it had been able to turn brother against brother and father against son. The emperor of Japan was now referred to as "Mr. Hero-hater." It seemed to *The Sporting News* more than a coincidence that when dictators rose to power one of the first things they did was to eliminate competitive sports like baseball. Such sports, because they taught such values as initiative, teamwork, sportsmanship, and fair play, were incompatible with dictatorship.

As the 1941 season came to a close, baseball had firmly established, at least in its own mind, the link between the National Game and the nation. It was ready for the eventuality of war. September, October, and November would see more players inducted into the service and occasional charges that baseball players were seeking to avoid the draft. The charges were duly refuted by the sportswriters. Then came December 7.

"Uncle Sam, we are at your command!" proclaimed *The Sporting News*, as it pledged baseball to full cooperation and dedication to the war. The game would even close down if that became necessary. Echoing these sentiments, Bob Feller volunteered for the Naval Reserve. He was quoted by the *New York Times* as saying, "There are many things more important than baseball these days....First we'll have to win the war to keep baseball." At the major-league meetings in Chicago, $25,000 was pledged to buy baseball equipment for the army and navy sports programs, and it was announced that the receipts of the 1942 All-Star game would be used for this purpose. As for the role of baseball in the war, the consensus seemed to be that baseball should go on with business as usual, serving as an escape and morale-builder for the nation. Naturally, many players would be drafted; that was as it should be. That was the way baseball wanted it to be, with no special favors.

Then there was Hank Greenberg. The former Tiger star was a sergeant in the army. Two days before Pearl Harbor he was released under the terms of a regulation discharging draftees over the age of twenty-eight. Hank Greenberg made a decision—to return immediately to active army service. He became the first ball player to join up, earning him the distinction that had belonged to Hank Gowdy of the Braves in World War I. Publisher J. G. Taylor Spink, in a page one feature story in *The Sporting News*, lauded Hank's decision, pointing out that Greenberg could have gone home and left the battle to younger men. But Greenberg was driven on by a picture of his parents who had emigrated from Rumania. They had not agreed with the way of life there, and in the United States they prospered. Their son had an equal opportunity with others and reached a high position in his profession. "We are in trouble," said Hank, "and there is only one thing for me to do—return to the service." By this decision, wrote Spink, "Hank Greenberg gave the game and the nation a special thrill."

The fact that the attack on the United States had come from Japan was especially galling to many connected with the National Pastime. Baseball had made a greater impact on Japan than on any other country outside the United States. Was it possible that a people who took so well to the game of democracy could now turn out to be the archenemy of the greatest democracy on earth? This turn of events called for an urgent rewriting of history. *The Sporting News* was equal to the task. It traced the history of baseball in Japan back to its introduction by American missionaries just after the American Civil War. The Japanese quickly became first-class fielders, but due to their small size they had never been able to develop into powerful hitters. This weakness "always was a sore spot with this cocky race," for they could not match the power of visiting American teams. The cockiness was seen as a cover for a "national inferiority complex." Furthermore, the Japanese had never really fully converted to the game. The people of this "treacherous Asiatic land" were unable to understand how Americans could question the authority of the umpire and harass their opponents. Americans would never say " 'So sorry' [behind] a grimacing yellow mask," nor would Americans ever "stab an 'honorable opponent' in the back" or "crush out his brains with a bat while he is asleep...." It was obvious to the careful observer that the Japanese, although they had acquired some skill at the game, had never acquired the "soul of our National Game....if the spirit of the game ever had penetrated their yellow hides," they never could have committed that "infamous deed" of December 7, 1941.

Dan Daniel's character, Snorter Casey, also expressed disappointment over the failure of baseball to influence the Japanese properly. Casey concluded that the Japanese were merely going through the motions and did not know any more about baseball than did Hitler. After hurling a number of colorful epithets at the "Japs," Casey issued a warning that some day in the near future they would find they had slipped themselves a "Mickey Finn" when they attacked Pearl Harbor. "Mr. Tojo will wake up some night with the feeling he got into this thing with two strikes against him, and Feller having one hell of a day. Nuts to the Nippons."

With the coming of the new year, J. G. Taylor Spink offered New Year's resolutions for the fans and for the major leagues. For the fans, it was resolved that they dedicate their full time and energies to defeating the Nazis and the Japanese and make the world free of any "impediments to the ways of living which are inherent in America, and in Democracy"; also, the fans were to work to strengthen the "bonds of union" of all the American people. The fans should do their best to help keep baseball alive, working as a force for national good and the maintenance of national morale. For the major leagues, it was resolved that the gift of baseball given to Japan be withdrawn and that more care be taken in the future when determining who should be given the gift of baseball. Furthermore, the major leagues should confess the error they made by allowing the Japanese to "share the benefits and the God-given qualities of the great game with us." The attention of all "civilized, democratic peoples of the world" should be called to the "unworthiness" of the Japanese to retain baseball. The revocation should be made effective as of December 7, 1941, when "the Jap agents of Hell treacherously attacked Pearl Harbor."

For the second time in a little over two decades the nation and the National Pastime prepared to begin yet another kind of World Series. For many in baseball the stakes remained the same—to make the world safe for both baseball and democracy. The world, and the world of baseball, would emerge from the war altered by the experience, facing even more rapid changes and the challenge of a rural game surviving in a world of automation and atomic power.

Bibliography

Allen, Lee. *The American League Story.* New York: Hill and Wang, 1962.
———. *The Cincinnati Reds.* New York: G. P. Putnam's Sons, 1948.
———. *The Hot Stove League.* New York: A. S. Barnes & Co., 1955
———. *The National League Story.* New York: Hill and Wang, 1961.
Allen, Maury. *Where Have You Gone, Joe DiMaggio?* New York: Dutton, 1975.
Andreano, Ralph. "Money and the Folk Hero." In *Sport and American Society*, edited by George Sage. Reading, Mass.: Addison-Wesley, 1970.
———. *No Joy in Mudville.* Cambridge, Mass.: Schenkman, 1965.
Angell, Roger. "Baseball, the Perfect Game." In *Ten Years of Holiday*, edited by *Holiday*, pp. 390–402. New York: Simon and Schuster, 1956.
Asinof, Eliot. *Eight Men Out: The Black Sox and the 1919 World Series.* New York: Holt, Rinehart, & Winston, 1963.
"Ban Johnson, the Teddy Roosevelt of Baseball." *Literary Digest*, March 18, 1919, pp. 78–83.
Barber, Red. *The Broadcasters.* New York: Dial Press, 1972.
Barrow, Ed. *My 50 Years in Baseball.* New York: Coward-McCann, 1951.
The Baseball Encyclopedia. New York: The Macmillan Co., 1969.
"Baseball and Football." *Nation*, December 1, 1920, p. 610.
"Baseball Is Honest." *Collier's*, October 23, 1920, p. 13.
"Baseball Scandal." *Nation*, October 13, 1920, pp. 395–96.
Beisser, Arnold R. *The Madness in Sports.* New York: Appleton, 1967.
"Benevolent Brotherhood of Baseball Bugs." *Literary Digest*, July 7, 1923, p. 68.
"Big League Baseball." *Fortune*, August 1937, pp. 36–45.
Black, C. M. "Carl Hubbell, the Master of the Screwball." *Scribner's Magazine*, April 1938, pp. 23–28.
Bonner, Mary Graham. "Birth of Baseball." *St. Nicholas*, October 1930, p. 931.
Boswell, Charles, and Thompson, Lewis. "Say It Ain't So, Joe." *American Heritage*, June 1960, pp. 24–27.
Boyle, Robert H. *Sport: Mirror of American Life.* Boston: Little Brown, 1963.

Bradley, Hugh. "McGraw." *American Mercury*, August 1932, pp. 461–69.

Brenner, A. "Why Is a Dodger Fan?" *New York Times Magazine*, May 11, 1941, p. 10.

Brown, Warren, *The Chicago Cubs*. New York: G. P. Putnam's Sons, 1946.

Browne, Ray; Fishwick, Marshall; and Marsden, Hael T. *Heroes of Popular Culture*. Bowling Green, Ohio: Popular Press, 1972.

Bulger, Bozeman. "Baseball Business from the Inside." *Collier's*, March 25, 1922, p. 7

Cain, Cullen. "The Rookie." *Saturday Evening Post*, April 3, 1926, p. 15.

Camp, Walter. "They Shall Not Pass." *Collier's*, October 13, 1923, p. 23.

———. "Truth about Baseball." *North American Review*, April 1921, pp. 483–88.

Chamberlain, J. "Safe at Home! Baseball Isn't All Sport for the Big League Club Owners." *Review of Reviews*, May 1935, pp. 47–49.

Cobb, Ty, and Stump, Al. *My Life in Baseball—The True Record*. Garden City, N.J.: Doubleday and Co., 1961.

Coffin, Tristram. *The Old Ball Game*. New York: Henden and Henden, 1972.

Cohen, Morris R. "Baseball." *Dial*, July 26, 1919, pp. 57–58.

Conley, G. H. "Here Baseball Was Born." *Rotarian*, June 1934, p. 25.

Connery, Thomas J. "Chain-Made Changes." *Baseball Magazine*, February 1940, p. 403.

Coover, Robert. *The Universal Baseball Association Inc., J. Henry Waugh, Prop*. New York: Signet Books, 1968.

Cozens, Frederick Warren. *Sports in American Life*. Chicago: University of Chicago Press, 1953.

Creamer, Robert W. *Babe: The Legend Comes to Life*. New York: Simon and Schuster, 1974.

Crowell, Chester. "Why Johnson Is the Best Loser and Best Winner in Baseball." *American Magazine*, November 1925, pp. 56–57.

Daley, Arthur J. "Baseball Pageant Thrills 10,000 at Game's 100th Birthday Party." *New York Times*, June 13, 1939, p. 1.

———. "Fabulous Yankees Through Fifty Years." *New York Times Magazine*, March 9, 1952, p. 16ff.

Daniel, Daniel M. "Baseball Follows the Flag." *Baseball Magazine*, June 1941, pp. 291–92.

Dayton, Stoddart. "What Baseball Has Taught Ty Cobb: An Interview." *Collier's*, July 19, 1924, p. 7.

DeGrazia, Sebastian. *Of Time, Work, and Leisure*. New York: Doubleday, 1964.

Dulles, Foster R. *America Learns to Play: A History of Popular Recreation, 1607–1940*. New York: Appleton-Century, 1940.

Durocher, Leo, and Linn, Ed. *Nice Guys Finish Last*. New York: Simon and Schuster, 1975.

———. "Candid Memories of Leo Durocher." *Saturday Evening Post*, May 11, 1963, pp. 26–28.

Durso, Joseph. *The Days of Mr. McGraw*. Englewood Cliffs, N.J.: Prentice-Hall, Inc., 1969.

———. "What's Happened to Baseball?" *Saturday Review*, September 14, 1968, pp. 138–39.

Dutton, William. "The House that Mack Built over Seven Cellars." *American Magazine*, June 1930, pp. 42–43.

"Editorial Comment." *Baseball Magazine*, June 1921, p. 296; September 1921, p. 450; February 1932, p. 386; October 1940, p. 482.

Farrell, James T. *My Baseball Diary*. New York: A. S. Barnes, 1957.

Farrell V. "Our National Pastime." *Recreation*, April 1938, pp. 25–26.

Finkelstein, Louis. "Baseball and Rivalry." *Dial*, October 4, 1919, p. 313.

Fitzgerald, Harold A. "All Quiet at Second Base." *American Magazine*, May 1936, p. 138.

Frisch, Frank, and Dexter, C. "Gas House Gang and I." *Saturday Evening Post*, July 18, 1959, pp. 28–29.

Frisch, Frank, and Stockton, J. Roy. "The Gas House Gang." *Saturday Evening Post*, July 4, 1936, pp. 12–14.

Fullerton, Hugh S. "Baseball, the Business and the Sport." *Review of Reviews*, April 1921, pp. 417–20.

———. "Baseball on Trial." *New Republic*, October 20, 1920, pp. 183–84.

———. "Baseball's Best." *North American Review*, May 1930, pp. 599–606.

———. "Matty's Tribute from the Fans." *Literary Digest*, January 15, 1921, p. 51.

Gallico, Paul. *Farewell to Sport*. New York: Knopf, 1938.

———. *Lou Gehrig, Pride of the Yankees*. New York: Grosset & Dunlop, Inc., 1942.

Graham, Frank. *The Brooklyn Dodgers*. New York: G. P. Putnam's Sons, 1945.

———. *Casey Stengel*. New York: The John Day Co., 1958.

———. *Lou Gehrig: A Quiet Hero*. New York: G. P. Putnam's Sons, 1942.

———. *McGraw of the Giants*. New York: G. P. Putnam's Sons, 1944.

———. *The New York Giants*. New York: G. P. Putnam's Sons, 1952.

———. *The New York Yankees: An Informal History*. New York: G. P. Putnam's Sons, 1943.

Halberstam, David. "Baseball and the National Mythology." *Harper's*, September 1970, pp. 22–25.

Henderson, R. W. "Baseball's Father: Are We Celebrating a Fake Centennial?" *Current History*, June 1939, pp. 53–54.

Henry, Jules. *Culture against Man*. New York: Random House, 1963.

Honig, Donald. *Baseball: When the Grass Was Real*. New York: Coward, McCann, and Geoghegan, Inc., 1975.

Hood, Robert E. *The Gashouse Gang*. New York, William Morrow, 1976.

Huizinga, Johan. *Homo Ludens: A Study of the Play Element in Culture*. Boston: The Beacon Press, 1962.

"Japanese Invade America." *Current Opinion*, August 1921, p. 254.

Jenkins, Burris, Jr. "No Longer Casey Now, It's Cohen at the Bat." *Literary Digest*, May 19, 1928, pp. 56–62.

"Judge Landis." *Literary Digest*, December 4, 1920, pp. 46–48.

Kaese, Harold. *The Boston Braves*. New York: G. P. Putnam's Sons, 1948.

Kahn, Roger. "The Real Babe Ruth." *Esquire*, August 1959, pp. 27–30.

Kaplan, Max. *Leisure in America: A Social Inquiry*. New York: John Wiley, 1960.

Kieran, John. "From Quadrangle to Diamond." *Literary Digest*, September 23, 1933, p. 25.

Kinnosuke, Adachi. "Attaboy Japan!" *Everybody's*, May 1919, pp. 68–69.

Kirksey, George, and Vander Meer, Johnny. "Two Games Don't Make a Pitcher." *Saturday Evening Post*, August 27, 1938, p. 42.

Klapp, Orrin E. *Heroes, Villains, and Fools*. Englewood Cliffs, N.J.: Prentice-Hall, 1962.

———. *Symbolic Leaders: Public Dramas and Public Men*. Chicago: Aldine, 1964.

Kofoed, Jack. "A Dirge for Baseball." *North American Review*, July 1929, pp. 106–10.

Koppett, Leonard. "Ex-National Sport Looks at Its Image." *New York Times Magazine*, December 20, 1964, pp. 18–19.

———. "Yankee Dynasty Can Never Come Back." *New York Times Magazine*, October 2, 1966, pp. 44–45.

Lane, F. C. "Base Stealing's Sensational Decline." *Literary Digest*, April 29, 1922, pp. 41–42.

———. "A Fallen Idol." *Baseball Magazine*, November 1925, pp. 558, 565.

———. "Why Babe Ruth Has Become a National Idol." *Baseball Magazine*, October 1921, p. 483.

Lewis, Franklin. *The Cleveland Indians*. New York: G. P. Putnam's Sons, 1949.

Lieb, Frederick. *Baseball as I Have Known It*. New York: Grosset & Dunlap, 1977.

———. *The Boston Red Sox*. New York: G. P. Putnam's Sons, 1947.

———. "Hard Times Hit Minors." *Literary Digest*, July 30, 1932, p. 37.

———. *The St. Louis Cardinals*. New York: G. P. Putnam's Sons, 1944.

———. *The Story of the World Series*. New York: G. P. Putnam's Sons, 1949.

Lucas, John A., and Smith, Ronald A. *Saga of American Sport*. Philadelphia: Lea and Febiger, 1978.

Luhrs, Victor. *The Great Baseball Mystery*. New York: A. S. Barnes & Co., Inc., 1966.

McDonald, John, and Dexter, C. "Fall of the House of MacPhail." *Saturday Evening Post*, April 17, 1943, p. 22.

McGeehan, W. O. "Baseball: Business as Usual." *North American Review*, March 1927, p. 120.

McGraw, Blanche. *The Real McGraw*. Edited by Arthur Mann. New York: McKay, 1953.

McIntosh, Peter C. *Sport in Society*. London: Watts, 1963.

Mack, Connie. *My 66 Years in the Big Leagues*. Philadelphia: J. C. Winston Co., 1950.

Mann, Arthur. "Baseball's Ugly Duckling: Durable Durocher." *Saturday Evening Post*, August 19, 1939, pp. 14–15.

———. "Rehearsing for Baseball." *American Mercury*, March 1933, p. 291.

Michener, James A. *Sports in America*. New York: Random House, 1976.

Novak, Michael. *The Joy of Sports*. New York: Basic Books, Inc., 1976.

Obojski, Robert. *The Rise of Japanese Baseball Power*. Radner, Pa.: Chilton Book Co., 1975.

Paxton, H. T. "Myths of Cooperstown." *Saturday Evening Post*, January 30, 1960, pp. 18–19.

Peterson, Robert W. *Only the Ball Was White*. Englewood Cliffs, N.J.: Prentice-Hall, Inc., 1970.

"Play Ball." *Literary Digest*, May 29, 1920, pp. 104–8.

Povich, Shirley. *The Washington Senators*. New York: G. P. Putnam's Sons, 1954.

Raignel, George E. "Fourth of July that Rang Round the World." *Ladies Home Journal*, July 1919, pp. 118–19.

Reed, Herbert. "Is Baseball Wobbling?" *Outlook*, June 5, 1929, pp. 208–10.

Rennie, Rud. "Changing the Tune from Gloom to Cheer." *Literary Digest*, June 16, 1934, p. 25.

Rice, Grantland. "The Coffeyville Express." *Collier's*, June 5, 1926, p. 21.

Riesman, David. *The Lonely Crowd*. New Haven: Yale University Press, 1950.

Ritter, Lawrence S. *The Glory of Their Times*. New York: The Macmillan Co., 1966.

Bibliography

Rumill, Edwin M. "Take Me Out to the Ball Game." *Christian Science Monitor Weekly Magazine Section,* April 15, 1939, p. 8.

Ruth, Claire Hodgson, and Slocum, Bill. *The Babe and I.* Englewood Cliffs, N.J.: Prentice-Hall Inc., 1959.

Ruth, George Herman. "Bat It Out." *Rotarian,* July 1940, pp. 12–14.

Ruth, George Herman, and Considine, Bob. *The Babe Ruth Story.* New York: E. P. Dutton & Co., 1948.

Russell, G. "Baseball as a Library." *St. Nicholas,* September 1923, p. 1201.

Sage, George H. *Sport and American Society.* Reading, Mass.: Addison-Wesley, 1970.

Sanborn, Irving. "Baseball Crusaders and the Sporting Spirit." *Literary Digest,* February 14, 1925, pp. 66–69.

Seymour, Harold. *Baseball: The Golden Age.* New York: Oxford University Press, 1971.

Shutts, John. "Youth Goes to Bat." *Rotarian,* July 1935, pp. 18–21.

Smelser, Marshall. *The Life that Ruth Built.* New York: Quadrangle, 1975.

Spink. J. G. Taylor. *Judge Landis and 25 Years of Baseball.* New York: Thomas Y. Crowell & Co., 1947.

"Sport of Lowbrows." *New Republic,* April 25, 1928, p. 286.

Stengel, Casey, and Paxton, Harry. *Casey at the Bat.* New York: Random House, 1962.

Stockton, J. Roy. "Bob Feller." *Saturday Evening Post,* February 20, 1937, pp. 12–13.

———. *Gashouse Gang.* New York: A. S. Barnes & Co., 1945.

———. "Me and My Public." *Saturday Evening Post,* September 12, 1936, p. 8.

Sunday, William A. "Sawdust Trail." *Ladies Home Journal,* November 1932, p. 17.

Terry, Bill. "Fly by Night." *Collier's,* April 20, 1940, p. 23.

"This Is a Night Baseball Crowd." *Life,* September 2, 1940, pp. 10–11.

Treat, Roger L. *Walter Johnson.* New York: Julian Messner, Inc., 1948.

Trevor, George. "The Spotlight on Sports." *Outlook and Independent,* January 27, 1932, p. 116.

Tunis, John. "Cornelius McGillicuddy." *Atlantic Monthly,* August 1940, pp. 212–16.

———. *Democracy and Sport.* New York: A. S. Barnes & Co., 1941.

Turesky, David S. "A World almost Apart: Baseball and American Life in the Twenties." Honor's thesis, Amherst College, 1972.

Turkin, Hy, and Thompson, S. C. *The Official Encyclopedia of Baseball.* Jubilee edition. New York: A. S. Barnes & Co., 1951.

Veeck, Bill, and Linn, Ed. *Veeck—As in Wreck.* New York: G. P. Putnam's Sons, 1962.

Voigt, David. *American Baseball.* 2 vols. Norman: University of Oklahoma Press, 1966, 1969.

———. *America through Baseball.* Chicago: Nelson-Hall, 1976.

———. "Reflections on Diamonds: American Baseball and American Culture." *Journal of Sport History,* Spring 1974, pp. 3–25.

Wallace, Francis. "College Men in the Big Leagues." *Scribner's Magazine,* October 1927, pp. 490–95.

Wallop, Douglas. *Baseball: An Informal History.* New York: W. W. Norton & Co., 1969.

Weaver, Robert B. *Amusements and Sports in American Life.* Chicago: University of Chicago Press, 1939.

Wecter, Dixon. *The Hero in America.* New York: Scribner, 1941.

"Why the Yankees Win." *Nation,* September 17, 1938, p. 258.

MANUSCRIPT COLLECTIONS

Columbus, Ohio. Ohio State Historical Society. Harding Papers. Microfilm edition, rolls 191, 239.
Cooperstown, N.Y. The National Baseball Museum and Library. Clippings files.
Hyde Park, N.Y. Franklin D. Roosevelt Library. Various files.
Washington. Library of Congress. Coolidge Papers. Microfilm edition, reel 88, series 1, no. 173.

NEWSPAPERS AND MAGAZINES

American Magazine
Baseball Magazine
Chicago Daily News
Cleveland Plain Dealer
Collier's
Detroit News
Literary Digest
Newsweek

New York Times
Outlook
St. Louis Post-Dispatch
Saturday Evening Post
The Sporting News
Time
Washington Post

Index

Adams, Henry, values of, 8, 20
Agrarianism, 54–57; Babe Ruth as
   example of, 92–93; Bob Feller as
   example of, 145–46
"Algerism," 30–31, 33–34, 74, 88, 123,
   128–29, 136, 138–39, 146–48
All-Star Game, first, 81, 111
Americanism, 162–63
American youth, 24, 39–42, 56, 82,
   84–87, 123, 141
Anti-immigrant feelings, 162–63
Anti-Semitism, 14, 165, 166, 167–68
Anti-urbanism, 57–63; toward aliens,
   58; toward New York, 59, 63
Arlin, Harold, 184
Arnovich, Morrie, 209
Bancroft, Frank, 150–51
Barber, Red, 188
Barnes, Jesse, 55–56
Barrow, Ed, 97, 175
Baseball Magazine: on Black Sox, 11; on
   democracy, 25; on Negroes, 168; on
   military, 207
Baseball Writers Association, 71, 169
Black Sox scandal, 8, 10–12, 41; reaction
   to, 12–17; trial, 17–19; Landis deci-
   sion, 18–20; and National Commis-
   sion, 20
Bolsheviks, 4–5
Boston Braves, 33, 44, 82, 100, 127, 155,
   192
Boston Red Sox, 2, 6, 46, 76, 91, 155,
   183, 192
Boxing, 42
Breadon, Sam, 33, 81–82
Brooklyn Dodgers, 44, 47, 51, 52–54,

112–13, 115, 157, 159, 164, 186–88,
   192, 205, 208
Broun, Heywood, 169
Bush, Guy, 82
Cannon, Ray, 156
Carter, Boake, 187
Cartwright, Alexander, 194
Centennial of baseball, 71–72, 193–95
Chance, Frank, 128
Change: in new player, 136, 149; in at-
   titudes to baseball, 191–92; in new
   fan, 192–93
Chapman, Ray, death of, 128–29
Character, 41, 128, 134
Chase, Hal, 19
Chicago Black Sox, *See* Black Sox scan-
   dal
Chicago Cubs, 2, 11, 16, 38, 51, 67, 76,
   78–79, 82, 96, 112, 127, 142, 161, 176,
   184–85
Chicago White Sox, 8–13, 17, 51, 76, 83,
   136, 147, 156, 170
Cicotte, Eddie, 12–14, 17
Cincinnati Reds, 4, 8–10, 29–30, 54,
   59–60, 112, 116, 127, 182, 187, 190–92
Class consciousness, 27–30, 153
Clean living, 45–47; and Babe Ruth, 86;
   and Christy Mathewson, 126–27; and
   Connie Mack, 130–31; and Walter
   Johnson, 134; and Pie Traynor, 136
Cleveland Indians, 3, 17, 128–29, 145,
   192
Cobb, Ty, 82–83, 133
Cochrane, Mickey, 37–38, 97, 147, 182
Cohen, Andy, 166
College players, 31–32, 57, 115–16

Collins, Eddie, 35
Colorful players, 116–18; Babe Ruth, 90; Pepper Martin, 137; Dizzy Dean, 139
Comiskey, Charles, 6, 12; and Black Sox scandal, 11, 16, 19
Community identity, 49–51; in Detroit, 51; in St. Louis, 51–52; in Brooklyn, 52–53; in Cincinnati, 54
Competitive spirit, determination, desire to win, 34, 37–39, 42–43, 108, 114–15, 202; of Babe Ruth, 88; of John McGraw, 129–30; of Connie Mack, 131–32; of Rogers Hornsby, 135; of Mickey Cochrane, 147; of Bob Feller, 147
Conscription, 206–8, 209
Continental League, 168
Cook County grand jury, 11–12, 16
Coolidge, Calvin, 70, 154
Cooperstown, 194
Corporate player, 114–25, 142–47, 148–49. See also Organization
Courage, 121, 122, 123, 147
Creel, George, 1, 4, 162
Dean, Dizzy, 32–33, 139–42; and Gas House Gang, 137; in 1934 world series, 139; in 1938 world series, 142; injury to, 142
Death, 126–29
DeCasseres, Benjamin, 25
Decline of baseball, 107–8
Deferments, 210–11
Democracy, 163, 216, 217
Depression. See Great Depression
Des Moines, Iowa, 188
Detroit Tigers, 37, 38, 51, 61, 97, 99, 115, 139, 142, 146, 147, 167, 183, 192, 201, 208, 210
Dillhoefer, William "Pickles," 36
DiMaggio, Joe, 119, 123–25
Doak, Bill, 157, 159
Doubleday, Abner, 193, 194–95
Douglas, Phil, 105, 160–61
Draft evasion, 209
Dreyfuss, Barney, 174–75
Durocher, Leo, 138–39
East-West conflict, 60–63
Ebbets, Charles, 44
Elson, Bob, 170
Europe, 199–200
Evers, John, 3, 153
Fan behavior, 47, 151
Far East tours, 200–201
Farm system, 108–10, 118–19
Farrell, James T., 14–16

Feller, Bob, 145–47, 215
Felsch, Happy, 12, 15
Ferrell, Wes, 46
Florida real estate boom, 157–59
Football, 26–27, 35
Ford, Henry, 165
Fournier, Jacques, 47, 157
Foxx, Jimmy, 99, 143, 183
Frazee, Harry, 6, 91
Frisch, Frank, 38–39, 137, 138
Frontier hero, 139–40
Fuchs, Emil, 99, 155
Fullerton, Hugh, 11
Gambling, 7–8, 135, 165
Gandil, Chick, 12
Gas House Gang, 137–42
Gehrig, Lou, 76, 80; as corporate player, 119–23; consecutive game streak of, 121; retirement of, 121–22; death of, 123; on Far East tour, 200
Gehringer, Charlie, 142–43
Gleason, Kid, 11, 18, 20, 136
Gomez, Lefty, 119–20
Gowdy, Hank, 3
Grant, Eddie, 3
Great Depression, 173–84; and Herbert Hoover, 70; and Franklin Roosevelt, 71; role of baseball in, 176; impact on baseball, 176, 177, 181, 182, 183; and Babe Ruth's salary, 178–80; New Deal, 181–82
Greenberg, Hank: Jewish hero, 167–68; and World War II, 208–9, 210, 215
Griffith, Clark, 2, 92, 110–11, 210–11
Grove, Lefty, 182
Haiti, baseball in, 197
Harding, Warren G., 67–69, 80
Harridge, Will, 214
Harris, Bucky, 199
Herbert, Tom, 3
Hermann, August Garry, 6, 20
Heydler, John, 6, 16, 169
Honesty, 41–42, 129, 132–33, 135
Hoover, Herbert, 70, 95
Hornsby, Rogers, 33, 35, 64, 134–35
Hubbell, Carl, 143–45
Huggins, Miller, 93, 129, 138
Hylan, John, 46–47
Immigration Act of 1924, 199
Independence, Kansas, 188
Individualism, 35; of Babe Ruth, 73–74, 91; decline of, 118, 142; of Pat Moran, 127–28; of John McGraw, 130; and unions, 157
Italians in baseball, 164–65

Italy, baseball in, 199–200
Jackson, Joe, 12, 15
Japan, baseball in, 197–98, 205–6, 214, 216
Jews in baseball, 165–68
Johnson, Ban: and World War I, 2–3; and National Commission, 6–7; and Black Sox scandal, 16, 20; clean living of, 46; retirement of, 132–33; and Prohibition, 151; and radio, 185; in Mexico, 197
Johnson, Walter, 55, 70, 72; in 1924 World Series, 133–34; in 1925 World Series, 134
Keeler, Wee Willie, 58
Kenny, William, 33
Koenig, Mark, 79
Ku Klux Klan, 163
LaGuardia, Fiorello, 129
Landis, Kennesaw Mountain, 6, 20–23; and Black Sox scandal, 18–19; and opportunity, 33; and American youth, 39–40; and character, 41; suspends Ruth, 91; and McGraw, 130; in conflict with Ban Johnson, 132; on Rogers Hornsby and gambling, 135; and Prohibition, 152; and Jake Powell incident, 170; on salary cuts and depression, 179–80; and dedication of Baseball Hall of Fame, 194; and World War II, 206, 208
Lange, Bill, 2
Lazzeri, Tony, 76, 96
Lively ball controversy, 103–5
Los Angeles Dodgers, 49–50
Lucas, Red, 82
Lyons, James J., 214
McCarthy, Joe, 97, 119–20, 124, 170
McGraw, John J., 129–30, 156, 158, 166
Mack, Connie, 72, 130–32, 176, 182, 183, 187
McMullin, Fred, 12
MacPhail, Larry, 112–13, 187–88, 190, 192, 209
Maharg, Bill, 12
Mann, Les, 105
Martin, Pepper, 137–39
Mathewson, Christy, 126–27, 153
Mays, Carl, 6–7, 128–29
Mexico, baseball in, 196–97
Mitchell, Miss, 161–62
Monroe, Lucy, 214
Moran, Pat, 127–28
Nasium, Jim (pseud. of Edgar Wolfe), 25–26, 132

National Baseball Museum and Hall of Fame, 194
National Baseball Players Association. See Unions
National Commission, 6–7, 20
Nationalism, 65–72
Navin, Frank, 97
Negroes in baseball, 168–72
Negro National League, 172
New Deal, 156–57
New York, feelings against. See Anti-urbanism
New York Giants, 3, 31, 33, 34, 37–38, 46, 51, 52–53, 58, 59–60, 61, 106, 109, 122, 126, 129, 134, 143, 156, 166–67, 186–87, 192, 193, 197, 209
New York Yankees, 6–7, 44, 52, 59, 61, 82, 83, 85, 87, 91, 92, 93, 95, 97, 99, 100, 106, 109–11, 117, 119–21, 124, 128, 129, 138, 148, 161, 170–71, 178, 180, 183, 186–87, 190, 192
Night baseball, 188–93
Nugent, Mae, 161
Opportunity, 172; and democracy, 26, 30–34; and immigrants, 163–64; and Hank Greenberg, 167–68
Optimism, 64–65
Organization, 104, 108–9, 124–25. See also Corporate player
Panama, baseball in, 197
Parker, Dan, 171
Pearl Harbor, reaction to, 215–17
Pegler, Westbrook, 169
Perry, Charles, 171
Philadelphia Athletics, 31, 35, 37, 58, 130, 137, 143, 145, 147, 148, 176, 182, 183, 192, 203
Philadelphia Phillies, 11, 16, 33, 76, 161
Philippines, baseball in, 198–99
Pittsburgh Pirates, 45, 134, 135–36, 141, 174
Powell, Jake, 170–71
Powers, Jimmy, 169, 171
Prohibition, 150–52
Promotional techniques, 111–14, 139
Radicalism, 5–6
Radio and baseball, 184–87
Rice, Grantland, 32, 134
Rickey, Branch, 35, 142; in World War I, 3; and American youth, 40; thought v. action, 64; and farm system, 109, 118; compares U.S. and Europe, 202
Risberg, Swede, 12
Robinson, Wilbert, 157
Roosevelt, Franklin D.: baseball during

the depression, 71; and baseball centennial, 72, 194–95; and night baseball, 190; baseball and war, 209
Root, Charlie, 79
Rowe, Lynwood Thomas ("Schoolboy"), 99
Ruch, Lewis, 33–34
Ruffing, Red, 148
Ruether, Walter, 4
Ruppert, Jacob: and National Commission, 6; on sportsmanship, 44–45; and Babe Ruth, 93, 178; and Negro National League, 172; and depression, 183; and night baseball, 190
Ruth, George Herman "Babe": and 1918 world series, 2; and American youth, 40; and agrarianism, 55; designated home run, 78–80; impact on baseball, 82, 93–94, 103; and middle-class values, 87; suspensions of, 91–93; and politics, 95–96; managerial aspirations of, 97; and Boston Braves, 99–100; and Prohibition, 152; depression and salary disputes, 178–80; on Far East tour, 200
St. Louis Browns, 18, 104, 145, 168
St. Louis Cardinals, 3, 33, 35, 36, 38, 39, 41, 51–52, 61, 64, 81, 87, 109, 115, 118, 134, 137–39, 168, 176
Santo Domingo, baseball in, 197
Schalk, Ray, 11
Sheridan, John B., 10–11
Simmons, Al, 147–48
Smith, Al, 95–96
Social Darwinism, 34
Spink, J. G. Taylor: on Pepper Martin, 138; on depression, 178–79; on Ruth's salary, 180; on World War II, 206, 216–17; on Hank Greenberg, 215
Sporting News, The, xi, 2; on World War I, 3–4; on Black Sox scandal, 10–12, 17; on fan behavior, 45–46; on agrarianism, 55; on nationalism, 66; on Franklin D. Roosevelt, 71; on John J. McGraw, 130; on Ban Johnson, 133; on Prohibition, 151; on Sunday baseball, 152–54; on Florida land boom, 158–59; on the depression, 174, 179, 183–84; on Ruth's salary, 180; on World War II, 207, 209, 214
Sportsmanship, 42–44, 202; and Miller Huggins, 129; and Connie Mack, 131; and Ban Johnson, 133; and Walter Johnson, 134
"Star-Spangled Banner," 66, 80, 205, 212

Stengel, Casey, 46
Stock, Milton, 157
Sunday baseball, 152–55
Television and baseball, 187–88
Terry, Bill, 192
Thought and action, conflict between, 63–64
Tinker, Joe, 151
Trautman, George, 113
Traynor, Pie, 135–36
Urban-rural conflict, 55–59, 73–74
Unions, 155–57
Vander Meer, John, 29, 30, 192
Vila, Joe, 169, 180, 181
Walberg, George, 31
Walker, Jimmy, 85, 129, 154–55
War: preparation for, 205–7, 212–14; baseball as substitute for, 202, 203
Washington Senators, 70, 133–34, 192
Watson, Edwin, 210–11
Weaver, Buck, 12
Weil, Sidney, 182
Weiss, George, 109–10
Williams, Claude, 12
Williams, Cy, 76
Williams, Joe, 207–8
Williams, Ted, 148–49
Williamson, Ned, 76
Wilson, Hack, 76
Winning. *See* Competitive spirit
Wolfe, Edgar. *See* Nasium, Jim
Women and baseball, 159–62
Work ethic, 36, 147
World Series
    of 1918, 2
    of 1919, 7, 8–12, 60, 105
    of 1920, 60
    of 1921, 60, 61, 91
    of 1922, 106
    of 1923, 46, 61
    of 1924, 66, 133–34
    of 1925, 134
    of 1926, 52, 61
    of 1928, 61
    of 1930, 37, 174
    of 1931, 137, 176
    of 1932, 78–80
    of 1934, 37, 38–39, 61, 137, 139, 140
    of 1935, 51, 201
    of 1938, 142
    of 1939, 148
World War I, 1–4, 24–25, 37, 66, 196
World War II, 203–4, 215–17
Wrigley, Phillip, 112
Wrigley, William, 184–85